MAVERICK LEADERSHIP

Embracing the Power of Constructive Disobedience

MAVERICK LEADERSHIP

Embracing the Power of Constructive Disobedience

Major General Anil Sengar

PENTAGON PRESS LLP

First published in 2023 by

PENTAGON PRESS LLP
206, Peacock Lane, Shahpur Jat
New Delhi-110049, India
Contact: 011-64706243

Typeset in Adobe Garamond, 11.5 Point
Printed by Aegean Offset Printers, Greater Noida, U.P.

ISBN 978-93-90095-93-3 (HB)

www.pentagonpress.in

DEDICATION

Inspired by the courageous 'Unsung Warriors' who defied authority for the larger cause. They did not wait for a martyr to be born in the neighbour's house. They took up the gauntlet and changed the world for the better, often at great personal cost.

Congo under King Leopold II 1885-1908: A man looks at the amputated foot and hand of his daughter for failing to meet the rubber plantation target.
(Image: Credit Internet)

♦ ♦ ♦

The tyranny that the 'Humanity' has suffered since time immemorial is not as a result of disobedience, but too much obedience and too quietly. For the first time, during the 'Nuremberg Trials', people were punished for Obeying. Blind obedience kills.

The Fate of the World is Everybody's Business.

♦ ♦ ♦

CONTENTS

Acknowledgement

The process of writing this book has been a wonderful journey. Most of the people that I interacted with were surprised by the theme itself. Many felt that there was no scope for disobedience in the military. Most were convinced that an organization needs amiable people to implement the orders of the authority. These perspectives reinforced the need for this book.

I thank my first commanding officer, Lt General Pup Mann, who agreed with me on the necessity of constructive disobedience and enthusiastically shared episodes from his experiences. I also thank Lt General Jagbir Cheema for his forthright assistance.

Above all, I sincerely acknowledge the invaluable contribution of Colonel Virender Singh of 2/4 Gurkha Rifles. He painstakingly read every word of the manuscript, provided a very honest critique and shared his perspectives that shaped the book immensely. I also thank Colonel Rajiv Anand and Captain Sanjay Gahlot (Indian Revenue Service) for their most useful suggestions.

Last but not least, this book would not have been possible without the ignorant, incompetent and self-serving commanders that I had the opportunity to serve under. They validated the law of stupidity and reinforced my belief in my concept of constructive disobedience in the interest of the mission, the men and the organisation.

Many actually wonder, with my belief in and practice of constructive disobedience, how did I reach this rank in the army which has no room for disobedience. My wild guess is that some wise men up there believed in the same philosophy and understood why I defied when I did.

Above all, my deep gratitude to the wonderful men of my battalion, 5 GUARDS, and others that I had the honour to command. It was the obligation to live up to their blind trust and loyalty that shaped my '**Time when not to**

care a damn' approach to safeguard their well-being and the organisation's interest.

For sure, it may have caused my superiors initial embarrassment but saved them many blushes and definitely many lives. I have no regrets.

Major General Anil Sengar

♦ ♦ ♦

Introduction

The theme of this book had many people raising their eyebrows with disbelief. The idea of disobedience as an essential leadership trait was unpalatable to them. They felt there was no scope for disobedience, particularly in the military, where there is misplaced belief in the dictum 'there is not to question why...' Some felt organisations need implicit obedience to function effectively. They are missing the point and it is for such people that this book is more important.

It is important to understand the following terms:

Constructive dissent. This refers to expressing disagreement or opposing views productively and respectfully within an organization, group, or society. It involves challenging prevailing opinions, policies, or decisions through logical critique and offering alternative perspectives or solutions. Constructive dissent aims to foster open dialogue, improve decision-making processes, and drive positive change for the organisation.

Constructive dissent is not combative in nature. It is characterised by respectful communication, constructive criticism, seeking common ground and commitment to the collective interest. Constructive dissent is necessary within an environment as it encourages and values differing viewpoints and obtains the unfettered contributions of others. This requires a culture that respects freedom of expression and appreciates the importance of constructive dialogue.

Constructive Disobedience/Positive Defiance. This refers to the act of intentionally and openly defying certain rules, norms, practices, policies, authority, and unlawful or lawful but awful orders to bring about positive change and prevent catastrophe by pre-empting fatal decisions. These decisions with potentially fatal consequences may be a result of many factors from incompetence, ignorance, personal interests, misplaced personal ambitions or expediency. The goal is not to disrupt for the sake of disruption but to prompt reforms through constructive dialogue, and critical thinking when clearly potentially disastrous.

Constructive disobedience can take various forms, such as peaceful protests, sit-ins, boycotts, and other acts of civil resistance. In institutions, individuals or a group of individuals can defy dangerous or illegal orders by circumventing them or simply declining to implement them in the shape and manner they are intended to. By engaging in such acts, individuals or groups aim to raise awareness about important issues affecting humanity, challenge systemic injustices, and promote human rights. They may intentionally break laws or regulations to draw attention to the flaws within the existing system and mobilize public support for necessary change.

Throughout history, constructive disobedience has played a crucial role in social movements and advancements in areas such as civil rights, gender equality, labour rights, and environmental protection. Prominent figures like Mahatma Gandhi, Martin Luther King Jr., and Rosa Parks are examples of individuals who practised constructive disobedience to challenge discriminatory practices and promote social justice.

It is important to note that constructive disobedience is not about rebellion or promoting anarchy by disregarding all rules and regulations. Instead, it seeks to navigate a balance between respecting the core values of a society and challenging unjust practices that contradict those values.

From the above, we see that constructive disobedience is about the spirit, the purpose and the context. The most defiant Indian leader, Subhash Chandra Bose, who resigned from the British Indian Civil Services, opposed Gandhi's approach to the independence movement. He raised the Indian National Army and fought the British. Seventy five years after his death, he was honoured with an imposing statute at the most iconic location in the country, the India Gate complex that also houses the National War Memorial. This gesture had universal public support.

Mahatma Gandhi himself, who was the apostle of peace and non-violence saw merit in mass civil disobedience and non-cooperation and practised it. So, the value of the concept of constructive disobedience is obvious. It is clear that if the leadership is competent and value-based this would not be necessary. (Compiled from different sources)

Count Axel Oxenstierna, Chancellor of Sweden during the turmoil of the Thirty Years' War in the seventeenth century under Gustavus Adolphus and

Queen Christina, to whom he was a First Regent, made this dying conclusion, "**Know, my son, with how little wisdom the world is governed.**"

This book shows how little has changed since then and why such people need to be held accountable, by defiance if necessary.

Contrary to what the title of the book may suggest, this book is not about engineering a revolution or a coup. It proposes the concept of 'Constructive Disobedience' or 'Positive Defiance', whatever one may choose to call it, as a necessary leadership trait for the long-term good of any organisation or institution. When you are certain that your disobedience and defiance will protect your country or your organisation from fatal decisions by ignorant or self-serving leaders, it is an obligation.

When you have superiors of good character, values and intentions, this will not be necessary.

Since time immemorial, individuals or small groups of men have charted the destiny of mankind to serve their personal ambitions or interests.

In historic times, wars were fought for political influence, name in history, territory and loot. As for the vanquished, either they accepted the diktat of the invader or they were massacred en masse. Those who survived were taken slaves with no accountability for what was done to them-rape, torture, and death for the entertainment of the victor and their people.

India, the most prosperous nation of that time, a peaceful country, suffered at the hands of the barbaric Muslim invaders from Central Asia and Afghanistan for centuries. They destroyed symbols of civilisation and progress—temples, libraries, universities and cities in the name of religion. People who could not or did not run away had only two options—convert to Islam or die. People were massacred by hundreds of thousands. Then followed India's brutal exploitation by the British colonialists, killing, plundering and sucking India dry reducing it from the most prosperous country in the world to a struggling poor country.

Europe has remained the main battleground for the better part of history. The two World Wars of the twentieth century were fought among Europeans that killed a hundred million people. The Ukraine war between white men has been raging in Europe for more than a year and a half as I write this in June 2023.

These Western countries have taken upon themselves the 'Burden of the White Man' as Rudyard Kipling put it, to civilise the rest of the world. They colonised most of the world, looting their wealth, keeping them illiterate and hungry, destroying their culture and dignity, keeping them in shackles as slaves and murdering them—the United Kingdom, Germany, France, Portugal, Spain, Netherlands, Belgium and others-all western white men country. America and Australia subdued the indigenous population to insignificance and the US dealt with the horrific slave trade for centuries. Hundred years after President Abraham Lincoln emancipated the US from slavery in 1864, and paid with his life for doing so, Martin Luther King was still struggling to fight racial discrimination and paid with his life too. Another half-century later, the world is still witnessing the 'Black Lives Matter' movement when unarmed blacks were killed by white policemen for no justifiable reason in America; defiance is coming to the fore.

There is hardly any war in the world where the so-called First World countries do not have a role to play, directly or indirectly. Nations across the world are exploited where people struggle for survival. Dictators and despots are acceptable as long as they are useful. Once inconvenient, they are disposed of in various ways, including regime change, political assassinations and local uprisings, often sending the region into turmoil for decades. Europe is suffering from refugee influx. Where are the refugees coming from—Iraq, Syria, Afghanistan, North Africa and now Ukraine? Why, because of the wars triggered by the West led by the US. Stop these unprovoked wars and the refugee problem will be over. War is good news for the West as it keeps their military-industrial complex growing. It also provides the laboratory to test their new weapons and dispose of their old inventory in proxy fighting.

Little has changed.

> '*I used to think that the causes of the war were predominantly economic. I came to think that they were more psychological. I am now coming to think that they are decisively "personal', arising from the defects and ambitions of those who have the power to influence the currents of the nation'.*
>
> ***—Liddell Hart***

Politicians in general remain the least trusted and most despised class of people across borders. Ironically, they are the ones responsible for people's well-being. According to various surveys, no more than 30 per cent of people trust them to tell the truth. In Europe, it is a dismal 19 per cent. And without research, I can say, amongst major professions, the least literate and educated by comparison. Every job application needs some qualifications and a CV, politics needs none.

US President Joe Biden, Donald Trump, Xi Zin Ping and Boris Johnson hardly inspire that they can make the world a safer place. These countries sit at the high table of the UNSC with veto power that sabotages even sensible proposals like declaring a proven terrorist as an UN-designated global terrorist when the world is suffering from global terrorism.

Politicians have been a necessary evil and they cannot be wished away. They are mostly part of the problem in some way and not the solution. It is time to demand that they also have a CV, which if nothing else, needs proven integrity and good character to find entry into the senate, parliament or state assembly.

In an era when international institutions like the UNO have been rendered irrelevant by superpowers, people need to take up the gauntlet and seek accountability from their leaders.

There are times when the Generals and people must protect their country from their own government. There are times when middle-level officers must protect their army from their own Generals.

Some things have begun to change. People like Edward Snowden and Julian Assange now question the rights of the government to control their lives.

It is the common man who is most powerful when they come together for a good cause. The common soldier forced Alexander the Great to retreat from India. It was the common man who brought down emperors and czars all over the world and today brings down dictators, politicians and government, as we saw recently in Sri Lanka and earlier during the Arab Spring movement. As I write, in Iran it is the women's 'positive defiance' which has shaken the despotic cleric rulers on personal choices of whether to wear or not to wear a Hijab. This movement has found traction all over the world as seen at the FIFA World Cup in Qatar and transforming into a movement against the government. This is the power of positive defiance. Those who have been entrusted with the destiny of the nation and its people must be held accountable when they fail to live up to their obligations.

Why This Book?

On December 1, 1955, during a typical evening rush hour in Montgomery, Alabama, a 42-year-old woman took a seat on the bus on her way home from work. Before she reached home, she had quietly set off a revolution when the bus driver instructed her to move back, and she refused.

Rosa Parks, an African American, was arrested that day for violating a city law requiring racial segregation in public buses. On the city buses in Montgomery, the first ten seats were permanently reserved for white passengers. When the bus became crowded, the driver instructed Rosa Parks and three passengers, all African Americans, to vacate their seats for the white passengers boarding. Eventually, three of those passengers moved while Rosa Parks remained seated arguing she was not on a seat reserved for whites. Arrested, and in police custody, she was fingerprinted, booked and convicted. This led to a bus boycott movement by the African community that lasted 381 days. This gave rise to the young Martin Luther King, the racial discrimination activist. Eventually, the court ruled that this discriminatory rule was unconstitutional. Rosa Parks came to be known as the "Mother of the Civil Rights Movement."

On that day, a simple act of defiance, by what would normally be seen as a frail and helpless lady, and not the obedience of millions of African Americans that changed America for good.

Lance Corporal Joe Glenton, UK, voluntarily joined the army to be part of the war on terrorism. He served a deployment in Iraq in 2006. In six months, he was convinced that it was an unjust war in which men, women and children were being killed who had nothing to do with terrorism, the Taliban or this war. He refused to return to the war on terror for he was convinced the enemies of the West were not the Afghans shooting at them; they were where their own planes came from. He went Absent Without Leave (AWOL) and then returned to fight his case against the establishment.

The events proved him right. The US made a disgraceful exit after two decades creating a humanitarian crisis in Afghanistan as the Taliban casually strolled back to power defeating the mightiest military alliance in the world. No different from Iraq, Syria, Yemen, North Africa, Ukraine etc. Some ISAF Force Commanders in Afghanistan said later in their interviews that there was a lot of tactics but they had no coherent strategy. So, what were the political and military leadership doing there without a strategy? Who was responsible to formulate it, if not them? This just proves that 'Constructive Disobedience' and 'Positive Defiance' are essential to hold the leadership accountable so we do not have more of Vietnam, Iraq and Afghanistan that killed millions of innocents.

I love the word leaders. But I am allergic to that word when it gets hyphenated with politicians—'Political-Leaders.' Leaders are meant to symbolise certain values, character, selfless service, wisdom and vision. Political leaders, in general, are far from it.

When Harry Truman was made the president after the death of his predecessor President Franklin D Roosevelt, his friend Sam Rayburn gave him this fatherly advice:

> *"From here on you will have many people around you. They will put a wall around you and cut you off from any other ideas except their own. They will tell you what a great man you are. But Harry, both you and I know that you aren't."*

And that is so true for Generals as well. Post-World War II, it is hard to find a shadow of Patton or Rommel who inspire others.

As I write, we see the 'Civilised West' fighting the Russians in Ukraine to the last Ukrainian, rather than saving Ukrainian lives by exploring peace. This was not a sudden development; the seeds of this war were sowed long back in the expansion of NATO hugging the borders of Russia. How had the US responded when the Soviet Union planted its missiles in Cuba in the sixties? What did they expect doing the same to Russia?

In the context of this book, the US has been the reference point, for, the US is a self-appointed policeman and has been at war all over the globe for the better part of its existence. I have often referred to the Vietnam War which lasted two decades, for two reasons. One, it does not meet any of the criteria of Jus ad Bellum and Jus ad Bello. Two, no other war has more lessons in the context of this book that seems to have never been learnt.

More so, Vietnam emerges as the most revealing example of 'folly' as defined by Barbara W Tuchman in her book *The March of Folly from Troy to Vietnam.* One, it was perceived as counter-productive in its own time, not merely by hindsight. Two, injury to self-interest was recognized by contemporaries. Three, a feasible alternative course of action was available. Fourth, the policy in question was that of a group of people and not an individual. In this case, five successive presidents over two decades with their close advisors, both politicians and Generals.

The developments in the Indochina region after the Second World War expose how five successive US presidents kept falling into the trap of their flawed logic and confirmation biases. Ignorance was not a factor in the American endeavour in Vietnam, although it was to become an excuse. There was no dearth of repeated contra-indications.

President John F Kennedy himself had said, "If it were ever converted into a white man's war, we should lose it as the French had lost a decade earlier." Here was a classic case of seeing the truth and acting without reference to it. This is exactly what happened.

Clark Clifford, presidential advisor on foreign intelligence to three presidents and the secretary of defence of the US from 1968-1969 said in an interview, "I know we were wrong. We should not have gotten involved in Vietnam. The domino theory was false. I have no hesitation whatsoever to accept that I could not have been more wrong in my attitude towards Vietnam." Easily said; two million Vietnamese and 58000 American soldiers dead. He also went on to state many facts that made it clear that the writing was on the wall, no matter what America did.

Source: The March of Folly, From Troy to Vietnam, Barbara W Tuchman

These foot soldiers validate the opinion of the secretary of defence above.

Captain Randy Floyd, a Vietnam bomber pilot, said, “These were people fighting for their own freedom. There was no civil war in Vietnam. It was a war with the foreigners, first the French and then the Americans. Americans have worked very hard not to see the criminality that the officials and the policymakers have exhibited in Vietnam.”

Edward Sowders, an Army deserter who returned said in the Congressional hearing for Amnesty, “Vietnamese were considered less than humans and inferior. Their lives were of no value to us whatsoever.... Instead of helping the Vietnamese people, we were party to the systematic destruction of Vietnam. Through our experiences, we came to understand the depth of lies and deception practised upon us and the American people by our country’s leaders. The supreme irony is that we are going to be prosecuted by the same very men who planned and executed a genocidal war in Indo-China.”

Source: Interviews, Hearts and Minds, 1974.

That the US seemed to have learnt little from Vietnam is evident by the fact they launched wars in Afghanistan in 2001 and Iraq in 2003 with similar characteristics and even worse results.

The Vietnam War was not supported by the UN. The Veto power of the permanent five made any intervention impossible. While the US Congress authorised troop deployment in Vietnam, it did not issue a declaration of war. So, technically speaking, Vietnam War is not considered a war in the US. Some paradox!

Why did the Vietnam veterans, who had suffered mentally and psychologically oppose the War, as did the public? Why did the American people deride the Vietnam veterans despite their sacrifices? America was made a better nation because just a few good American soldiers in Vietnam defied authority and exposed the My Lai massacre in which over 500 unarmed, unresisting old men, women and children were massacred in cold blood by the professional US army.

Tragically, at the end of it, not one in the chain of command was held responsible and punished. The hope that this tragedy will not happen again, was belied. We will examine more of this later.

General Peers, a forthright officer was nominated to conduct a deep investigation when the lid on My Lai was blown off in 1970. He found the entire command chain from the division commander downward guilty of incompetence or deliberate cover-up. Col Henderson, the Regiment commander was found guilty of a deliberate cover-up and falsification of reports. However, after a court-martial hearing, he too was cleared of all charges.

General Peers expressed his disapproval, writing "**I cannot agree with the verdict. If his actions are judged as acceptable standards for an officer in his position, the Army is indeed in deep trouble.**"

Prosecutor's Letter to the President

Army Prosecutor Aubrey Daniel proved beyond doubt that Lt Calley was guilty on all counts as charged and responsible for at least 100 murders. He was sentenced to life in the longest court-martial in US history.

When he was ordered to be taken out of the stockade and eventually acquitted under the orders of President Nixon, the prosecutor wrote to the President.

"I truly regret having to write this letter and wish that no innocent person had died at My Lai on 16 Mar 1968, but innocent persons were killed in circumstances that will always remain apparent to my conscience. Well in some respects, what took place at My Lai has to be considered a tragic day in the history of our nation. The greatest tragedy of all will be if political expediency dictates the compromise of such fundamental moral principle as the inherent unlawfulness of the murder of innocent persons, making the actions and the courage of six honourable men, who served their country so well, meaningless."

—*Army Prosecutor Aubrey Daniel*

Like the Vietnam War, the US-led invasion of Iraq in 2003 (Operation Iraqi Freedom), was neither in self-defence against an armed attack nor supported by the UN Security Council authorising the use of force by member states. It thus constituted the crime of war of aggression, according to the International Commission of Jurists (ICJ).

More than 31 countries joined the 'coalition of the willing' as the US decided to call it. This unauthorised aggression plunged the world into chaos that continues. Hundreds of thousands of innocent lives have been lost as a consequence of the US invasion of Iraq and new challenges have emerged starting with the birth of the Islamic State (ISIS) and other Islamic extremism threats. It further reinforced the existing hatred of the West amongst Muslims in the world leading to long-term problems.

The trumpeted cause for which the US invaded Iraq, the Weapons of Mass Destruction (WMD), turned out to be false and fabricated, as many experts were warning even then. Hans Blix, the Executive Chairman of the UN Monitoring, Verification and Inspection Commission (UNMOVIC) in Iraq reported that till the 18 Mar 2003, when they were withdrawn, a day before the US-led coalition invaded Iraq, the inspectors had found no evidence of WMD. Neither did the US during or after its invasion.

Extracted from https://www.un.org/press/en/2003/sc7777.doc.htm

Should the military leadership become an accomplice to or acquiesce in creating humanitarian crises based on the unjustified war of choice? Is the justification of civilian supremacy over the military tenable as an argument? The fact that obedience of orders was held untenable in the Nuremberg trials and people were, for the first time, punished for obeying orders, gives the emphatic answer.

In 1971, Pakistan Army let loose a reign of terror in East Pakistan, killing and raping over a million women. Ten million refugees fled to India creating a serious humanitarian and security situation. Distant Asian war, it made no difference to the international community. Indian efforts to resolve the issue through the international community made no headway. India decided to intervene militarily to address the humanitarian crisis. The US supported the perpetrator of the genocide Pakistan by sending the Seventh Fleet in their support to the war zone.

The powerful Indian Prime Minister Indira Gandhi directed the Army Chief, General Sam Manekshaw to move in immediately by April 71. The army was not prepared to launch so quickly and the campaign timing did not suit on many counts.

General Manekshaw stood firm against hurriedly launching the army into East Pakistan, till he was materially ready and the climatic factors were favourable. When pressured, he firmly told her that he was prepared to put in his resignation if he was pushed into launching the army without adequate preparation. He gave sound reasons for his decisions and stood by his convictions. He went to war on his terms and the Indian military created history in two weeks in difficult terrain full of rivers and marshes; a new nation was born in less than a fortnight to live at peace with itself and its neighbours. A case of perfect positive defiance.

Every year, the month of October is a stark reminder of the tragedy of the Indo-China War in 1962, when the Indian military leadership failed to stand up to the ignorant political authority for pushing them into a war for which they had not been equipped and prepared. It has become a wound that hurts badly. On the other hand, 16 December is a cause for a nationwide celebration of the grand victory in 1971; the difference between the two was the quality of military leadership – positive defiance of the political authority when in the interest of the country. No US General stood up during the entire course of the Vietnam War or Iraq War. On the contrary, General Westmoreland was a willing party to the Vietnam folly perpetrated by successive US presidents. It was the defiance from the bottom that brought the brutal war to an end. General Mark Milley, the US Chairman of the Joint Chiefs of Staff demonstrated positive defiance during the tumultuous Trump Administration to ensure nothing untoward takes place both within and outside America. More of this later.

As we shall see, the US Military had seen the writing on the wall as they approached the end game in Afghanistan, but it still went ahead with the hasty withdrawal with disastrous consequences. It took them two decades to realise what was evident at the beginning based on the Russian experience in Afghanistan. The famous term, 'the graveyard of empires' too did not ring bells in the White House or the Pentagon.

Today, Ukraine is the sacrificial lamb being reduced to rubble as a result of Western power politics. The US has manipulated the EU leadership, for its own agenda in Ukraine, as Doug Bandow wrote in his article '*Washington will fight Russia to the Last Ukrainian*'. *https://www.cato.org/commentary/washington-will-fight-russia-last-ukrainian.*

The US Army General Jack Keane, ex-Chief of Staff of the US Army said, "We paid only 66 billion for Ukrainians to die for US interests in the war with Russia." Many American thinkers are squarely blaming the Joe Biden Administration for the Ukrainian crisis, pushing their own agenda through Ukraine and NATO.

The US, ironically, is blaming Russia for the invasion forgetting that it invaded Iraq on fabricated evidence without UN sanction and has been perennially involved in regime change.

Powerful nations manipulate or simply disregard international regulations where their national interests (or fabricated national interests) are involved and quote the same regulations when other countries are in question. The US now is calling for an investigation of allegations of genocide against Russia in Ukraine, while the US itself is not a signatory to the ICC. Many observers believe they did so to avoid investigations of war crimes in Iraq where hundreds of thousands of civilians were killed. US arguments on this issue contradict the fact that the US has participated in various international courts including the International Tribunal for the Far East, the Nuremberg and Tokyo trials and the tribunals for the former Yugoslavia.

The institutional safeguards, as we have seen above, have become redundant, and the world blunders along at the whims of the political leadership of the Western countries. The West has taken upon itself the 'White Man's Burden', to civilise the rest. The white man has been the cause of most miseries and exploitation inflicted throughout the world during and after the colonial era. There is hardly any conflict in the world in which the West does not have a role to play, under the fig leaf of democracy, rule of law, human rights and freedom.

It is individuals like Rosa Parks, Martin Luther King, Mahatma Gandhi, and now the likes of Julian Assange and Snowden who change the world through defiance of authority and seeking accountability. Today there are unknown warriors, who, powered by their conscience are questioning the high and mighty. Foot soldiers like Corporal Joe Glenton and Lt Colonel Scheller demand accountability from the political and military leaders on the Afghanistan fiasco that claimed tens of thousands of innocent Afghans' lives and thousands of their own soldiers.

India suffered humiliation in the India-China War of 1962 because of the ignorance and arrogance of the political leadership and the unwarranted obedience of a lawful but awful order of the government by the military at a critical juncture. In India-China border War of 1967, India emerged glorious and buried the ghosts of the 1962 debacle because of the defiance of one army General who refused to obey the disastrous directions of his superiors. During the Indo-Pakistan War of 1971 for the liberation of Bangladesh, it was the defiance of General Sam Manekshaw against political pressure that created history that India is proud of today.

Politics: Contemptible Beyond Compare

GBS Sidhu, a former Research Analysis Wing (RAW) officer, who was deeply connected with the developments has put on record, what has always been known.

In his book, *The Khalistan Conspiracy*, he has unravelled the path to the 1984 'Operation Blue Star', a military operation to clear the Golden Temple Complex in Amritsar of the militant Bhindranwale and his terrorist group.

He writes how the whole Bhindranwale - Khalistan conspiracy was hatched and curated by Prime Minister Indira Gandhi and her gang, as Sidhu calls them, for political expediency. The purpose was to discredit the government in Punjab and win the election on the Bhindranwale-Khalistan plank. They deliberately created and nurtured Bhindranwale into a monster. Even when he seized the Golden Temple, he was allowed to become a big threat, so it could be claimed as a big accomplishment when he was liquidated.

The developments devastated the nation. Thousands of Hindus and Sikhs were killed during that period of Khalistan militancy. Indira Gandhi was shot dead by her Sikh bodyguards, as was the former Army Chief. In the resultant anti-Sikh riots, thousands of Sikhs were killed. It alienated the Sikh community and created a Khalistan monster that remains a threat to national harmony even today.

Indira Gandhi had also imposed the uncalled-for Emergency in 1975, the darkest chapter in Indian democracy. She was awarded Bharat Ratna, the highest national award.

Politics has no ethics. They need to be held accountable and periodical five-yearly elections are not the answer.

Apropos, the destiny of the world is in the hands of a class of people who are among the least trusted in the world and amongst the least educated—the politicians. Can this state be allowed to continue and put the lives of millions hostage to their whims and fancies? The militaries world over are being steered and led by Generals, who are trained but not educated. They grew up in a world which is history, biased by thoughts three decades old and now irrelevant to the VUCA (Volatile, Uncertain, Complex and Ambiguous) future. The majority lack Phronesis and what Jack Welch calls Edge, so essential at that level for the future world. Moral courage at that level is mostly conspicuous by absence, lost somewhere on their competitive journey to higher ranks. Organizations and institutions are mostly led by people, who are prepared to sacrifice values and lives for dollars, as we shall see. They all need to be held accountable within the system.

Author's Notes

I am an army veteran and I have been a proponent of the 'Doctrine of Disobedience'. I practised the philosophy of 'Positive Defiance' all through my career and am convinced of its value in the interest of organisational effectiveness. I have talked of this philosophy in my earlier books too and have shared my experiences later in the book.

In the military, there is a definite price to pay for questioning the authority, simply because of the authority the superior wields over the subordinate which makes it an unequal battle on an unfair playing field.

I have been privileged to experience most of the operational challenges and combat situations that the Indian army has been in during my service from 1979 to 2016. I have seen the enemy at close quarters and I have seen unworthy commanders at close quarters too. It takes greater courage to take on your own system than the enemy.

It is also true, that every time I did this, I put my career on the line and hurt my personal cause. That I still rose to be a General; just proves the point, that if you are defying for a good cause, it is hard to put that man down.

When people fail to defy authority when they should, there is a very heavy price someone pays. When politicians have a free run, the country and part of the world suffer. In the military, it is the nation itself and the junior rank and file. Over 156,000 Allied soldiers in the Second World War did not question their nation's decision to land on the beaches of France on D-Day or tried to evade military service because of the justification that a blind man could see. They were prepared to pay the ultimate price. Their families too, while praying for the safety of their children, knew it was for the right cause. When the corporate leadership defies ethics, people pay with their money, health and lives.

There are courageous people all over the world who are questioning and demanding accountability from institutions and unscrupulous political leaders who will go to any extent for political expediency.

This book is inspired by the courageous men and women who defied authority at great personal cost to change the world for the better and continue to do so.

In every walk of life, we need people who can defy their ignorant or self-serving leaders and seek accountability, so we do not have more of the Vietnam, Iraq, Afghanistan, Bangladesh, and Ukraine tragedies or the Aurangzeb and ENRON saga.

The purpose of the book is to promote an awareness of constructive disobedience/ positive defiance as an important leadership trait. It is important to internalise it in organisational culture for the long-term good of every institution. It is critical, for the future of the world and the good of humanity is everybody's business.

For those who may find this concept hard to stomach, let me remind them that the 'Right to Information Act, 2005' by the Indian Parliament and the 'Citizen's Charter' in the Indian governance statutes precisely are aimed at enforcing accountability from the government office bearers.

> *The most striking contradiction of our civilization is the fundamental reverence for truth which we profess and the thorough-going disregard for it which we practice.*
>
> —***Vilhjalmur Stefansson, Adventures in Error, 1936***

♦ ♦ ♦

Chapter One

The Necessity of Positive Defiance

The purpose of 'Constructive Disobedience' is to enforce accountability in the superior authority and disempower those who misappropriate their legitimate powers and use them illegitimately, intentionally, through ignorance or expediency.

Defiance is necessary because we are governed by people, most of whom are self-seeking and corrupt and cannot be trusted. Politicians worldwide in general are concerned with just two things: how to get into power and then stay there by means fair and foul and to make money. Politics can easily be a synonym for corruption, deceit, lies and distrust. They are not concerned about people, values or ethics. If it needs young girls like Greta Thunberg to challenge the world leaders on climate change, the effects of which Europe experienced first-hand in the summers of 2022, says it all. If it needs a global 'Black Lives Matter' movement to bring justice and dignity to blacks in the twenty-first century, a hundred and fifty years after President Abraham Lincoln died for this cause, says it all.

Based on the available information, the world has been at peace for 268 years out of 3400 years or just eight per cent of its history. The US has been mostly dictating the narrative of the world over the last hundred years. Since its birth in 1776, the US has been at war for 225 years out of 243 or more of its existence or 93 per cent. Barring the four years of the American Civil War from 12 April 1861 to 9 April 1865, it has fought in other's territories. Civilian casualties have been entirely on the other side except for the 9/11 terrorist attack. Since 1816 there hasn't been a single point in time when the world has not been in a state of war somewhere that includes civil wars.

Some of these wars may have been justified, but most were not. Even if there was a reason to go to war, statesmanship lies in preventing a war. Today, America maintains more than 800 military bases across the globe! Has it preserved peace?

We will see that a handful of people governing some countries have been keener on waging a war, rather than finding a peaceful way out. A glaring example is the Iraq War 2003. The US launched an absolutely unprovoked and illegal war against international law that sent the region into turmoil. More than 30 countries joined them as a coalition of the willing. What about Syria? It was a war engineered by the US to overthrow Bashar-al Assad and not because of local protests. Can these leaders be allowed to take decisions that kill millions of people and threaten world peace without oversight? These political leaders need to be held accountable, for life in Vietnam, Iraq, Afghanistan and Africa or anywhere else is as precious as it is in the West. Wars beget more violence and hatred and it is peace that is the test of statesmanship and the need for humanity. The human capital and wealth need to be spent on what makes humanity better—poverty, health, education, global warming and peace and not on wars that kill innocents.

Power corrupts, absolute power corrupts absolutely. Most global political conferences are high on optics and photo ops and low on substance, whether it is the UN, G7, G20 or anything. What have the world leaders done to control global warming or hunger or poverty, except hold conferences and set academic targets? What equality or compassion was demonstrated by the world towards poor nations during the Covid pandemic?

Is the world a better place today than it was half a century ago? Should millions of people have died or gotten displaced in the last half-century? Should millions around the world be suffering from hunger, illness, exploitation and indignity? Have the high and mighty nations done more for peace or to perpetuate war?

How many political leaders around the world come across as people with practical wisdom, common sense and vision that current and future challenges demand?

The net assessment is that we do not have leadership in any department that can be blindly trusted with the destiny of humanity. It is, therefore, necessary that the concept of constructive disobedience and positive defiance be inculcated as part of the necessary character traits for higher leadership.

Let us start by looking at what people think of political leadership across the globe.

PEOPLE WHO GOVERN THE WORLD

Image: Credit Internet

"In politics nothing is contemptible," warned Benjamin Disraeli, a novelist, essayist, Conservative politician and twice the Prime Minister of England.

The world is governed by a small group of people who are at the helm as part of some system that varies from democracy to a dictator. In most countries, there is no laid down educational qualification required to be a legislator, congressman or member of parliament though all have a laid down qualification even for a peon.

Plato said, as we understand clearly today, the government is a special art in which competence, as in any other profession, could be acquired only by the study of the discipline and could not be acquired otherwise. His solution was philosopher-kings. "The philosophers must become kings in our cities, or those who are now kings and potentates must learn to seek wisdom like true philosophers, and so political power and intellectual wisdom will be joined in one." Until that day, he acknowledged, "there can be no rest from the troubles for the cities, and I think for the whole human race." And so, it has been.

However, Plato began to have doubts and concluded that laws were the only safeguard. Whilst there is supposed to be institutional oversight, they often overlook what they must not, and rarely are laws enacted or implemented that seek accountability from the political leadership.

Source: The March of Folly... Barbara W Tuchman

Plato has simply highlighted that if politics remains the last resort of scoundrels, as the saying goes, the future will be full of misery as we have seen for centuries.

Throughout history, there have been innumerable cases of military folly that spelt disaster for humanity.

Four of the most eventful represent policy decisions at the government level and involve the US. They were, the German decision to resume unrestricted submarine warfare in 1916, the Japanese decision to attack Pearl Harbour in 1941, the Vietnam War and the US attack on Iraq in 2003. In the first two cases, sane counsel warned against the fatal consequences of the course taken. The folly in both cases was self-imprisonment in their beliefs, disregarding the contrarian view and in the most frequent and fatal of self-delusions—underestimation of the opponent. We will look at the other two in greater detail separately.

Admiral Yamamoto, the Chief of the Japanese Navy and the architect of Pearl Harbour, while fully convinced of the fatal consequences of this decision, went ahead with the attack. He is known to have said, "I fear all we have done is to awaken a sleeping giant and fill him with a terrible resolve." He was so prophetic. At a time, when the US was bitterly divided on war and wanted to stay out of it, Japan did the only thing that could bring the nation together and dragged them into the war with the greatest resolve.

Germany was no different in the Second World War. They attacked the Soviet Union and expected the Bolshevik regime to collapse like a rotten door the moment it was kicked open. Why did Hitler and his advisors learn nothing from the failures of Charles XII and Napoleon's disastrous campaigns in Russia a couple of centuries earlier? Why did the US blunder in Vietnam despite the French debacle just a decade earlier?

No matter the form of government, in the normal course, the politicians ride roughshod over the military advice when their self-interest is served by the war unless there are Generals like Milley and Manekshaw. Often, by the time a person reaches those exalted ranks, very few have the moral courage to confront the political authority, which in the best of times is not easy, unless the army owns the country like Pakistan does! Here comes the importance of positive defiance.

However, these examples demonstrate that positive results can be achieved when Phronesis prevails over ego, vanity and self-interest.

If the mind is open enough to perceive that a given policy is harming rather than serving self-interest, self-confident enough to acknowledge it, and wise enough to reverse it, that is a summit in the art of government. Israel has been at war with its neighbours for the better part of its existence. Late Shimon Peres, who held the offices of the defence minister, the prime minister and the president of Israel, understood the necessity of peace for the well-being of his people. All his life, he strove for that elusive peace. I suppose President Anwar Sadat took a leaf from his book which I will mention a little later.

The policy of the victors after World War II, in contrast to the Treaty of Versailles after World War I with Germany is an actual case of learning from experience and putting what was learned into practice—an opportunity that does not often present itself.

The occupation of Japan according to a post-surrender policy drafted in Washington, approved by the Allies and largely carried out by the Americans, was a remarkable exercise in conquerors restraint, political intelligence, reconstruction and creative change. Keeping the Emperor as the head of the Japanese state prevented political chaos and supplied a footing for obedience through him to the army of occupation and an acceptance that proved amazingly docile. Apart from disarmament, demilitarization and trials of war criminals to establish blame, the goal was the democratization politically and economically through constitutional and representative government and through the breaking up of cartels and land reform. Political democracy, which ordinarily would be impossible to achieve by occupation and only gained by inches through the slow struggle of centuries, was successfully transferred and on the whole, adopted. The army of occupation ruled through offices of liaison with Japanese ministries rather than directly. A philosophy, regrettably forgotten or disregarded by the US in Iraq.

The rarest kind of reversal—that of a ruler recognizing that a policy was not serving self-interest and daring the dangers of reversing it by 180 degrees—occurred only yesterday, historically speaking. It was President Sadat's abandonment of a sterile enmity with Israel and his search, in defiance of outrage and threats by his neighbours, for a more useful relationship. Both in risk and potential gain, it was a major act, and in substituting common sense and courage for mindless continuance in negation, it ranks high and lonely in history, undiminished by the subsequent tragedy of his assassination.

Source: The March of Folly... Barbara W Tuchman

Anwar Sadat's wisdom is validated by the developments in the Middle East today. Several Arab and Islamic countries have opened up bilateral relations and mutually beneficial initiatives with Israel. It is never too late to acknowledge the folly and turn the corner, for war rarely brings lasting peace. Anwar Sadat set a glowing example of how to avert folly.

India is a manifestation of Plato's wisdom and his worries. Here, a traditional housewife with a school education of the 8th class can be catapulted from the kitchen to the cabinet and replace her husband as the chief minister of a state, and an illiterate gun-toting dacoit queen can become a member of parliament. Anyone with vote-catching potential, be it a criminal, actor, sportsperson or anyone else is parachuted in as a member of parliament. There is no laid down qualification to hold a political office. It is touted as the strength of Indian democracy. I do not agree.

Well, nothing in the world will be perfect. The fate of humanity is a serious business and people in power need to fear that they will be held accountable and dealt with if they do not measure up.

Corruption has been endemic in Indian politics, as elsewhere in most parts of the world. The Indian anti-corruption movement, popularly known as **Anna Andolan**, after the social activist Anna Hazare, a former soldier of the Indian Army, was a series of demonstrations, protests and hunger strikes across India that began in 2011. It was intended to establish strong legislation and enforcement against endemic political corruption through the introduction of the Jan Lokpal Bill. The movement was named one of the "Top 10 News Stories of 2011" by *Time* magazine. Eventually, the government had to give way and the parliament enacted the Lokpal and Lokayukta Act of 2013.

The Lokpal and Lokayukta Act, 2013 seeks to provide for the establishment of Lokayukta for States to inquire into allegations of corruption against public functionaries and for related matters. It is an anti-corruption authority or ombudsman. Justice Santosh Hegde was the Lokayukta of Karnataka state in 2011. His investigation of illegal mining led to one of the three chief ministers he had named, going to jail. Recently, in an interview with the *Indian Express*, on the level of commitment of various political parties to fighting corruption with institutions like the Lokayukta, he said:

"The truth is that none of the political parties wants this institution to function effectively, but the fact is that none of them also has the courage to abolish it. What they are trying to do is denude the institution of its powers so that it loses credibility. Fighting corruption is only a slogan for political parties. In 2011, when we submitted the report on illegal mining... it was not implemented by the ruling BJP... At the time, the Congress marched from Bengaluru to Ballari, saying the Lokayukta report should be implemented. They came to power in 2013 on this plank of illegal mining but did not implement the report.... On the contrary, they took away the powers of the Lokayukta..."

Source: https://indianexpress.com/profile/author/johnson-t-a/

So, here we are. The biggest beneficiaries of corruption and misgovernance are the politicians themselves whose fortunes change overnight. In the 76th Independence Day speech, on 15 August 2022, the Prime Minister of India described corruption as the biggest menace facing the country and promised to fight it. Well, the ruling Bhartiya Janata Party (BJP) has the largest number of members of parliament with criminal records, as have all other parties.

A number of investigations for corruption against the political heavyweights were initiated when the ruling BJP party came to power in 2014; sadly they are not heard of anymore. Some investigations are going on presently against the political heavyweights; we have to wait and see, or like in the past, it is theatrics for public consumption to be forgotten when the political purpose is served. There are skeletons in every party's cupboard, so, a lot of noise for effect and little else. The public would seriously hope things change and corruption is brought under control. Political debates on Indian TV are theatrics at their noisiest best. Allegations are not countered by clarifications but by digging skeletons from the accusing party's cupboards and out-shouting them. The next day is another day.

GLOBAL TRUST IN PROFESSIONS

Trust is the greatest asset between people and between the leader and the led. The trust rating of politicians across the globe, charged with the destiny of humanity is disappointingly low. Here are a few surveys.

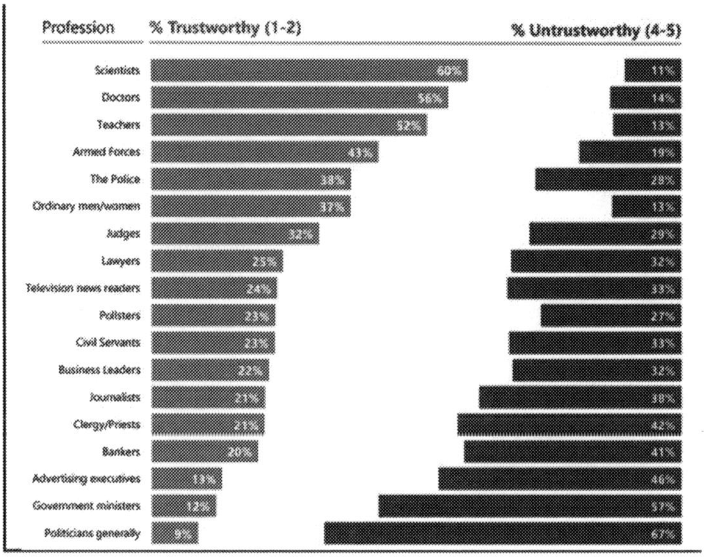

Profession Trustworthiness Index

Top three:
#1 most untrustworthy
#2 most untrustworthy
#3 most untrustworthy

	TOT	ARG	AUS	BEL	BRA	CAN	CHN	FRA	GB	GER	HUN	IND	ITA	JAP	KOR	KSA	MEX	POL	RSA	RUS	SPA	SWE	TUR	USA
Politicians generally	67%	79%	64%	64%	74%	61%	38%	64%	63%	56%	77%	59%	67%	54%	69%	-	75%	73%	79%	73%	76%	57%	65%	69%
Government ministers	57%	71%	55%	62%	67%	46%	15%	58%	57%	50%	70%	52%	53%	48%	45%	-	65%	65%	77%	67%	71%	34%	52%	41%
Advertising executives	46%	40%	55%	59%	37%	48%	32%	55%	55%	50%	53%	41%	42%	35%	53%	30%	33%	46%	39%	64%	44%	52%	42%	49%
Clergy/Priests	42%	60%	42%	47%	34%	42%	29%	44%	37%	38%	45%	32%	55%	31%	37%	-	50%	60%	27%	44%	68%	27%	44%	27%
Bankers	41%	50%	52%	49%	52%	27%	24%	50%	53%	43%	64%	24%	45%	30%	20%	20%	37%	45%	27%	58%	70%	29%	43%	34%
Journalists	38%	46%	41%	36%	38%	27%	19%	40%	46%	31%	52%	38%	42%	38%	40%	31%	30%	35%	35%	39%	39%	49%	51%	39%
Civil Servants	33%	71%	19%	23%	33%	23%	22%	17%	24%	25%	40%	26%	42%	24%	40%	20%	68%	54%	37%	51%	26%	19%	25%	13%
Television news readers	33%	45%	27%	22%	42%	26%	18%	37%	19%	19%	45%	38%	43%	26%	27%	26%	43%	39%	22%	58%	31%	26%	46%	35%
Business Leaders	32%	45%	34%	26%	31%	30%	18%	23%	34%	26%	38%	30%	26%	23%	42%	22%	23%	39%	29%	48%	50%	28%	41%	32%
Lawyers	32%	45%	38%	34%	40%	36%	19%	25%	29%	24%	44%	39%	34%	18%	33%	23%	38%	33%	37%	26%	30%	21%	35%	42%
Judges	29%	61%	17%	23%	36%	18%	15%	21%	16%	14%	38%	21%	29%	17%	42%	-	47%	36%	25%	47%	36%	17%	31%	15%
The Police	28%	41%	15%	17%	32%	20%	9%	12%	18%	14%	34%	35%	15%	21%	28%	-	63%	30%	60%	41%	20%	16%	30%	21%
Pollsters	27%	24%	35%	26%	33%	25%	20%	17%	34%	18%	31%	31%	23%	29%	32%	19%	19%	31%	31%	19%	25%	25%	33%	35%
Members of the Armed Forces	19%	35%	10%	15%	23%	13%	11%	10%	12%	27%	16%	11%	16%	14%	31%	-	30%	27%	33%	9%	26%	15%	24%	11%
Doctors	14%	9%	8%	8%	16%	12%	15%	10%	8%	10%	22%	18%	10%	13%	23%	19%	7%	24%	10%	19%	10%	12%	17%	11%
Teachers	13%	11%	9%	11%	14%	12%	14%	11%	10%	11%	12%	12%	14%	26%	20%	17%	12%	17%	13%	7%	11%	13%	13%	9%
Ordinary men/women	13%	9%	10%	9%	18%	13%	16%	10%	11%	8%	19%	12%	15%	15%	16%	15%	8%	11%	16%	4%	10%	21%	23%	12%
Scientists	11%	6%	8%	11%	15%	12%	14%	9%	7%	8%	11%	12%	9%	11%	17%	15%	8%	10%	13%	12%	8%	11%	10%	9%

Top three untrustworthy Professions

https://www.ipsos.com/sites/default/files/ct/news/documents/2019-09/global-trust-in-professions-trust-worthiness-index-2019.pdf

The World and Europe

The chart below shows a comparative table of trust between various professions including politicians between the world in general and Europe. It is based on a survey from 28 countries as indicated at the bottom of the table.

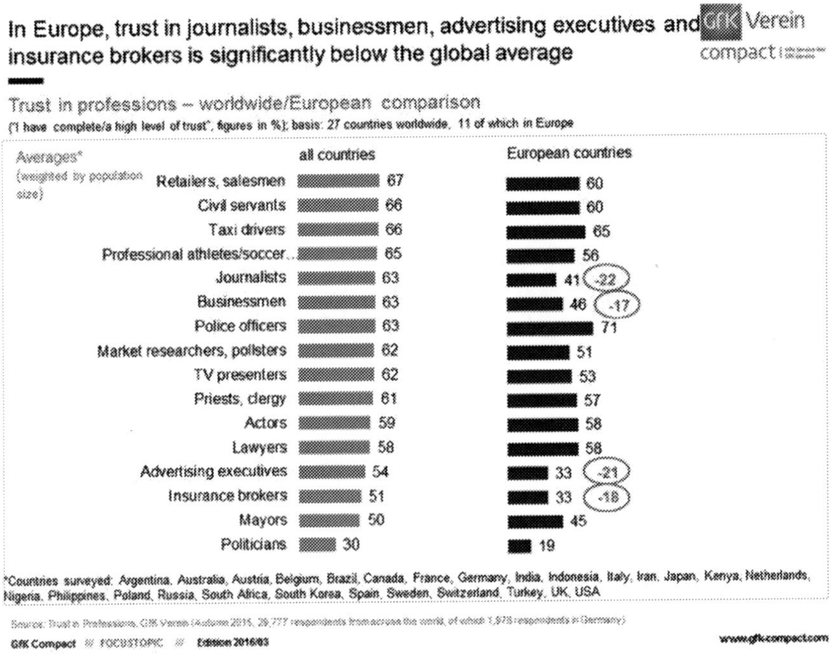

United Kingdom

Just **21% of Britons trust politicians to tell the truth** compared with 25% trusting journalists and estate agents and 42% who trust builders. Despite this, the picture for politicians has improved since last year, when just 16% of the public trusted them to tell the truth. This question has been asked consistently since 1983, making it the longest-running series on trust in key professions in the UK. It shows that public trust in politicians has always been low: at no point since 1983 have more than a quarter of the public ever trusted politicians, to tell the truth. The lowest trust score was recorded in 2009 in the wake of the expenses scandal when only 13% said they trusted politicians.

New polling by Ipsos shows that politicians remain the profession least trusted by the British public, below estate agents, journalists and bankers.

Source: Worldwide ranking: trust in professions, March 2016 https://www.nim.org/en/compact/focustopics/worldwide-ranking-trust-professions

The politicians are at the bottom of the table. In all countries, only 30 per cent of people trust them to tell the truth. In Europe, it is a dismal 19 per cent.

America

Let us have a look at America. The bar chart below shows the rating in terms of honesty and ethical standards in 2018

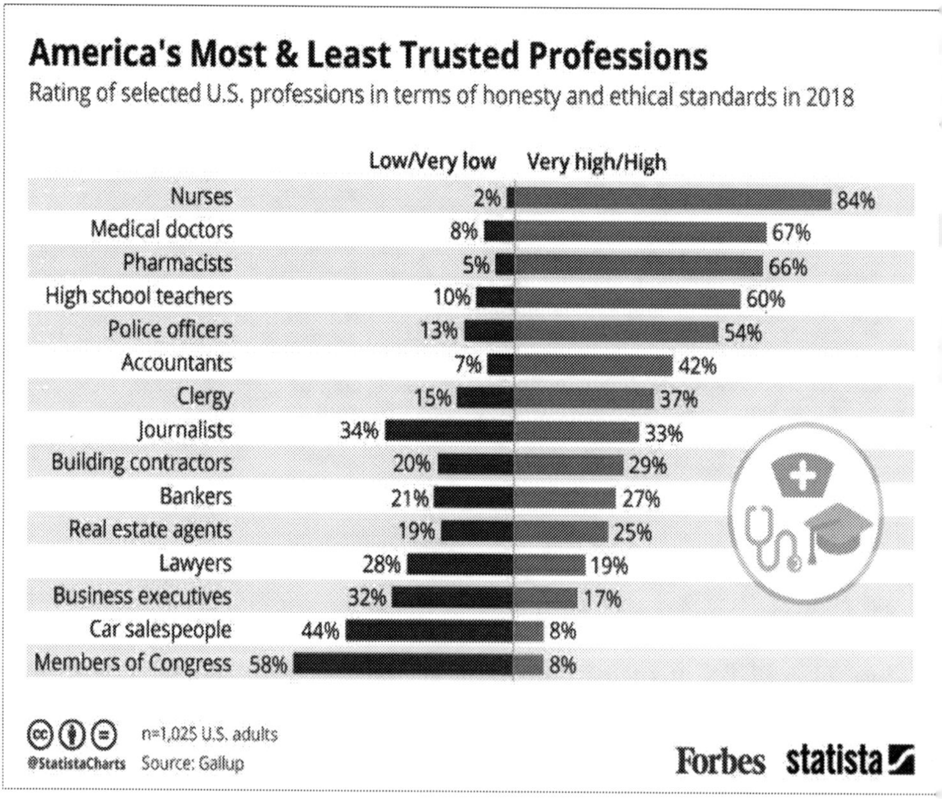

https://www.forbes.com/sites/niallmccarthy/2019/01/11/americas-most-least-trusted-professions-infographic/?sh=f99efe67e94e

Table: Confidence in Institutions in America-2019-2021

Confidence in Institutions, 2019-2021

% Who have "a great deal" or "quite a lot" of confidence

	2019	2020	2021	Change, 2021 vs. 2020
	%	%	%	pct. pts.
The public schools	29	41	32	-9
The medical system	36	51	44	-7
Small business	68	75	70	-5
The church or organized religion	36	42	37	-5
Banks	30	38	33	-5
The U.S. Supreme Court	38	40	36	-4
The criminal justice system	24	24	20	-4
The military	73	72	69	-3
Technology companies	--	32	29	-3
Organized labor	29	31	28	-3
Newspapers	23	24	21	-3
Television news	18	18	16	-2
The presidency	38	39	38	-1
Big business	23	19	18	-1
Congress	11	13	12	-1
The police	53	48	51	+3

Source: Gallup's Institutional Trust Poll, 18 July 2021 / Jack Marshall https://ethicsalarms.com/2021/07/18/gallups-institutional-trust-poll/ accessed on 11 June 2022

India

India is described as a vibrant democracy. It is so vibrant, noisy, unpredictable, accusative, opportunist and often unethical that one is always guessing which politician will jump the orbit and join another party. A party will ditch its ideological alliance to join another with an entirely different ideology—all for power. It is difficult to understand what most stand for. Nowhere else in the world is this saying more applicable than in India-politics makes for strange bedfellows and they change to suit one's interests.

That politics is the last resort of a scoundrel, as they say, is applicable in Indian politics as you shall deduce from the statistics below. It is funny; when high-end resorts and hotels get booked by a political party in one remote part of the country, we know that a state government is going to fall in the opposite end of the country.

The state of criminalisation. Nearly 50 per cent of members of parliament (MPs) in the Lok Sabha (Lower House of Parliament) in India have criminal records. That the system permits them to stand for elections and that the gullible people elect them time and again does not augur well for the country.

Out of the 539 winners analysed in Lok Sabha 2019, 233 MPs have declared criminal cases against themselves. This is an increase of 44 per cent in the number of MPs with declared criminal cases since 2009. This goes across all parties.

The chances of winning for a candidate with declared criminal cases in the Lok Sabha 2019 was 15.5 per cent whereas for a candidate with a clean background was 4.7 per cent.

29 per cent of the cases related to rape, murder, attempt to murder or crime against women according to the Association of Democratic Reforms. One of the MPs has 204 criminal cases against him including culpable homicide, house trespass, robbery, and criminal intimidation. When we remember leaders of the independence movement, Sardar Patel, Nehru, Lala Lajpat Rai, Dr Rajagopalachari, Rajinder Prasad and others, one wonders where are we headed. In the end, you get the government you deserve; the people are voting for these criminals.

Source: Nearly 50 per cent of MPs in new Lok Sabha have criminal records, Anand Patel, 25 May 2019
https://www.indiatoday.in/elections/lok-sabha-2019/story/50-per-cent-mps-new-lok-sabha-criminal-records-1534465-2019-05-25

We are in a system where the fence has been eating the grass for long and now started devouring the soil too. In the Maharashtra state of India in 2021, an extortion case was filed against the state home minister who asked the top police cop to extort Rs 100 crore (approximately 15 million dollars) every month from hotels, bars and restaurants in Mumbai. Both are in jail and under investigation. Businesses have one single-minded mission to make money, hospitals also set business targets that result in malpractices. Where does a common man go?

Bank employees join in huge bank frauds. In India, people like Vijay Mallya, a Rajya Sabha MP conned the country of tens of thousands of crores and fled the country as did others with the help of senior office bearers. Similar examples abound all over the world, as we shall see.

Nothing can be more depressing than these statistics. One wonders why countries fail to find ethical people for public service. Maybe the cesspool of politics keeps them away.

Can you trust such people with your destiny?

Getting back to the Iraq War. Many people in the UK have accused Tony Blair of telling lies and misleading the nation into war in Iraq. And a whole lot of people in the US have bluntly accused George Bush of lying to the American people concerning Iraq and held him responsible for the deaths of American soldiers and hundreds of thousands of deaths in Iraq. No wonder conscientious people like Julian Assange and Snowden rose against such leadership and exposed their doing.

The statistics above validate my contention that the world, in general, is being led by unethical and untrustworthy people. Thus, the spirit of constructive disobedience/positive defiance seeks accountability from those elected to chart their destiny and make this world a safer place. This is a necessity for the good of humanity.

Julian Assange became famous for WikiLeaks and put his life on the line when he brought out in public the true face of the war in Iraq. It started with a video in 2010 where an Apache attack helicopter shot a group of suspected terrorists standing at a street corner in Baghdad. They claimed that some of them were armed, while others claimed that two in the group were Reuters journalists carrying cameras. About twelve people were killed including some bystanders. Assange described the indifference of the helicopter pilots as if they were playing a video game. Then on, a trove of documents was published on multiple sources like WikiLeaks, *The New York Times* etc. That brought the wrath of America and he has been hounded ever since in their attempt to extradite him to the US to punish him on 18 counts of charges. As of today, he is in a British prison in very poor health.

Fast forward a decade. 29 August 2021, in the aftermath of the chaotic withdrawal of the US from Afghanistan, the US claimed that its drone killed ISIS-K terrorists and prevented a terrorist attack. After initial justifications and denials, Gen. Frank McKenzie, the top General of US Central Command, finally acknowledged that they made mistakes. The strike killed ten civilians including seven children.

A decade after Assange had released the video of the attack helicopter strike on innocents in Baghdad, little had changed—innocents were being killed the same way with little accountability.

General said that when his forces launched this strike, it was with an honest belief that they had prevented an attack on their forces. There lies the rub. One side launches a strike with full honest belief and the result is ten innocents dead, who had nothing to do with the Taliban, Al Qaeda, ISIS or the 9/11 attack. It demands accountability, not forgetting that in that complex war, mistakes will occur despite the best intentions.

How many such unreported strikes would have taken place over two decades in Iraq, Syria and Afghanistan killing an unknown number of civilians? Isn't this what Corporal Glenton was saying—why he won't return to the 'War on Terror.'

Does this not demand that the truth of the inhuman wars anywhere in the world be brought to the notice of the world?

Source: US military admits it killed 10 civilians and targeted the wrong vehicle in Kabul airstrike, Anna Coren, Julia Hollingsworth, Sandi Sidhu and Zachary Cohen, CNN, 17 September 2021
https://edition.cnn.com/2021/09/17/politics/kabul-drone-strike-us-military-intl-hnk/index.html accessed on 18 June 2022

These days, the only time politicians tell the truth is when they call each other a liar.

—Alfred E Neuman, Mad Magazine

Defiance

The word defiance seems to convey a negative sentiment. Normally, it won't be necessary if the organisation has a value-based culture of free discussion and constructive dissent. It won't be necessary if people in positions of authority are competent and responsible and discharge their duties selflessly. This is Utopian. A human is easily corruptible and selfish. The world is run by politicians and bureaucrats, and as the survey shows, they are among the least trusted people.

Since there is civilian control over the military, very few Generals have shown the courage to stand up to political indifference, interference or ignorance.

Many countries in the African continent are perpetually at war within themselves inflicting all kinds of misery on the common people, Yemen, Nigeria, and Sudan are the current ones. Africa remains the most exploited continent by the West for wealth and natural resources.

In the modern day, every profession is driven by the lure of wealth. Even noble professionals like doctors have been affected by corporate greed and lost the trust and faith of people. Pharmaceutical companies will not hesitate to follow unethical practices to make more money. Recently, a pharmaceutical company was in the news for bribing hospitals and doctors with 1000 crore freebies to prescribe Dolo 650 paracetamol for Covid patients. Hospitals have become corporate houses with business targets to be achieved.

The Covid Pandemic demonstrated the discriminatory nature of the global world. Barring India, hardly any country came forward to help poor countries. The West has been involved in most of the wars in some or the other manner—most innocently providing weapons and ammunition, making wars a business enterprise. Post-World War II, Europe saw the war in former Yugoslavia, Armenia-Azerbaijan and now Ukraine.

In the garb of war on terror, the state has intruded into every aspect of citizen's life. Edward Snowden, a soldier of conscience felt that the state had no right to peek into his e-mails expressing love for his near ones. He chose to leak how the US was spying on every aspect of their citizens' life. A whole lot of other countries like China and others are doing worse. They are not only controlling their today but their very future.

Chelsea Manning (born Bradley Edward Manning) is an American activist and whistleblower. She is a former US Army soldier who leaked a trove of classified and unclassified documents to WikiLeaks. What did she leak the information for; for no personal gain, no money, political, or other ambition? She too was a soldier of conscience.

What do these warriors achieve by their sacrifice? They spread awareness and enforce accountability on the authorities—political, bureaucratic and military. They enforce caution on the governments and make the lives of innocents who have nothing to do with war safer. In the US-Vietnam War, it took the courage of three Americans to expose the horrors of My Lai, which all up in the chain of command cowardly covered up. Three decades later, the US recognized the service of Warrant Officer Hugh Thomson and his two brave colleagues by the award of the Soldiers Medal.

Well, President Barrack Obama was conferred with the Nobel Peace Prize; the world, including Obama, wondered why. One day, hopefully, they will realize the services of Edward Snowden, Julian Assange and Chelsea Manning and reward them too.

THE FUNDAMENTAL PROBLEMS WITH MILITARIES

The importance of the idea of positive defiance can be seen in the character of military upbringing. The militaries world over are value-based organisations. The foundation of these organisations is the military values of loyalty, selfless service, camaraderie, brotherhood, integrity, moral courage and discipline.

Militaries mostly suffer from a serious drawback of their own making that they do not, in the true sense, encourage free discussion and dissent. Blind obedience is the unstated expectation. A common dictum is '*A young officer is meant to be seen and not heard.*' The majority of senior officers are uncomfortable with constructive dissent in a discussion. In the military, rank equals wisdom—a great fallacy. Given the steep promotion pyramid, just one above-average report could end one's career. Thus, over time, losing one's voice and remaining silent becomes a deep-seated and self-preservation trait; and moral courage evaporates. An officer who questions the status quo or challenges the beaten track or templated thought is an unwelcome presence.

Isn't that disappointing that these Generals who would not flinch in sacrificing their lives for the country as young officers, cannot speak truth to power for the next rank?

Where character and integrity are the foundations of leadership, positive dissent and constructive disobedience naturally emerge as essential leadership traits, unfortunately, conspicuous by absence.

Dealing with Politico-bureaucratic Combine

In democratic systems, the military is most likely to be relegated to the back burner by the combination of the politico-bureaucratic combine despite false public demonstration of goodwill.

The investment in the military is seen as a dead investment that has no visible dividends – prosperity, public good or political mileage. They choose to ignore that without national security, there can be no economic progress. India learned its lessons yet again during the Galwan clash with the Chinese in 2020.

In India, the military is rightly seen as being consistently relegated in every aspect since independence—status, protocol equivalence and pay, despite the demonstrated respect by both.

The biggest shortcoming at that level is the inability of the senior military hierarchy to positively deal with the politico-bureaucratic combine and preserve their genuine interests. The reasons for this are many.

General George C Marshall (1880-1959) became the US Army Chief of Staff in 1939. He knew he needed to change the army from what it was in the period between the two wars to one that was prepared for the future challenge. In this position, he knew that he had to learn new things and do entirely different things than he had done in his career. He said, "In this position, I am a political soldier. I have to learn the art of persuasion and guile. I must become an expert in a whole lot of new skills." Most Generals lack this skill and hence fail in this department.

Professional Dissent. Every organization must realise that genuine and constructive dissent is the vehicle of growth and preempting catastrophic decisions. They must be encouraged. This is even more important in the armed forces since its exclusion would only encourage mediocrity and predictability.

> *'Blind conformation is not loyalty, nor independent thinking, dissent.'*
>
> *Source: Military Leadership for the 21st Century, Lt Gen A K Singh*

Norman Dixon, in his seminal book *The Psychology of Military Incompetence,* after analysing wars over a hundred years concludes that Generals are mostly a set of incompetent people, ill-equipped to deliver at that level. They are trained but not educated. An analytical study of military history validates that deduction.

Having served almost four decades in the army myself, I have come to believe that conformist mediocrity will outshine non-conformist brilliance because of human frailties. This mostly produces pedestrian leadership. Since most armies select their Generals essentially based on peacetime performance of varying nature which does not factor the intangibles of combat leadership, as such, most fail to measure up to the challenges of higher wartime leadership when confronted with it. Higher military leadership requires the perception of the intangibles, a broad-based intellect and multi-faceted skills that cannot be taught in a school of instruction. That is a personal endeavour and needs a long-term devotion to developing that art through analytical study and self-development. Very few do it.

Professional accountability is an essential requirement to promote a culture of excellence. Unless we do so, the incident-free mediocre commander will outshine a risk-taking commander who might falter. In the military, senior officers are rarely sacked for professional incompetence and 'good chaps' outlast 'good commanders' in the rat race for promotion. In any organisation, the best talent will not rise if there is no accountability for incompetence and no incentive for performance. Army, despite its steep promotional pyramid, has evolved into such an organisation because of the redundant performance evaluation and promotion system that is deeply flawed and in need of an overhaul. The other government organisations are worse for many more reasons where the promotional pyramid has become a cylinder and now growing into a mushroom. We will see this in detail in respect of Indian civil services.

Moral Courage

Given the very steep promotion pyramid, ambition kills moral courage and compromises with values as Captain Liddell Hart wrote long ago.

> *A different habit with worse effect was the way that ambitious officers, when they came in sight of promotion to the General's list, would decide that they would bottle up their thoughts and ideas, as a safety precaution, until they reached the top and could put these ideas into practice. Unfortunately, the usual result, after years of self-repression for the sake of their ambition, was that when the bottle was eventually uncorked the contents had disappeared.*

Generals mostly come across as lacking professional military education and tact to successfully navigate the politico-bureaucratic friction, and the Phronesis or practical military wisdom required at the strategic level.

The civilian discretion on promotion to the higher ranks, the service chiefs and the chief of defence staff, dangle a carrot that effectively silences a dissenting voice.

The Indian government has gone a step further. First, they superseded two very competent Generals to appoint the third in seniority, General Bipin Rawat as the Army Chief in December 2016 and later the chief of defence staff. Their rationale convinced no one. It had definite undesirable consequences from the military point of view as we saw during the period of General Bipin Rawat. Now, they have unpleasantly surprised everyone by making all Lt General equivalent in the three services below 62 years, including retired officers, eligible for the post of the chief of the defence staff. That puts a large number of three-star Generals in the same competing basket as their chiefs for this all-important post. So, you could have an officer who is two rungs below becoming senior to the service chiefs if he can convince the political establishment of his loyalty and pliability. The dangers are too obvious to be stated. This also effectively gags a contrarian view, reflective obedience or a dissenting voice against the government policies when required, a pattern we have seen in the Indian Army ever since the two competent Generals were superseded in 2016. This, in my view, is a recipe for disaster as three-star General rank officers are in policy and decision-making positions that impact the future of the military, hence the national security.

It will trigger the race for political favours that is destructive to the apolitical nature of the military. This leads to a dangerous situation, as happened when 700 officers and men bypassed the command chain to approach the Supreme Court in the case of the Armed Forces Special Powers Act (AFSPA). When the leadership fails to measure up to their responsibilities, the onus of constructive disobedience or positive defiance then passes down to the middle-level officers and men—a very dangerous situation. Militaries must evolve top-down; when it happens the other way, it is not evolution, it becomes revolution and that is bad news.

The army leadership does not seem to question this disruptive decision.

While the supremacy of the political authority over the military is unquestioned, that does not mean bureaucratic control. Two, it does not mean blind obedience and dog-like loyalty. The military leadership has a responsibility to safeguard national interests and their organisation's because that impacts national security. Sometimes it may be from their political executives themselves as demonstrated by incidents covered in this book. In India, the politicians have exploited the military for political mileage and in the process affected the apolitical nature of the military. Generals who dare to stand by their convictions are far and few, a rare breed as they say.

This has a serious impact and that must not be allowed to happen by the military.

Courage - Defiance – Generalship

Climate change has mutated genes; they do not make such Generals anymore

Amritsar - 1959. Some Indian Army Officers and their wives went to the Railway Station to see off one of their colleagues. Some goons made lewd remarks against the women and tried to molest them. The Army Officers chased the goons who took shelter in a nearby cinema theatre.

On learning about the incident, the Commanding Officer ordered the cinema hall to be surrounded by troops. All the goons were dragged out and the leader of the goons, heady and drunk with power was the son of the Chief Minister of Punjab, Pratap Singh Kairon, a close associate of the then Prime Minister, Jawahar Lal Nehru.

All the goons were stripped to their underwear, paraded in the streets of Amritsar and later interned in the cantonment. The next day, the Chief Minister became furious and tried to release his son from Indian Army's incarceration.

His vehicle was not allowed to enter the cantonment as a VIP Vehicle. He was compelled to walk all the way to meet the Colonel. The infuriated Chief Minister complained about the whole affair to the Prime Minister.

The perplexed Prime Minister, instead of questioning his confidante Pratap Singh Kairon on his son's conduct, sought an explanation from the Army Chief General Thimayya on the conduct of his Officers.

The Chief replied, "***If we cannot defend the honour of our women, how can you expect us to defend the honour of our Country?***"

Nehru was dumbfounded.

—Major General Dhruv Katoch, 'Salute to the Indian Soldier.'

♦ ♦ ♦

Chapter Two

The Doctrine of Disobedience

This chapter explains why I feel I have the credentials to write on this subject.

When I was a Major in my battalion, the Corps Commander, Lt General SS Sangra, as the senior reporting officer in my chain of command wrote in my annual confidential report:

> *"This officer will prove dysfunctional to the organization if promoted to higher ranks."*

Why will such a senior officer be so critical of a Major? The reason is simple, in the army, superiors in general, are uncomfortable with an independent-minded and dissenting subordinate. They are comfortable with blind conformation bordering on subservience, which they tend to see as loyalty. Dissent, so necessary for growth and effectiveness is an alien concept with most superiors in the military. Today, I can say with conviction that a large number of officers are inspired by the values that I served with and stood for, long after my curtains were drawn on my career. It is just that he was in a position to write my report and I had no way to respond. And he did that quietly, not even informing me as he was required to do as per regulations. While that man became an army commander, not many had heard of him before and no one has heard of him since.

I am a veteran soldier and commanded an Infantry division. I have never believed in blind obedience. I believed in verified obedience and when necessary defied illegitimate, unlawful or lawful but awful orders. In my books on command and leadership, I have propagated the 'Doctrine of Disobedience', as an important command function.

As a commander responsible for a mission and the lives of hundreds of men, one is expected to have his own mind and the ability to analyse the given order. A commander must be prepared to represent against illegitimate, illegal or immoral orders, and if necessary, disobey them; orders that will dishonour their country, and bring a bad name to their organization and uniform, if implemented. Orders that will expose your men to unwarranted risks; orders that cannot be implemented in the given timeframe, orders that negatively affect your command, orders that are used to 'Cover Your Ass' (CYA) by the superiors or higher headquarters etc. This is easier said than done, for, in all armies the world over, there are neither adequate safeguards nor much hope of finding support from the establishment, even when you have a case. The officer in most cases is likely to come out battle-scarred at the end of the day.

It is always an unequal battle and it has consequences in many forms, from career to mental peace and the resultant impact on the family. It all depends upon the conviction of the man and the readiness to accept the battle and the consequences.

UNDERSTANDING DEFIANCE

On the face of it, it might seem that defiance has no place in any organization, least of all in the military, where success is measured in life and death, honour and dishonour, where there is no prize for the runners-up. So, in the military, it must be 'theirs is not to reason why, theirs is but to do or die.' This extract of a poem from *The Charge of the Light Brigade* by Lord Tennyson, while praising the unflinching courage of soldiers also offered a timeless reflection on the senselessness that accompanies much of war. When one is being led by a set of incompetent and self-serving superiors like the 'Fighting Generals' of the First World War, this cannot be without a caveat.

It would be acceptable if the world was an ethical place. We know, it is not. It would be okay, if people leading international institutions, their government, their armies or their organization were righteous like King Dashrath of Ramayana or King Leonidas of Sparta. It would be okay if people in positions of authority and responsibility lived by the values that their organizations and constitution propagate and stand for. Starting from the highest organization, let us say UNO to the lowest on the earth, every organization has some kind of ethics monitoring and enforcement mechanism. Why, may I ask? They are not there to monitor the error of judgment; they are there because of the frailty of the human character.

Men are inherently greedy, selfish and untrustworthy. Thus, they cannot be left on their own without checks and balances. Look around, how many people can you trust your money and wife with when there are no consequences? Those you won't trust are under every pebble.

In any good organization, there should be a free exchange of ideas. Dissent during the planning stage is a tool for growth. Where dissent is discouraged, the boss loses the advantage of different perspectives. So, discussion, debate, disagreements and dissent are part of the planning process to evolve the best course of action.

In the army, one is taught that, if you disagree with your superior, put across your point and then accept his decision and implement it wholeheartedly. Sounds good in theory. My experience is that this cannot be accepted as gospel. While the superior may have his perspective, it is not necessarily right every time. Some incidents that I have narrated prove the point.

Army

During a casual discussion, a few officers who had read my book on *Battalion Command: Dare to Lead,* appreciated how I repeatedly stood by my conviction and when necessary defied authority for the larger good. A Brigadier who was listening to this discussion said, Colonel Sengar's command philosophy is a recipe for getting sacked.

Very interesting; the point he was inadvertently making was that if you cross paths with your superiors and stand for what you should as a commander, you are likely to get sacked, even if you are right. He is right. For a commander to stand by his conviction, he has got to be one hundred per cent certain he has a case and be prepared to be sacked, notwithstanding who is proved right in the end. That is not a reason to back down.

Here I am a Major General, respected by superiors, colleagues and juniors alike. My books still inspire the next generation of officers and are making them more effective and conscientious leaders. It is through positive defiance that you make a positive difference. By no stretch of the imagination is this dysfunctional to a competent professional soldier. I never found it to be one either as a superior or a subordinate.

PROTECT YOUR COMMAND FROM INCOMPETENT SUPERIORS

When a veteran writes a controversial piece, the serving fraternity's first response is, "Oh, they all start doing this after retirement. What did he do when he was in service?"

So, what did I do during my time in service?

I would like to narrate my experiences that border on defiance in different ranks and circumstances spanning more than three decades. Post-retirement I continue to do so, through my writings. I can do so because I had practised what I preached all my service.

Incident 1

May 1983, Infantry Brigade Exercise: I was a young Captain with less than four years of service.

The commander of the Infantry Brigade, an Infantry officer himself, ordered a 40-kilometre inter-battalion endurance competition. This was immediately after the brigade had finished 40 kilometres forced march through the rocky hills in searing heat in the garb of exploitation exercise. For the endurance competition, a milestone on a road was given as the finish point which would be manned by the brigade staff to take the report.

The exercise itself was a professional joke, asking the infantry battalions to exploit an objective 40 kilometres away after a night attack on a water obstacle.

The men had been on rationed water for the last 24 hours-one water bottle in that hot summer in Punjab. My commanding officer's request to give the men a refill of water bottles before starting was denied by the commander on the grounds that there was enough water en route.

In the searing heat of the lower Shivalik ranges near Hoshiarpur, there was not a drop of water. Every single man from the commanding officer downwards was just about staying on their feet and trudging along nearly dehydrated. We came across a small cement tank full of muck, made for wild animals. The men rushed to drink that crap. When I stopped them, my commanding officer asked me to let them drink. I said, "Sir, this is no water, it is all muck, they will fall sick if they drink a drop." He said, "They will die of dehydration if they don't."

The exercise, unrealistic as it was, was effectively over after the overnight attack on the canal. The troops had been on man-pack rations for three days. The cookhouse lorries which would have brought hot meals after three days, which marked the end of the exercise, were declared destroyed by the commander. This order to hold 40 kilometres endurance competition within hours of 40 kilometres exploitation exercise meant that the units would walk over 80 kilometres in twenty-four hours in peak summer without food and water.

Throughout the night, the battalions pushed themselves to the limits, as happens in an inter-battalion competition, only to find no brigade staff at the designated finish point to take the report, nor any sign of the commander. Finding no one, the battalions broke off and the competition was forgotten most unceremoniously.

The summing-up of the exercise was to be conducted by the commander personally. To everyone's surprise, I stood up to make my points, when none were solicited. I insisted that I come to the front of the gathering to speak.

I directly addressed the commander, "Under the conditions in which certain activities were conducted in this exercise, I would like to ask four questions.

One, given the capability and limitations of infantry battalions, is it a viable task to ask the units to exploit an objective 40 kilometres in-depth or did the commander have some different purpose under this garb?

Two, immediately after this, the commander ordered the competition, which meant that the brigade force-marched 80 kilometres in 24 hours without food or water in this heat. Does the commander believe that men can operate effectively in combat this way?

Three, having ordered an inter-battalion endurance competition, how does the commander explain that his staff was missing from the finish point when the battalions reached there after the whole night on the move?

Four, and the most important, under the circumstances, was the commander not expected to show up and meet the troops at the finish point, or somewhere during the 80 kilometres route march rather than be in his caravan?"

The commander, visibly shaken, attempted lame justification and questioned my physical and mental robustness. He asked me, "Have I answered your questions?" to which I replied, "No sir. The issues that I have raised are very basic. They are on leadership, the viability of the task and the basics of soldiering. You have not answered any of my questions."

In private, he promised to fix this 'bastard'. As the saying goes, 'fortune favours the brave'; I was posted out of the battalion. He did endorse in my confidential report that the officer needs to improve his sense of self-discipline.

Author's Notes

What an irony! A man who lacked the courage to accept that he and his staff made serious mistakes, for which he should have taken full responsibility and held his staff accountable, was telling me to be self-disciplined. All because I, a young Captain, dared to point out major follies in his art of command when those who should have, remained silent. The seniors in the army, mostly, try to shoot the messenger rather than read the unpleasant message that will make them better people. That is the irony, the senior can write anything on a subordinate and get away. In a 360-degree assessment, I would have had a view on his competence and leadership abilities.

Four decades later, when this issue came up during a battalion social event, the commanding officer of that time said, someone had to tell him. No one wants to be that someone. Everyone wants a freedom fighter but wants him in the neighbour's house.

In a brigade of almost forty officers, it took one young officer to seek accountability from the commander, something the commanding officers should have done.

Forget my methodology, was I wrong in questioning him?

♦ ♦ ♦

Incident 2

The Prevailing Environment. I commanded my battalion from 1999 to 2002 in Jammu (J&K). During this period, Jammu was the target of increased terrorism by Pakistani-sponsored terrorists. The famous Raghunath temple was subjected twice to suicidal attacks in 2002 and so was the Jammu railway station. The terrorists had launched two suicidal attacks on two army units resulting in many casualties. The terrorists had also struck the soldiers' family quarters resulting in the deaths of over two dozen army families and soldiers.

It was under these circumstances that the incident below happened.

I was having a blissful sleep one night. Past midnight, the army phone came alive. We were not at war, so this unearthly call was a surprise; it had to be important, I thought. Colonel GS (the senior operations officer of the division) came on the line. He asked me to send one company (about 100 men) to secure the famous Vaishno Mata shrine by seven in the morning, as a VIP was landing by helicopter the next day to visit the shrine. In effect, he was giving me seven hours, when we had no prior warning of the task.

This is a very holy place and tens of thousands of people from across the country, young and old, walking, on ponies and palanquins swarm up to pay obeisance to the shrine every day. It is a maddening place during religious festivals; a perfect chaotic environment for terrorists to strike a VIP. In terms of time and distance, it was over 50 kilometres by road to the road head at Katra from my unit location. From Katra to the shrine at 5200 feet, is 12 kilometres walk on a paved footpath. This takes five to six hours. The soldiers then have to deploy on the hills dominating the helipad to secure the landing approach of the helicopter. This would take another two hours; in total about 11 to 12 hours of movement time alone.

"That cannot be done," I replied.

"Why not?" asked Colonel GS, taken aback.

"It is past midnight. You have given me no prior warning for this task. The time and distance themselves indicate that even if my company was to start right away, they will not be there before mid-day. My men are asleep, they need to be selected, organised, briefed, draw weapons and ammunition, for which the armoury and the magazine need to be opened in the middle of the night. We need to ensure the vehicles have adequate fuel, etc. They will be out for the whole day in small teams and need to be self-contained for food and water. All this needs time, more so when you are giving me this task at midnight without any notice. This cannot be done by seven in the morning," I said.

"Are you disobeying my orders?" asked Colonel GS quite irritated.

"No, I am not. I am telling you that your orders are unimplementable in the given time frame. I will be committing a bigger sin by accepting the unimplementable task and risking the life of the visiting VIP," I replied.

"I am sure you realise that when I pass orders, I do that on behalf of the divisional commander. Should I tell him what you are telling me?" retorted the Colonel GS.

"Most certainly, the issue does not change, never mind who ordered it," I replied.

He then asked me to order the party to start preparing for the task in anticipation, while he sought clarification. I politely refused, stating that I saw no reason in creating panic in the battalion when the task itself was unacceptable. I told him that I will wait for his call, and only then will I take further action.

The Colonel GS, possibly realising the futility of pushing me, said he will get back and disconnected the call. Half an hour later, he was back on the line cancelling his last directions and asked me to stand down.

Author's Notes

The higher headquarters tend to cover up their faux pas by putting the ball in the subordinate's court. Sometimes they will put impossible timelines on the unit. In the army, for routine helicopter commitments, the process is initiated a minimum of two days in advance for the approval of the competent authority, which is the General Staff Branch at the command headquarters. This means someone in the chain had forgotten to pass the instructions down and was trying to do the CYA by giving me an impossible timeline at midnight that would leave me in the dock and then pass the blame if things went wrong.

The commanders must weigh the task, and if it is impractical, have the courage to stand up and, if necessary, refuse to execute an impossible order.

I am told that the VIP, in this case, the army commander, was informed of my stand. He cancelled his plans.

What my defiance did was that it did not endanger the life of the VIP and avoided severe embarrassment to the army. For sure my troops could not have reached their positions in the given timeframe. It also conveyed a message to the higher headquarters that there was a commanding officer who will not obey stupid orders and you better do your homework before you engage him.

Two, I did not put my men in an uncalled-for misery on a task that simply could not be done in the given time. This was not an urgent operational mission; this was a personal trip. The visit could be planned again without detriment to anything or anyone.

If the person who created the 'faux pas' of failing to inform the battalion in time paid for it, I couldn't care a damn. I won't put my men to misery for someone else's incompetence nor risk the life of a three-star General officer when there was nothing at stake. I have no doubt a confrontation with the divisional headquarters was worth the cause.

Would I have suffered professionally? Hard to say; that would depend on whom the blame was pinned by the staff for the cancellation of his trip. I will never know, whether the blame was dumped on my doorstep. If it was, chances are, I would have paid the price. Am I concerned? No, I am not. When a commander's decisions are guided by his career, he ceases to be a leader and will let his men and organization down and make wrong decisions. When they are guided by professional integrity, he has nothing to worry about and nothing to fear.

Whilst we are at this, let me narrate another incident for exactly the same mission a few months later that proved how right I was in defying the order earlier.

My troops had secured the same helipad near the Vaishno shrine for the same purpose. The first helicopter crashed about 200 metres short of the helipad as it approached to land. All five persons aboard, the two pilots, a brigadier and two commandos perished in the crash. The second helicopter with the army commander aborted the landing and returned to base.

Then started the hunt for the scapegoat. A court of Inquiry was ordered and the winds of accusation started filling the sails of my ship. It was to be my battalion, which means I the commanding officer, for not marking the helipad properly. Well, it was a permanent tarmac helipad also used by civilian helicopters. It was well marked as permanent helipads are. It was visible from as far as the eyes could see because of the shrine buildings in the vicinity. There was nothing to be marked, except a windsock to be placed on a permanently fixed pole and a smoke candle to be lit as the helicopter was sighted. My experienced second-in-command, with almost twenty years of service, was present at the helipad to receive the army commander.

I walked up to the divisional commander and firmly but politely told him that this court of inquiry is witch-hunting and I will not participate in this inquiry, till the aviation court of inquiry is completed. He agreed with me and the court of inquiry to find the scapegoat in my battalion was dropped at his insistence. The aviation court of inquiry concluded that the cause of the crash was the loss of power due to some technical reason that had nothing to do with the helipad.

The lesson is that well-directed and rational moral courage is indispensable for good command and leadership.

♦ ♦ ♦

Incident 3

On December 13, 2001, Pakistan-sponsored terrorists attacked the Indian Parliament in Delhi in which nine persons were killed. The perpetrators belonged to Lashkar-e-Taiba (LeT) and Jaish-e-Mohammed (JeM)-two Pakistan-based terrorist organisations.

After the terrorist attack, the Army was mobilised in Jan 2002 under the name of "Operation Parakram". I was commanding a specialised battalion at that time which gets deployed in contact with the enemy in company groups over a vast frontage.

Two things happened that brought me into conflict with the divisional commander. First, my state of equipment was poor. Despite my best efforts, because of the lack of spares for the imported legacy equipment, nothing changed. My high decibel protests resulted in the MGEME (General rank officer from the technical maintenance service) from Command Headquarters visiting my battalion to take stock. He seemed least interested. He told me, "Why don't you try the TATRA vehicle engine in the BRDM combat vehicles?"

TATRA is a Czech Republic-produced tank transporter prime mover vehicle, and BRDM is a small-size Russian missile launcher vehicle of 1958 vintage with nothing in common.

I was surprised at this suggestion. I said, "Sir, I thought you are here to solve my problem. You are asking me to do a thing I have no means, resources, technical skill or the authority to do. You should be doing that. Isn't that the reason you have come to my battalion?"

That was the end of the higher headquarters' effort to resolve my problems. My officers were doing their best to do *'jugaad'*. They tried to make oil seals from the soles of military boots, but they never lasted.

During my briefing on deployment, I apprised the General Officer Commanding (GOC) of the poor state of my equipment and said, from the equipment point of view, my battalion is only partly fit for war. He expressed shock saying what had I done to address the situation. I politely suggested that he should ask the staff of his headquarters what efforts I had made and why they did not keep him informed.

He deputed the Commanding Officer (CO) EME battalion to fix the problem. I told the GOC that the CO EME cannot influence anything. I have my full-fledged workshop of 120 men. All that I need are spares which are not forthcoming for the last two years, being obsolescent imported equipment.

No spares came. All that happened was that this CO EME battalion started giving false reports of my equipment readiness to show his progress. Once the GOC mentioned to me that I did not know the state of my equipment and that the CO EME knew better. I said, no one is more concerned about my equipment than me, for my men have to fight with them in this looming war; neither does anyone know my battalion better than I do. That the CO EME was giving him false reports.

It would not only be unethical but dangerous for me to give an inflated report of my equipment readiness, as the GOC will then task me accordingly. That will put the mission and the lives of my men in danger. I would appreciate that the GOC trust the commanding officer's word and ask me and not anyone else.

I then told the Colonel GS of my conversation with the GOC and that my battalion was out of bounds for the CO EME battalion for wrong reporting. Either he conveyed that to the GOC in a manner he deemed appropriate or I will tell the GOC myself. The CO EME never ventured again into my battalion but got a Vasishta Seva Medal (VSM) all right and went on to become the Director General of the Corps of EME.

The possibility of war at that stage was high. The units were all geared up and on the starting blocks, awaiting orders. Recce and Support battalions have unique organisations and roles. There is a vast variety of imported legacy equipment and they were in a poor state for lack of spares and vintage.

The companies were decentralised to the brigades and deployed in platoon entities. The battalion was deployed over a frontage of one hundred and fifty kilometres. This meant decentralised control and necessitated the full-time commitment of the battalion and the company commanders.

Much against my protest, I and my second-in-command were employed full-time to establish and run the divisional surveillance centre in the divisional headquarters which kept me away from the unit for days. A few days later, unknown to me, the company commanders of my battalion, deployed in the forward zone, were ordered by the GOC to establish and run the brigade surveillance centres in the brigade headquarters.

One of my company commanders told me that his brigade commander was directing him to establish and take over the brigade surveillance centre. I told him to flatly disobey that order and that he will do no such thing unless I approve. I directed him to tell the commander in the same words, which he did.

Not used to defiance, the commander spoke to me very agitated and said, "Your company commander is disobeying my orders and refusing to take over the brigade surveillance centre."

I replied, "My company commander is not disobeying your orders, he is obeying my orders and I told him to tell you what he did."

"He is under my command and I can employ him the way I want. He cannot disobey my orders, and these orders have the GOC's approval," he retorted.

I told him, "All this is news to me. I am the commanding officer, and I have direct responsibility and accountability for their operational effectiveness, safety and well-being. My company commanders cannot be taken away from their command functions without my concurrence. Even if these are the GOC's orders, I am afraid I cannot implement them unless I discuss them with the GOC." I told him I will revert in 24 hours.

As the officer in charge Division Surveillance Centre, I was briefing the divisional commander every morning and politely represented against the GOC's directions. I explained that given various operational and equipment-related factors, and based on my experience in the divisional surveillance centre, I am convinced that my company commanders will get sucked in neck-deep if they were employed for this time-consuming staff job in the brigade headquarters. They will be seriously handicapped to do justice to their primary tasks as company commanders at this critical time. The General hardly heard me and rejected the request summarily. He directed that the company commanders will take over the brigade surveillance centres and find time to command their companies as well.

I chose not to argue at that time in front of the divisional staff officers. I went back and deliberated over the issue. I decided that we were talking war and there was simply too much at stake. I had a responsibility to my mission, unit and my men. My battalion was indispensable to the success of the division, and my company commanders were indispensable for the success and well-being of my companies. The decision of the divisional commander was neither in the interest of the division nor my battalion. The issue, I was convinced, needed to be represented in writing.

The same day I made a written representation to the divisional commander.

The extracts of the representation are reproduced below:

> *"The GOC's directions have resulted in my unit becoming headless; all command elements having been pulled out for staff functions in the brigade and divisional headquarters. The unit has serious issues with the serviceability of equipment and the serious nature of tasks of the unit.*
>
> *That the unit, deployed along the 150 kilometres forward zone in platoon detachments will fire the first shots of the battle and take the first casualties of the looming war. The unit has been effectively reduced to a staff officers' battalion. In the absence of command elements, the companies have been left to inexperienced lieutenants and JCOs to fight the war under. My tasks directly impact the ability of the division to accomplish its tasks. In the absence of the command elements, I regret my inability to accomplish the tasks given to me by the GOC. I owe it to my battalion, that in this warlike situation, I strongly request for re-consideration of GOC's directions and the order be rescinded. I and my company commanders be reverted to lead the unit in the looming war. I will provide suitable officers to perform the tasks at the formation headquarters."*

The representation was handed over to the Colonel GS of the division, who was stunned by the tone and tenor of the letter. He saw this as suicidal, given that the GOC had already overruled the request the same morning. He asked me to reconsider.

He also mentioned that my confidential report was with the GOC. I replied that I would rather go home as a Colonel who had the balls to stand up to the unjust order than be part of battalion history as the commanding officer who got his men killed in pursuit of the next rank. Victory in case of a war, meaning the unit's professional reputation was more important than anything else, not to mention the casualties bound to be suffered without the command elements.

I was summoned by the GOC.

"I have gone through your letter. I am disappointed that despite giving directions on this issue earlier, you still represent in writing," said the GOC.

"You are right sir; you gave the decision in the morning. I felt that I did not have the opportunity to present my case properly and arguing there would have been improper. The fact that I have decided to represent shows how adversely, I feel, the decision is going to impact my battalion's ability to accomplish the mission the GOC has given me. We are talking war and not an exercise, and therefore, I felt it was my moral duty to put forth my point clearly and unambiguously as it has serious consequences for the division and my battalion, in case the conflict breaks out," I replied.

"I have deliberated on your case. I have decided that you cannot be relieved from the task at the divisional headquarters, but your company commanders need not take over the tasks at the brigade headquarters," said the GOC.

I thanked the GOC. I was happy that I had the courage to place the interest of the battalion and the division above my own, at a time when my annual confidential report was to be initiated. With my company commanders back with the companies, I was confident in dealing with the enemy.

As for my report, it was of no consequence under the circumstances. Did it impact my unit? Yes, it did. Everyone's appraisal report including mine was well below what they genuinely deserved. Do I regret my action? No, I felt bad for the few company commanders, who richly deserved to command the unit but never made it to colonel. At that stage, war with Pakistan looked imminent. If the war had broken out, my battalion would have suffered grievously in every way if I had not questioned the divisional commander's orders. I would have never been at peace with my conscience if my men had suffered due to my lack of moral courage.

I am certain the GOC realised that I was right in what I was demanding; it was his ego that prevented him from rescinding his orders completely and relieving me too from the divisional surveillance centre.

> *'Tell the King that after the battle my head is at his disposal, but mean time, I hope he will permit me to exercise it in his service!'*
>
> ***—General F.W. Seydlitz to Frederick the Great, quoted in Christopher Duffy, The Military Life of Frederick the Great, 1986.***

Attila the Hun was a young accomplished king who achieved great military successes. His military chief, a middle-aged hugely experienced man was rather curt and rudely frank in his advice to Attila. When Attila pointed this out to his chief, his General said, "This way I serve you better, my King."

♦ ♦ ♦

Incident 4

I was commanding a division in 2013. One day, my agitated corps commander called me up. He said that he had just got a call from the agitated army commander, saying the Army Chief, General Bikram Singh, is very unhappy with the GOC 22 Infantry Division. He has got reports that the commanding officers and the brigade commanders are being called to the division very frequently, leaving them no time to discharge their command functions.

Well, my entire chain of command was annoyed with me for factually wrong and fabricated reasons without even seeking clarification from the accused.

I told the corps commander, "Sir, the report, whichever way given to the Chief, is factually wrong. It is incorrect of him to have poisoned the whole command chain without confirming the facts. In my four months of command, these people had been called to the division headquarters only four times, none of which was avoidable given the prevailing norms, and none of which was for more than half a day. I now seek the corps commander's permission to write to the Chief and clarify his misperceptions."

Surprised at my suggestion, he said, "You sure, you want to write to the Chief?"

I said, "Yes sir, he needs to know the truth and realise that his sources are feeding him false inputs for reasons that sound mischievous."

I wrote a letter to the Chief with a copy to the Corps Commander. The gist of my letter is reproduced verbatim:

> *"...I was informed by my Corps Commander of the Chief's concern, passed down by the Army Commander that the commanders and the commanding officers of 22 Infantry Division are being called to the divisional headquarters too often. The information of the Chief is factually inaccurate and the facts were clarified to my corps commander. As a conscientious officer, I need to apprise the Chief of the facts. I also have a bigger reason to write. That deals*

with the inaccuracy of the report and hence the reliability of the source dealing with the highest office of the Chief himself. Unverified inputs could become a cause of embarrassment to the Army if the Chief continues to rely on such sources and hence my letter to the Chief.

Since this input relates to my formation, I am certain of the facts. At the time of the Chief's observation, I was in command of the division for four months. The officers came to my headquarters four times, not one of which could be avoided as per military norms. The commanders and the commanding officers were called to the divisional headquarters on the following occasions...

To be fair to my commanders in New Delhi, I must mention that the capital, as is well known, has many commitments of great national importance for which my brigades are responsible. They demand thorough execution and thus a significant involvement of my commanders, commanding officers and men. ... I give it my hundred per cent. My commanders and the commanding officers share my passion and my command is highly motivated and fully prepared to undertake any task with the assurance of success in peace or war.

I would request the Chief to give me an audience to clarify the issue which has been of concern to the Chief."

Sometime later, the MA to the Chief called me to tell me that the Chief had received my letter and he has conveyed that there was no source, it was an anonymous letter. Not convincing at all. Well, if there was one, which I doubt, is this the way to dispose of an anonymous letter? The regulations on anonymous letters are very clear and the Chief did not follow them. Biasing the entire chain of reporting against me without seeking my clarifications on the allegations, as is always done on an anonymous letter, can only be seen as mal-intended and deliberate by the Chief.

♦ ♦ ♦

Incident 5

The second incident, a serious one, happened with the same actors in the larger frame.

I had one battalion from the SIKHLI Regiment under my command, based in Delhi. The Army Chief belonged to the same regiment.

There was an incident of mass insubordination in the unit in October 2013, closer to mutiny, a term the Army was shy of using. During this incident, the unit was undergoing an annual training camp in the proximity of the divisional headquarters.

The troops of the battalion rebelled against their officers creating a very dangerous situation in the unit. This unit was already in a state of distrust between the officers and the men, as it had emerged after my talk with the men. The rebellion was triggered when an enthusiastic young officer manhandled a soldier of his platoon who had refused to fight in the boxing ring.

The commanding officer, instead of controlling the men and restoring order, abdicated command. Along with his subedar major (senior-most warrant officer), he went into hiding in the surrounding undergrowth, displaying the worst form of cowardice and leadership, leaving the unit in a state of disarray and anarchy. Seeing him disappear, all the officers ran away too. The leaderless troops resorted to violence, burnt the commanding officer's tents, ransacked the mess and destroyed the officers' personal property. The second-in-command was beaten up and landed in the hospital, as did another officer.

As I learnt of this, I rushed to the unit and found the officers of this unit gathered safely away from the unit. I asked one JCO to get the men together for me to speak to them. I addressed the men, many in an inebriated state.

I heard them for fifteen minutes and then spoke to them. I said I am here to save the unit's honour, not for my sake, but for their sake. That this matter, while very serious, will not leave the boundary of the training area.

They realised they had made a great mistake by crossing the threshold. They agreed that this matter must be contained in-house. As I was saying this, I got a call from home to say that the news of this incident is being flashed all over TV channels.

I told the men of this and said there is little that I can do to contain the damage in-house anymore. Some soldiers had leaked the incident to outsiders, and in no time, it was public information.

During my efforts to restore the authority of the commanding officer, the men in unison refused to have this commanding officer back. Very bluntly, they said, he is not acceptable to us and we will not have him back. They said, of this lot, only one young Captain Chikara can come back to the unit.

After issuing the necessary directions, I asked the men to have their dinner and go back to their tents. Later, when I told the commanding officer what his men thought of him and his officers, he looked surprised, stating he was born and brought up in this battalion and his men respected him.

Many like him have a false sense of their standing with the men. So much for the confidence that the commanding officer and the officers enjoyed amongst the men.

Rugbying the Battalion Back to Order.

The next morning, it was pouring heavily. I had the battalion fall in and got all the officers of the unit back. The next hour was a no hold barred rugby game, with me rubbing shoulders in ankle-deep slush with the combined team of officers, JCOs and the men of the battalion. The battalion was back on its feet and training the next day with the unit command authority restored.

Based on my personal witnessing of the events, I was convinced of the incompetence of the commanding officer and that he needed to go. I recommended that he be attached for a court of inquiry and also not be given the second command of a battalion.

My recommendations were also endorsed by the corps commander.

When the report was perused by the army commander, his deputy military secretary called me up to convey the army commander's strong reservations against my recommendations on the commanding officer of this unit. He wanted me to revise my recommendations in his favour.

"On what grounds, may I ask?" I inquired.

He said the army commander says that the officer has a good record of service and my recommendations will ruin his career. I said, "The officer has failed the basic test of leadership. He has displayed not only absolute failure of command but also cowardice of the most shameful kind, running away from the men he served with for a decade-and-a-half. What record of service are we talking about?"

I told him, "I am not convinced and cannot consider this at all."

"What is the second point?" I inquired.

"The army commander says that you have convicted the officer without the court of the inquiry being completed, hence your recommendations are not justified," he replied.

I said, "I have made recommendations as required vide Defence Services Regulations Para 120, and they are independent of the court of inquiry. They are based on my personal witness of the events and not on staff officers' recommendations. The court of inquiry has its mandate and is in progress. If the court finds anything contrary to what I have stated and recommended, the army commander, as the superior commander has the authority to overrule me if he has the justification and I will have no problem with that. Why should he be asking me to change my recommendations?"

I told him, I was fully convinced by my recommendations and cannot morally bring myself to change them. He can convey my view to the army commander.

After I relinquished the command of the division, the corps commander was pressurised to change his earlier endorsement of my recommendations. Sadly, with nothing at stake, he buckled under pressure. Eventually, no one in the battalion was given any serious punishment. The commanding officer was given the second command.

The Chief had spoken to me after the incident and conveyed that strict action be taken, notwithstanding that this battalion belonged to his regiment. In the end, not one in the chain including the Chief acted in a manner that will inspire confidence in their leadership. It was business as usual for the commanding officer despite grave command incompetence and command failure.

Author's Notes

There were two similar incidents of mass insubordination within about a year in two units. In the other incident, the CO stood his ground and faced his agitated and violent men in an attempt to restore order, getting injured in the process. Very strict action was taken against him, while the commanding officer under me, who abdicated command in similar circumstances was let off with minor action because he belonged to the same regiment as the Army Chief. It was a poor reflection on the judgement of our senior leadership and set the wrong precedence as regimental affiliation was allowed to overshadow their rational judgement on military necessity.

The issues are not so much with what happened in this unit. My concern is with the way the command hierarchy—the commanding officer of the unit, the corps commander, the army commander, the chief and their advisors responded to this. The commanding officer ran away. The corps commander changed his initial recommendations under pressure. If the army commander genuinely believed what I was conveyed by his Deputy MS, I would expect him to overrule me, if he had the justification, rather than fire the gun from the subordinate's shoulder.

If he was doing that at the behest of the Chief, then I would have expected him to have the moral courage to tell the Chief that this was too serious a case to be glossed over on regimental consideration.

In the whole chain, I was the only one who had his career at stake, and I was the only one to stand by my conviction and suffer in the end, for which I have no regrets, whatsoever.

Such parochial actions weaken the army by destroying its institutions and values. The senior officers are the face of the military. When they fall short in values and courage, the men lose faith in the system.

Someone had to stand up for the values of the Army; I am proud I did even when there were severe consequences for me. Even though they found a way around my defiance, they could not do it while I was in command. My positive defiance had lessons in leadership that many in my division took home.

♦ ♦ ♦

Incident 6

Sometimes, the higher headquarters do the CYA act by issuing stupid orders to the battalions to cover their follies and incompetence. In the battle of Somme in the First World War, more than 30,000 soldiers died on day one alone in frontal assaults under devastating fire. At the end of this, the gains and losses were measured in yards. The armies were led by what was known then as the 'Fighting Generals' and not thinking Generals.

I am narrating yet another incident of my battalion to which I was a personal witness. Answer my question given at the end of the episode.

In 1991, my battalion 5 GUARDS, as part of 192 Infantry Brigade, 8 Infantry Division was deployed in a counter-infiltration role in the Poonch sector, 25 Infantry Division sector. This meant a second-tier deployment in company groups extended over thirty kilometres in mountainous and high-altitude terrain. The cross-border fire was a daily affair. The Pakistan Army in a surprise move occupied an Indian village Kirni on the Line of Control which was the responsibility of 19 PUNJAB, of the holding infantry brigade, 93 Infantry Brigade. The villagers fled to the safe hinterland.

All peaceful efforts to restore the situation failed. The cross-border fire escalated to the exchange of intense artillery fire. It was decided to attack and take back the village. 10 MAHAR, also from the 192 Infantry Brigade, in the neighbouring sector, was tasked to capture the village with adequate time to prepare for the attack. My battalion, located in close vicinity of the area of operations was not given any task of any kind. My Commanding Officer was neither informed of the day of the attack nor asked to attend the orders. Having informally learnt of the attack that day, he chose to attend the commander's orders of his own accord as an observer. He appreciated that as his companies were deployed in the area from where the attacking troops would pass, he could be required to assist in many ways.

On 31 Aug 1991, the D-Day for the attack, the commander of the holding brigade, 25 Infantry Division, was giving orders to his 'O' group that included officers of 10 MAHAR Regt for the attack. A most bizarre thing happened during the orders.

The commander was interrupted by a phone call from his divisional commander. He returned and announced that the attack would now be launched by 5 GUARDS and not 10 MAHAR.

The Commanding Officer of my unit, sitting there as an observer, was struck by a thunderbolt. The first thought that crossed his mind was, what kind of Generals do we have in our army? When he sought clarification on the D-Day for the attack, he was told the attack would be launched as scheduled, on the same day. He did not protest there but spoke to his own commander, the commander 192 Infantry Brigade. He projected his problems and the major equipment deficiencies and sought adequate time for preparation. The commander said that his requirements will be provided in location and he must launch the attack as directed.

It was past midday. With the battalion stretched over thirty kilometres in mountain/high altitude terrain, concentrating two company battle group, organizing them for attack from a counter-infiltration mindset to an assault mindset without prior warning and minimum essential reconnaissance and preparation was an impossible task. Add to that the fact that the battalion was short of major weapons and communication equipment.

The dynamics of a battalion going into an attack—physical, material and psychological are complex. The machine guns and the radio equipment pooled and provided to the unit were not tested by those who would use them in the attack. Ordering the unit to launch the attack in this fashion was plain lunacy. Notwithstanding the challenges, the battalion took the task in its stride. But, clearly ill-prepared in every way, the battalion launched the attack. The radio equipment failed and the battalion was mostly out of communication in no time.

Cutting the story short, the battalion captured the village and held on tenuously and beat back counter-attacks over the next forty-eight hours. In less than twenty-four hours, the battalion had travelled a long journey; from a sedate counter-infiltration role to an assault on the enemy, having been launched into the attack most atrociously. There was nothing that indicated that the attack could not be postponed by another day, or, if that was not possible, the battalion that was tasked and had prepared should have launched the attack.

What role did the two brigade commanders play in this fiasco? Neither the holding brigade commander, who was giving orders nor the brigade commander of 5 GUARDS took up the cause for minimum preparatory time for the unit for the attack. A case of despicable moral and professional bankruptcy!

I also wonder where the corps commander was during this all-important operation in the corps zone.

Full credit to 5 GUARDS for the successful attack in the most difficult circumstances. And later, having the courage to reflect in the after-action report, the truth of the shocking manner in which the battalion was shoved into the attack, despite pressures from higher headquarters to change the report.

Both brigade commanders went on to become Generals and the divisional commander became Lt General—so much for our assessment and promotion system.

Might sound incredible, but it was our considered opinion that this was a deliberate act to let down another formation commander and the unit, in which both the holding brigade and the division commander was a party.

Author's Notes

As professional military leaders, whose major concern should be the lives of their men while accomplishing the mission, they were blatantly prepared to let down another commander and unit. And this means more casualties. Hard to believe that in an institution whose survival lies in military values, some senior officers are prepared to sacrifice those very values in pursuit of petty selfish interests.

Now my question is, 'What would you have done as the Commanding Officer 5 GUARDS if you were wearing his boots?'

What did his responsibility as the commanding officer demand? Would he have been justified in defying that order and saying he will attack after 24 hours after getting basic preparation time?

If the attack could not be postponed, why change the battalion that has been tasked and prepared for the mission?

What did I do? Unfortunately, when I was away from the unit for an interview at the Army Headquarters, these developments suddenly snowballed. I was thus unfortunate to miss the attack. I joined them a few days after the attack and took charge of the two companies in that tense environment for the next two months till the withdrawal.

What would I have done? If I was there, I would have persuaded the commanding officer to insist on 24 hours for the attack. I would have suggested that he directly speak to corps commanders if others in the chain were refusing to listen. In the worst case, if he had declined, I would have rung up the corps commander myself, after volunteering in writing to lead the attack the next day. There is no way that you can allow such unprofessional commanders to risk the lives of your men without justification.

Why were 24 hours so critical? The battalion was starting from zero—no prior 'be prepared' order of any kind, not even informed or asked to attend the orders. We needed to organize a cohesive task force of two assault companies from the battalion deployed over 35 kilometres in mountainous terrain. The companies needed to be battle grouped with attachments and detachments. We needed this time to psychologically gear up troops from a sedate counter-infiltration mindset to an assault mindset in a very active environment. We needed to deliberate, reconnoitre and plan every detail. We needed to check out the equipment pooled by other units. We needed to organize, rehearse and attack in an organised manner rather than rush the battalion into attack as happened. That neither the two brigade commanders nor the GOC understood or disregarded these very basics speaks volumes of the incompetence of these commanders. This also casts a serious aspersion on the competence of the army hierarchy at large.

The reader may well ask that in each of these incidents, if the commanding officer had a perspective strong enough to defy authority, the division commander could also have a perspective, from a higher vantage point. That is a fair question and that will always be the case. In the incidents that I have narrated above, do you agree with me? You may disagree with my aggressive approach; how do you find my perspective unjustified and the divisional commander's perspective justified? If the divisional commanders had a case stronger than mine, and if they were so convinced about their case, they should have overruled me the second time too. When you take a position on my question, you should remember that I did not have the benefit of hindsight or the comfort that you have—no responsibility or accountability for the decision that you may now suggest.

♦ ♦ ♦

Incident 7

This is an interesting episode where I as the commanding officer had to make a difficult choice—**obey orders and risk mission failure or defy orders and ensure mission success.**

A seminar was to be conducted at Jammu University on the Kashmir situation. Many military and civil VIPs were to deliver talks. That was a very sensitive period as I stated before. Several terrorist attacks had taken place in Jammu inflicting scores of military and civilian casualties. A short while after I finished command of the battalion, terrorists struck army family quarters that left 31 dead and 47 injured, including 18 army family members killed and 12 family members injured. Such was the prevailing environment.

My unit was made responsible for the security of the venue with many constraints. In that university, no students or cars were to be frisked. No internal roads of the university were to be closed. No restrictions on the movement of students were to be imposed. No police detachments were deployed to assist in any manner.

No soldier would carry a weapon and the like. It was a perfect recipe for disaster under those circumstances.

Universities can be a hotbed of politics and violence. I strongly represented that in the prevailing security environment, it is important that some of my men were armed. My representations were overruled.

I then decided what was best under the circumstances, prepared well and executed it. I armed my men against orders. I put my men through intense pistol handling and firing practice and posted them at important places in civil dress with pistols tucked under their shirts. A Quick Response Team had thoroughly reconnoitred the site in civvies and prepared a response plan in the event of a crisis. They were moving around the area as a routine troop movement.

On the day of the seminar, I sat nonchalantly near the entrance reading a newspaper. The brigadier in charge walked up to me and said that he cannot see any signs of security arrangements and seeing me sitting without a worry, made him very worried indeed.

I told him that I was given a task to be executed with both hands tied behind the back. Over the last few days, I have done what I thought should be done and my time to worry was over. If the terrorists are smarter than me today, it will be their day, and the army would be looking for a head to roll and that head was mine. No sweat; worry won't help.

I also told him, against all orders, I have armed my men and he could either report it or keep quiet about it.

He said, "You have not told me." That was fine with me. The brigadier said he liked my attitude and left me alone—how much assured, only God would know. The point is, that I was given a task with unrealistic terms of reference. To accomplish that task, I had to defy stupid orders and I did. God forbid, if a terrorist suicidal incident had taken place as many before and later, I could have done little with unarmed men.

Author's Notes

The episodes above may appear small. You have to put yourself in the shoes of those commanding officers to appreciate the challenges of defiance. The courage, the concern for their men and above all preparedness to put your neck on the line. All that is not as easy as it appears reading these here.

Thus, it is a call that is not easy to take, yet must be taken when the Rubicon is crossed. I avoided embarrassment and saved lives by constructive disobedience; blind obedience would have been disastrous and in some cases could have been fatal as we saw.

♦ ♦ ♦

Chapter Three

Historical Context: The Deafening Silence that Destroyed a Kingdom

MAHABHARATA

The Mahabharata is an ancient Indian epic where the main story revolves around two branches of a family—the *Pandavas* and the *Kauravas*—who, in the *Kurukshetra* Battle, 140 kilometres northwest of Delhi, battle for the throne of Hastinapura. The war lasted eighteen days with massive casualties on both sides. Interwoven into this narrative are several smaller stories about people dead or living, and philosophical discourses. While the views on the period of the battle vary, it is widely believed that the Mahabharata battle took place around 3100 BC.

It is a battle of good over evil, right over wrong.

The poem is made up of almost 100,000 couplets, about seven times the length of the *Iliad* and the *Odyssey* combined, divided into 18 *parvans*, or sections.

The authorship is traditionally ascribed to the sage *Vyasa*, who appears in the work as the grandfather of the *Kauravas* and the *Pandavas*.

Here, the purpose is to dwell on those aspects of the epic that has relevance to the theme of this book. Let us recapitulate important aspects of the epic for a better perspective.

Kunti was a princess, later the mother of *Pandavas*. Rishi *Durvasa* visited the palace of *Kunti*. She looked after him with great devotion. Pleased with her devotion, Rishi *Durvasa* blessed her that she will be blessed with Dev Putra, roughly meaning sons of God. To try that blessing, she worshipped the Sun God. As a result, she was blessed with a son, *Karan*. Afraid of castigation for having a son while being unmarried, she decides to quietly discard the baby.

She puts the baby in a basket and puts it in the river to float away. *Karan* was found by a Shudra (lower caste) family. *Karan*, thus, despite being a prince grew up in a Shudra family and came to be known as *Shudra putra* (Son of Shudra).

A great warrior himself, *Karan* pledged his life and loyalty to *Kauravas* for being made the king of a small kingdom and for the respect he received from *Duryodhan*, despite being a shudra putra. At one stage of the battle, he became the commander of the Kauravas army.

Dhritrashtra and *Pandu* were two prince brothers. *Dhritrashtra* was born blind and was the elder brother.

Kunti was married to Prince *Pandu* and was blessed with three great warrior sons. *Yudhishthira*, *Bhim* and *Arjun*. Twins *Nakul* and *Sahdev* were born to the second queen of *Pandu*, *Madri*. They were known as *Pandavas*.

Dhritrashtra was married to *Gandhari*. His wife *Gandhari* decided to spend her life blindfolded to experience the pain of her husband and support him.

With the blessings of *Rishi Vyas*, they were blessed with hundred sons. *Duryodhan* was the eldest of the hundred sons and *Dussasan* was the next. They came to be known as *Kauravas*.

Bhisma Pitamah (*Bhisma*), also known as *Ganga putra* and *Devavrata* was the son of King *Shantanu*. He was the eldest member of both clans and the most gifted warrior. His father King *Shantanu* fell in love with fisherwoman *Satyavati*. Her father would allow her marriage to King *Shantanu* on the condition that her son would become the king and not his son *Devvrata*. For his father's pleasure and happiness, *Devavrata* ceded his rights to the throne and promised to put the son of *Satyavati* on the throne of the kingdom. *Satyavati's* father was not assured as he claimed that disputes were likely to arise between *Satyavati's* son and *Devavrata's* children regarding the rights to the throne. To satisfy him, *Devavrata* took the vow of lifelong celibacy, thus denying himself the pleasures of marital life. He also dedicated himself to the service of the kingdom of *Hastinapur* and played an important role in its statecraft. He was blessed with *Ichha Mrityu* (self-willed death) by his father for his great sacrifice and came to be known as *Bhisma* for this terrible vow. Related to both, the *Pandavas* and the *Kauravas*, he was respected by both camps.

Because of the blindness of the elder brother *Dhritarashtra*, the younger *Pandu* was crowned as the king. *Pandu* renounced the throne and retired to the Himalayas as a hermit. *Dhritrashtra* then became the king.

Both the *Kauravas* and the *Pandavas* were trained by the same accomplished guru, *Dronacharya*. *Arjun* was the most accomplished and the favourite of the guru.

When the *Pandavas* came of age, the eldest, *Yudhishthira* demanded the throne from his uncle *Dhritrashtra*. *Bhisma* advised that *Yudhisthira*, the eldest of all *Pandavas* and the *Kauravas* be crowned as the King. However, the *Kauravas* brothers were not prepared to accept this and treacherously plotted against the *Pandavas* and tried to kill them by burning their palace when they were inside. They managed to escape to the forest and started living there in anonymity.

Duryodhan proclaimed himself the heir to the throne of *Hastinapura* and declared that the *Pandavas* were dead.

Five years later, King *Draupad* organised the swayamwar (ceremony to choose the groom) of his daughter *Draupadi*. The *Pandavas* emerged from their hiding to participate in this swayamwar. *Duryodhan* also participated in the swayamwar but failed, whereas, *Arjun* won at the *Swayamwar* by shooting an arrow into the eye of a moving fish. *Duryodhana* became a laughing stock here. The *Pandavas* jointly married *Draupadi*, who herself was born of sacrificial fire.

The *Pandavas* returned to *Hastinapur* and demanded their share of the Kingdom. On the advice of *Bhisma*, *Dhritarashtra*, divided the kingdom between the *Kauravas* and the *Pandavas* to avoid war. Shakuni, the cunning maternal uncle of *Duryodhana*, played smart and the Pandavas were given the arid, barren part of the kingdom, *Khandprasth*, and kept the fertile part *Hastinapur* with them. Through prayers and hard work, they transformed the land and started living in prosperity.

Duryodhana visited their palace where he felt humiliated as he could not understand the unique construction. He kept falling into the water which looked like a floor or banged against the walls which appeared to him like doors. He was further antagonised when Lord *Krishna* married his sister *Subhadra* to *Arjun* and not him. They were blessed with a great warrior son *Abhimanyu*.

The *Kauravas* challenged the *Pandavas* to a great dice match, at which they won the entire kingdom of the *Pandavas* by devious means. The *Pandavas* in a last-ditch attempt to recover their kingdom, put their wife *Draupadi* on the line. Because of the treachery of *Shakuni*, they lost *Draupadi* also.

To humiliate the *Pandavas*, *Duryodhan* and *Dussassan* dragged *Draupadi* into the royal court and tried to disrobe her. Lord *Krishna* came to her rescue as her sari, the traditional five-meter Indian wear became a never-ending cloth covering her body. The sari kept piling up and *Dussasan* eventually fainted, but she could not be disrobed.

India has always had a special place for women. A large number of Goddesses worshipped are women deities. The women of the warrior clan Rajputs valued their honour and would not fall into the hands of the enemy. The women would voluntarily and collectively perform what is called '*Jauhar*', self-immolation to prevent falling into the hands of the enemy. In some parts of the country, there was a practice of women voluntarily dying on the pyre of their husbands to prevent exploitation after the death of their husbands, called '*Sati pratha*'. In such a society, what happened to *Draupadi* was of monumental significance.

Subjected to a shocking humiliation in a full royal court, *Draupadi* took a vow that till she washes her hair with the blood of *Dussasan*, she will not tie her hair.

The Silence of the Mighty. Now, here is the relevance of the episode to this book.

During this entire episode, *Draupadi* kept pleading for the intervention of the high-profile presence that included the great *Bhisma*, King *Dhritarashtra*, Queen *Gandhari*, guru *Dronacharya*, the minister *Vidur* etc. No one intervened and looked helplessly as she was humiliated in full court.

We also need to look at the acquiescence of the *Pandava* brothers to *Yudhishtra's* decision to stake *Draupadi* in the dice game. This is the folly of most people in higher positions in all organisations; rather than firmly opposing fatal decisions, they acquiesce. In doing so, they become party to the crime, like the *Pandava* brothers, who in my firm view share the responsibility for that fatal decision by *Yudhisthra*. This is a case of tyranny through respect and too much obedience.

As per the terms of the game, the *Pandavas* were exiled for twelve years, *vanvass* (life in the forest) and one year of *Agyatvaas* (life in disguise). During *Agyatvaas*, they were to live in disguise and if found, the *vanvaas* would recommence.

After the completion of the *vanvass*, the *Pandavas* returned with their friend

Lord *Krishna* to reclaim their kingdom, but the *Kauravas* refused to oblige and declared that land not even the size of the tip of a needle will be given. All the efforts to provide justice to the *Pandavas* failed and the stage was set for the great battle of Mahabharata.

Deployed for battle, *Arjun* was facing an internal struggle and does not want to take up arms and kill people who included his cousins, gurus and elders of the family whom he greatly respected. He could see the great destruction and loss of lives that this war would bring. Lord *Krishna* preached the exalted *Bhagavad-Gita*, convincing *Arjun* of the righteousness of this war and his duty to do so.

The *Pandavas* won; the entire family of *Kauravas* was decimated. *Yudhishthira*, the eldest of the *Pandavas* ascended the throne. After a long and peaceful reign, he and his brothers abdicated with their wife *Draupadi* and set out for the Himalayas, where they entered the blissful city of the Gods.

When we look around and see large parts of the world engulfed in conflict, perpetrated primarily by the US and the West, there are great similarities. There are lessons in Mahabharata, which we will refer to in the book later.

- *Yudhishthira* was the eldest of the *Pandavas* family. He was responsible for the family. What right did he have to put the entire kingdom and his entire family on the line? What was the duty of the other four Pandava brothers to intervene and stop the disaster at some stage? (Positive defiance.)
- What was the moral duty of the *Pandava* brothers in preventing *Yudhisthra* from staking even *Draupadi* in the game?
- The result of the dice game being what it was, the greatest travesty was the humiliation of *Draupadi* in the grand durbar. In this episode, none of the distinguished personalities, King *Dhritarashtra* or other elders including the wise man *Bhisma*, while fully pained and distressed by the happening, failed to intervene in support of righteousness. (Positive defiance.)
- While the younger generation of *Kauravas* led by *Duryodhan* was leading the kingdom up the path of destruction, the elder generation with all the authority was more culpable for their failure to prevent the doom, which they clearly saw coming.

It was the murderous silence of those in authority and their lack of courage to intervene that led to the destruction of the kingdom.

Dhritrashtra helplessly says, "***I know what is wrong, but I am not able to stop it. I know what is right, but I am unable to do it.***"

In this book, I have quoted officers and men of relatively junior or insignificant positions in the army, rising to the call of their conscience and speaking up against their country's unjustified wars that were killing hundreds of innocent civilians. The senior officers and political heavyweights, who should have and could have made a positive difference to their countries did not.

It is important to recapitulate and examine the reasons why these great men failed to intervene.

After the war is over, *Bhishma* is lying on the deathbed of hundreds of arrows that have pierced his body, still alive because of the boon of *Icha mrityu.*

The *Pandavas* go to seek the blessings of *Bhisma. Yudhisthira* seeks his advice on the matters of life, spirituality and statecraft. While speaking about these subjects, *Bhishma* says:

"One should not stay silent when injustice is happening. One should try and stop it; if they cannot stop it, they should at least leave that place and go."

On listening to these words, *Draupadi* laughs and this makes *Yudhishthira's* face go red.

Here Bhishma says to *Yudhishthira*:

> *"I know why Draupadi is laughing. She is laughing because, I, who am speaking these good words now, was silent when she suffered the* ghor apmaaan *(great dishonour) in Duryodhana's court. Draupadi, I was silent then because my blood was polluted. I was eating the food of Duryodhana and that food polluted me and my thought process. Your husband Arjuna has pierced my body with so many arrows that I cannot even bend my thumb. All the polluted blood is out of my body and my mind can think clearly now. Hence, I am able to speak all this."*

This story is routinely taught in many households in India to signify the importance of being with good people. Good people relate to the behaviour and character of the person and not to their caste, creed or religion.

It is taught that a person who does not care for his parents, who earns without putting in the effort, who eats before his guests, a person who constantly thinks of stealing others' property, a person who is not able to give up a feud and makes it a long-standing enmity, who eats without offering food to God, who enjoys killing etc ... are papatmas (sinful) and food from such houses is bound to make you lose your wisdom.

Bhishma cites this and says that his mind was polluted as he lived on the food given by Duryodhana who wanted to take away others' lands and properties.

In the same fashion, *Karan* the great warrior, who was also the eldest brother of *Pandavas*, maintained his loyalty to *Duryodhan* despite his actions because of the favours that he had accepted from him.

So, when Generals, or for that matter anyone else is promoted over others, they come under obligation, and their blood gets polluted as was the case with *Bhisma* and *Karan*. Often, this prevents them from performing their righteous duty.

RAMAYANA

Different views notwithstanding, based on astronomical information such as the position of constellations and time of eclipses available in scriptures, it is believed that events in the Ramayana took place 7,000 years ago.

In short, the story goes like this.

Dasharatha was the King of Ayodhya and had three wives and four sons. *Rama* was the eldest and his mother was *Kaushalya*. *Bharata* was the son of *Dasharatha's* second and favourite wife, *Kaikeyi*. The other two were twins, *Lakshmana* and *Shatrughna* whose mother was *Sumitra*. The four sons grow up into fine young men and were tutored by the greatest rishis, including *Vasishtha*, the raj guru.

In the neighbouring kingdom, King *Janak's* daughter was named *Sita*. In the legend, *Sita* is said to be the daughter of *Bhudevi* or mother earth, and *Janak* is said to have found her while tilling the land.

When it was time for *Sita* to choose her bridegroom (at a ceremony called a swayamvara) princes from all over the land were asked to string a giant bow which no one could lift. *Rama* picked it up with ease; he not only strung the bow but also broke it. Seeing this, *Sita* indicated that she had chosen *Rama* as her husband by putting a garland around his neck. Their love became a model for the entire kingdom as they looked after the kingdom under the watchful eye of his father the king.

A few years later, King *Dasharatha* decided it was time to give his throne to his eldest son *Rama* and retire to the forest. Everyone seemed pleased, save Queen *Kaikeyi* since she wanted her son *Bharata* to rule. Earlier, during a fierce battle, *Kaikeyi* who was acting as *Dashrath's* charioteer had saved his life when he was injured and his chariot was immobilised. Happy with her service, he offered her two boons, which she chose to ask for later. Because of this oath, she got the king to agree to banish *Rama* for fourteen years and to crown *Bharata* as the king, even though the king pleaded with her not to demand such a request. The devastated king could not face *Rama* and it was Queen *Kaikeyi* who told *Rama* the king's decree. *Rama*, always an epitome of virtues, was content to go into banishment in the forest. *Sita* and *Lakshmana* accompanied him in his exile.

Having succumbed to the pressures of Queen *Kaikeyi* and being plagued by regrets, King *Dashrath* fell sick and died.

Bharata never forgave his mother for her selfishness and ruled in the name of Lord *Rama*. During his absence, he placed *Rama's* wooden footwear on the throne, always longing for his return.

In the forest, *Surphanaka*, a female rakshasa (demon) princess is attracted to *Rama* and tries to seduce him. She threatens and attacks *Sita*. Seeing this, *Lakshmana* cuts off her nose and drives her away. She returned to her brother *Ravana*, the ten-headed ruler of Lanka. In retaliation, *Ravana* devised a plan to abduct *Sita* after hearing about her incomparable beauty. He sent one of his demons disguised as a magical golden deer to entice *Sita*. To please *Sita*, *Rama* and *Lakshmana* went hunting the deer. They drew a protective circle around *Sita* and told her that she would be safe as long as she did not step outside the circle. After *Rama* and *Lakshmana* left, *Ravana* appeared as a holy man begging for alms. The moment *Sita* stepped outside the circle to give him food, *Ravana* abducted her and carried her to his kingdom in Lanka (modern-day Sri Lanka).

Rama then sought the help of a band of monkeys to help him find *Sita*. *Hanuman*, the general of the monkey band could fly since his father is the wind. He flew to Lanka and, finding *Sita* in the grove, comforted her and told her *Rama* would come to save her soon. *Ravana's* men captured *Hanuman*, and Ravana ordered them to wrap *Hanuman's* tail in cloth and set it on fire. With his tail burning, *Hanuman* escaped and hopped all over setting Lanka on fire. He then flew back to *Rama* to tell him where *Sita* was.

Rama, *Lakshmana* and the monkey army built a bridge from the southern tip of India to Lanka and crossed over to Lanka where a cosmic battle ensued. *Rama* killed several of *Ravana's* brothers and eventually confronted the ten-headed *Ravana*. He killed *Ravana*, freed *Sita* and after *Sita* proved her purity, they returned to Ayodhya where *Bharata* returned the crown to him.

Source: summary adapted from www.indhistory.org

Author's Notes

Respect for superiors and elders should not prevent a person from doing his moral duty, however unpleasant.

I wish to highlight a few important aspects from these two epics which I will be relating to some issues later.

The lessons of Mahabharata apply today. The silence of those who had the responsibility to intervene resulted in an unavoidable war that killed an unknown number of people on both sides. A whole generation of princes and youth were killed.

While the *Pandavas* ruled for apparently four decades in a peaceful environment post their victory, the magnitude of casualties was so high that it is presumed that they would have presided over a desolate kingdom of war-widowed women, orphaned children and old men. In the same manner, the world lost over 100 million people in the two World Wars. In the Second, because of one man, fanned by a circle of sycophants and evil men, Russia lost most of the young generation and six million Jews were killed. Two million Vietnamese were killed in the US-Vietnam War and the Iraqis lost hundreds of thousands of people in the US-led war on false and fabricated evidence, based on primarily the decision of one man—George Bush. So, what these misplaced 'righteous' wars inflicted by the West left were countries of widows, orphans and grieving mothers.

Bhisma tells *Draupadi* on his deathbed of arrows that his blood was polluted because he was eating the food of the evil-minded *Duryodhan*. Similarly, political leaders surround themselves with people who cocoon them from outside advice and that can lead to disaster. Their blood is polluted by selfishness and a false sense of loyalty, which becomes disloyalty to the country and its people—like *Karan*. More of this later.

So, when the government institutes a policy where chiefs are selected on their whims, superseding meritorious officers, the Bhisma explanation comes into play. Their blood gets polluted because of the obligation, like *Karan*, and they fail to discharge their duty desirably.

Both Mahabharata and Ramayana were righteous wars fought for the victory of good over evil.

Let us examine a very important aspect of Ramayana. Should King *Dashrath* have declined to keep his promise when he saw that Queen *Kaikeyi's* intention was devastatingly evil, resulting in gross injustice to many?

It was a great injustice to the entire people of his kingdom who loved *Rama* and wished to see him as their king. If he had done so, would it have been unethical on his part or justified? Would he have been considered unrighteous? How would history have judged him? In fulfilling his promise to an evil-minded Queen, he inflicted misery on a whole lot of people including Queen *Kaushalya* for no fault of hers, *Rama* and his subjects.

The other aspect is the righteousness of *Bharata*, who understood that the throne was not his by right. His righteousness led to peace and harmony and a peaceful return of the kingdom to the rightful owner Lord *Rama* under whom a peaceful reign prevailed. Compare this with the Mughal rulers in India who killed their brothers and fathers for the throne. In the modern-day, the great depths to which political leaders can go for power are despicable. The siege of Capitol Hill by Trump supporters in a country that prides itself on its democracy and values is unprecedented.

In the Indian context, it was the charitable General Nathu Singh, who was the modern-day *Bharata*, who not only questioned PM Nehru on appointing a British General as the Indian Armed Forces Chief but declined the post of the Chief and recommended General Cariappa.

What are the lessons here for the present world?

These epic battles have impacted the Indian psyche very strongly. It led to the concept of '**Dharma**' and of fighting only the righteous wars. Perhaps, this is the reason, why no Indian King ever went on an expansionist war beyond the subcontinent or failed to act proactively against perceived threats.

However, all that legacy of righteousness means nothing today. Everything is dusted under the carpet by two simple statements, 'I was misunderstood or quoted out of context' or 'political vendetta and conspiracy' etc. The very One Rank One Pension (OROP) that was promised by the government on the floor of the Parliament was fiercely contested by them in the Supreme Court.

Source: India's Battlefields, From Kurukshetra to Balakot, Ajay Singh.

Which modern war except World War II would qualify as a righteous war? Righteous because the Nazis had an inhuman and destructive ideology that had no place in the world and had to be fought. Wars that are not supported by the UN will never fall into this category, and neither will all the wars sanctioned by them because of the manipulation that this organization is subjected to by the powerful countries.

The present world is intricately interdependent. No country is isolated and no one can survive alone. One incident impacts the whole world, and we have seen that in Ukraine. The political leadership will be guided by their own narrow agenda and that invariably brings immense misery to humanity all over the world. I wonder why has the US and Europe not fought climate change, poverty and African humanitarian crises with a fraction of the zeal with which they are fighting Russians to the last Ukrainian. If Russia prevails in Ukraine, the world will not come to an end, but if the world fails to prevail in climate change, many countries will be wiped off the face of the earth and the consequences for the world are too terrifying to think.

So, it is here that the people must rise when their governments and political leaders are climbing the wrong pole, as the Americans did against the war in Vietnam and many other countries.

> "*The only thing necessary for the triumph of evil is for the good men to do nothing.*"
>
> —***Anonymous***

♦ ♦ ♦

Chapter Four

In Search of Morality in Warfare

The Laws of Conflict are Silenced by the Roar of the Artillery guns.

—***Anonymous***

EVOLUTION OF LAWS OF CONFLICT AND MILITARY ETHICS

The wars till the middle 19th century were essentially fought without rules. Means did not matter. Might was right and brutality was the accepted norm. There was no such thing as humanism in war, barring individual exceptions. Wonder, if it is there even today! Conquest of territory, loot and plunder, brutal massacres, rapes and slaves were the order of the day. The losers had no rights of any kind. If it was a Muslim invader, there were some more choices—convert to Islam or die.

The law of armed conflict is based on our customs and traditions and our experience of armed conflict throughout the ages. A good example is a universal ban on poisoning as a form of warfare, which dates back to ancient times when, for example, the military on both sides would issue orders not to poison wells, as much for their benefit as for that of the civilian population.

Although the foundations of the modern law of armed conflict are very old, it was only in the second half of the nineteenth century that the customary principles began to be codified in specific binding multilateral agreements.

The states saw the need to lay down precise written guidelines that provide greater clarity.

The first treaty was born quite literally on the battlefield of Solferino in 1859. Here some 30,000 soldiers were left wounded or dead within the space of a few hours. Army medical services were virtually non-existent at the time. The scene of carnage was witnessed by a Swiss businessman, Henry Dunant, who happened to be in the region. He postponed his business trip and with the help of local villagers, did what he could to assist. On his return to Geneva, Dunant wrote a book on his experience, *A Memory of Solferino*. In it, he suggested that the States should "formulate some international principles sanctioned by a Convention inviolate in character" and give legal protection to wounded soldiers in the field. His proposals received enormous support all over Europe.

Dunant's practical experiences of battle led to a diplomatic conference in Geneva, Switzerland, which resulted in the initial Geneva Convention of August 1864 for the Amelioration of the Condition of the Wounded and Sick in Armies in the Field. For the very first time, States agreed to limit, in an international treaty open to all, their own power to wage war in favour of the individual, and for the first time, the war gave way to the written law. Modern international humanitarian law or the law of armed conflict had been born.

The twentieth century saw the two most brutal wars, World Wars I and II. World War I led to the establishment of the League of Nations and World War II led to the establishment of the United Nations Organization to prevent and manage conflicts and facilitate the rule of law. The 21st Century saw many serious conflicts that killed millions, despite these organizations and the law of armed conflict.

The 1949 Geneva Conventions became the core of humanitarian law and have been accepted by almost every member State of the United Nations that defined that the prisoners of war (PWs), the non-combatants, the medical personnel and establishments and the civilian population had to be protected and treated with dignity.

Over the years, with the changing character of warfare, new conventions banning weapons of mass destruction i.e. biological and chemical weapons and regulations regarding the proliferation of nuclear weapons etc. were introduced.

Source: The Law of the Armed Conflict. https://www.icrc.org/en/doc/assets/files/other/law1_final.pdf

Shortly after this, in 1868 in St Petersburg, Russia, an international treaty was drawn up prohibiting the use of certain types of weapons and explosives. The St Petersburg Declaration, as the treaty is called, was the first to limit the use of a weapon of war. It also codified the customary principle prohibiting the use of weapons that cause unnecessary suffering or superfluous injury, which is still valid today.

These two international conferences were therefore the starting point of the contemporary law of armed conflict. Both dealt with practical aspects of war: the first, which protects the victims of armed conflicts, has generally become known as Geneva Law; the second, which contains restrictions and prohibitions on the means and methods of warfare, is known as the Hague Law. The terms derive from the fact that the relevant treaties were drafted primarily in those cities.

Geneva Law

Geneva law comprises the four Geneva Conventions drawn up in 1949 (which supplemented the earlier Conventions of 1864, 1906 and 1929). They concentrate on protecting the victims of armed conflict:

- The First Geneva Convention protects the wounded and sick on land;
- The Second Geneva Convention protects the wounded, sick and shipwrecked at sea;
- The Third Geneva Convention deals with the status and treatment of prisoners of war;
- The Fourth Geneva Convention protects civilians in times of war.

THE LAWS, THE ETHICS AND THE FARCE

A code of ethics is necessary to regulate human behaviour. There are two ways to do so, one is the influence of conscience and character, and the other is the fear of deterrence. The first is often conspicuous by its absence. The second is mostly ineffective as we shall see in this book. Only a negligible percentage of humanity is ethical by choice and it is for this reason that every organization worth the name has an institutionalised code of ethics and ethics committee.

Politicians across borders and oceans, as a class, have earned a universal reputation that they cannot be proud of. Unfortunately, they chart the destiny of humanity. Across countries, they will go to any depth to win an election; we saw a manifestation of this in the siege of Capitol Hill, in a country that sees itself as the trendsetter in human values and democracy. In India, out of over 535 members of parliament (MP), about 40 per cent have serious criminal cases against them. In India, you need to be a high school pass to get the job of a peon; you need no qualification to be a member of parliament (MP) or a minister or a member of the State Legislative Assembly (MLA). In India, politicians declare with pride the number of times they have been in jail. It is India's misfortune that the politicians, when released after the jail term for corruption or other crimes are welcomed along the road by lakhs of people.

It is no different in spirit in most parts of the world.

For unscrupulous politicians, human lives do not matter, neither of their countrymen nor others and we shall see this.

Madeline Albright was the US Secretary of State from 1997 to 2001. During an interview, she was asked "Half a million children have died in Iraq, more than children who died in Hiroshima. Is the price worth it?"

Madeline replied, "I think, it is a very hard choice, but the price, we see the price is worth it."

What sanity could be expected from her if half a million children's lives can be dismissed without batting an eyelid? Would it be the same if half of them were American or European children? And, she held the important position of Secretary of State in the US.

Given her and by extension the Western world's indifference to the deaths of half a million children, hate and violence are only to be expected from those affected.

In a speech on 26 Mar 1997, Madeline Albright talked of Iraq meeting international standards. Which standards was she talking of? Standards of American unilateralism and exceptionalism, the standards of Western colonialism and exploitation, and the standards of the US and British governments that defied the UN to attack Iraq on the baseless charges of weapons of mass destruction. The 31-nation coalition of the willing joined the US in its illegal invasion of Iraq. Standards of Western Civilisation where two World Wars killed over 100 million people. The American standards of regime change killing innocent people all over the world in the name of democracy and freedom by defying the United Nations? The Western world policies have led to the destruction of Ukraine in the ongoing war.

What about the prolonged NATO bombing of Yugoslavia without the sanction of the UN Security Council? As long as there is White Man's exceptionalism and unilateralism there will be defiance. It will take place in some form, terrorism, asymmetric warfare, and the 9/11 type of attacks.

This was an unethical world and will remain so. As in the past, might is right today as well.

The behaviour of the Western World comes from its aggressive past. They have exploited the world since time immemorial and doing it now. The rise of Asia as an economic and military power is shifting their balance of exploitation and it is hurting them.

Compare that with India. The battles in historic India were fought based on rules. It started with the sound of a conch shell or trumpet at sunrise and ended at sunset with the sound of a conch shell. A soldier fought a soldier, the king fought the king, and no one attacked from the rear. At night, they were safe to look after the dead and the wounded and stay in peace. Indian customs prevented the killing of fleeing enemies, unarmed soldiers and the civilian population. The great Indian Epic, the Mahabharata and the Ramayana were battles for the victory of good over evil. In these epics, the Indian culture of tolerance, brotherhood, and respect for all living beings shaped the Indian Values that are reflected in the conduct of the Indian Army. No Indian ruler in its history ever went on an expansionist campaign beyond the geographical India of the times. They never killed anyone off the battlefield or those who surrendered. They never destroyed any religious structures, libraries or buildings. They never forced anyone to convert to Hinduism. The Muslim Kings did exactly this over centuries in India and it shows in their thoughts and actions today. The ancient Bamiyan Buddha statues in Afghanistan, dating back to 544 AD were destroyed by the Taliban in March 2001. In 2016, parts of the Palmyra historical and other structures in Syria were destroyed by the ISIS.

The US and the Western powers are invariably fighting some kind of war somewhere or the other in some capacity, as we have seen earlier. The My Lai massacre in Vietnam on 16 Mar 1968 was a landmark and shameful incident. While the armies seriously attempt to train their men in ethical conduct, there are often gaps in the practised and stated values on the ground. We need to examine this aspect, as it is related to the theme of the book.

I am a soldier and have been in combat situations. Thus, I must say something in defence of 'soldiers. The vast majority of soldiers are proud professionals who pride in being soldiers and live by the highest values of their military. They have very challenging tasks, particularly when dealing with civilian people in counter-insurgency operations. No Rules of Engagement (ROE) can cover all the situations that they encounter and the minimal time they have to decide on their response makes it extremely difficult. Often, even a slight delay in the decision could cause the loss of their lives and the lives of their comrades and many times innocent civilians.

Having said that, there are a few who intentionally violate military ethics and human values, which are simply unacceptable as soldiers, for it is an honourable profession. When such deliberate incidents are not prevented and reported when they happen, the soul of soldiering gets a hit.

The paradox and the painful aspects are that the same hierarchy that touts ethics and ROE often disregards such acts and overlooks those crimes with an eyewash punishment, as we shall see in some cases mentioned in the book.

Army ethics are a reflection of the country's culture and past experiences. Essentially military ethics are guided by a combination of the following concepts.

Virtue Ethics. Character is the foundation of ethical conduct, thus building the character of soldiers is critical. It leaves a fair degree of freedom for the individual to make decisions. It is a practical approach that does not require the soldier to memorize all the rules and regulations to deal with different situations.

Deontological Concept. Ethics must be governed by the rules i.e. actions that are permitted, forbidden or required. If the action is within the laid down rules, the action is ethical. Every military lays down ROE which serves as a guide to making decisions in critical situations.

Pragmatism. That is avoiding fixed norms and providing flexibility since all situations cannot be covered by rules. Pragmatism bridges the gap between theory and practice.

The action itself must be ethical.

Consequentialism. The morality of an action is judged according to the results without considering the actor's intentions or his character. The consequences define the ethical standards of action.

The end justifies the means.

Experiential framework. Ethical conduct is based on what has worked best for the organization and the country in the past.

The Utilitarian Concept. Everything is justified in the interest of the country.

Hybrid theory. It is based on the realization that no single theory meets the demand of the complexity of military ethics. The hybrid theory combines the best practices of two or more theories. A soldier with poor character will subvert the rule book and the conscience is not part of his vocabulary.

Combat is characterised by many constraints and uncertainties. These uncertainties multiply in counter-insurgency operations where soldiers come in contact with the civilian population. These include situational constraints i.e., lack of or inaccurate information, acute stress as a result of some quick developments and chronic stress due to prolonged deployment.

The biggest challenge is the need to be compassionate to the civilian population, knowing well that they are collaborating with the terrorists. Marcus Schulzke mentions in his book that "10 per cent of soldiers and marines report mistreating non-combatants or damaging their property when it was not necessary. Only 47 per cent of soldiers and 38 per cent of marines agreed that the non-combatants should be treated with dignity and respect." (Chapter 6, Ethics in American, British and Israeli Counterinsurgency.) This demonstrates a total lack of understanding of counter-insurgency operations.

So, half a century after My Lai, the mindset of the US soldier, essentially remains the same. What comes to your mind if I ask you a question? The civil population that they are talking about are the people whose country they have invaded and not vice versa.

Thus, a soldier faces intense combat dilemmas, which essentially come down to the decision of whether to shoot or not. So often, they are split-second decisions and that is the difference between who dies and who survives. In the era of suicidal bombers, when one religious fanatic has chosen to die, there is only one loser, he is the soldier-doomed if he shoots and doomed if he doesn't, at least in India.

Either decision can have serious consequences. In counter-insurgency, the problems arise because of the proximity of the combatants and non-combatants, women and children and child soldiers. Aggressive tactics can have serious derogatory effects. A soft approach leads to other kinds of problems. The right balance is always difficult to achieve. One wrong decision can undo all the good work as it alienates the fence-sitters. The failure to align the cultural differences can have serious effects. For example, in Arab and many other countries, celebratory gunfire during a marriage ceremony is a common practice. On one occasion, in Iraq, it was mistaken for hostile fire that led to many innocent civilians' deaths. This is poor training; a well-trained soldier can differentiate threatening fire from such celebratory fires through many indicators.

The Vietnam War showed the harm that could be inflicted on a powerful military because of poor ethical preparedness. The My Lai massacre by a large number and three good soldiers risking their lives to save the Vietnamese, and then reporting the incident led to the US military reinventing itself. Did they reinvent themselves effectively or do Abu Ghraib and Guantanamo Bay tell different stories?

Marcus Schulzke's interview of twelve brigade commanders who commanded brigades in Iraq and Afghanistan concludes that the army does not do justice to ethical training. Is it by design? The fact that serious and intentional omissions and commissions are overlooked and no one is held accountable proves the point.

Ethics is a non-contact weapon of great influence. In the infamous My Lai massacre over 500 old men, women and children were massacred. As a proportion of over two million Vietnamese who died in the whole war, it is an insignificant proportion, but the impact of these 500 may have been the point at which the Americans lost the war. This would have multiplied the resolve of the Vietnamese like nothing else and turned the vast majority of the people against them, not only in Vietnam but back home in America. Their own Vietnam veterans protested the war. A war like the Vietnam War cannot be won by a foreign power without the goodwill of the people.

The soldiers are seen as an ethical and trustworthy class of people.

Armies all over the world are conscious of the high pedestal on which the public places them and they make all efforts to live up to that expectation. The irony is that the unscrupulous politicians decide where and when to fight and the soldiers fight and die.

The military, particularly the army operates in a very challenging environment. The armies are organized, structured and trained for conventional warfare, but mostly operate in asymmetric, sub-conventional, counter-insurgencies and counter-terrorism combat. The 'White Man's Burden' has taken them to civilize the world, and therefore they fight on other's lands and kill innocent people there, and then like Madeline Albright, justify the killing of half a million children as a price worth it.

COUNTER INSURGENCY OPERATIONS

Counter-insurgency operations pose multiple challenges. The ethical codes required here are far different from conventional war. These cover aspects such as operating among own people where one incident can have a severe fallout. Conflicts arise out of constraints and caution imposed by ROEs and the ground realities, use of minimum force, human rights et al. An environment where a plethora of agencies is only looking for sensationalizing military errors—the human rights organization will blame the army without verification, round-the-clock media competing for the breaking news and the political parties just waiting to pounce on anything that can give them political mileage. Above all, pressure to perform in a competitive environment where success is measured by the number of terrorists killed. Maintaining an incident-free environment may not necessarily mean good performance.

The units are caught in a paradox. A soldier's task in war entails the use of maximum force against the enemy. Here he is asked to use minimum force. In war, he is not asked questions if civilians die during the battle. Here he may land up in big trouble if that happens, even if inadvertently. In war he can shoot first even without seeing the enemy, here he is only sure of the enemy when he is first shot at. In war, he gets rewarded for killing the enemy. In India, the unit is required to prove that the individual they have killed is a recorded terrorist. He knows the conventional war will be short. Here it is a long haul and he will be back here again.

In war, the whole nation rallies behind him. Here, part of his countrymen are against him. In war, he does not have to worry about what lies behind him. Here, the enemy is all around. In war, there is little chance that he will have to answer in a court of law. Here, he may be defending himself in court even for false allegations. In war, the enemy's culture and beliefs are of little relevance during combat. Here, he is told to be sensitive to local culture and customs all the time, even fighting terrorists barefoot sometimes. A unit is required to transform from an aggressive fighting unit to a people-friendly one.

The militaries on one hand formulate an Ethics Code for their men and train them, on the other, they overlook even serious and intentional violations of the same ethics. Here are some examples.

The US Experience

The US experiences have been referred to at different places, hence not being repeated here. The My Lai massacre, Abu Ghraib and Guantanamo Bay incidents are well known. The worst form of soldierly conduct in recent times was American soldiers urinating on dead Taliban fighters, an incident that brought disgrace to the US Army and their country and would have alienated the Afghans.

British Army

The Bloody Sunday. The famous 'Bloody Sunday' incident in Northern Ireland on 30 January 1972, where the British Para battalion shot dead 14 peaceful protesters and injured an equal number. The Widgery Tribunal, held in the aftermath, largely cleared the soldiers of blame. It described some of the soldiers shooting as 'bordering on the reckless' but accepted their claims that they shot at gunmen and bomb-throwers, whereas the protesters were throwing stones and bottles. The report was criticised as a whitewash.

The Saville Enquiry was instituted in 1998 to investigate the incident thoroughly. Following a twelve-year investigation, the Saville report was made public in 2010 and concluded that the killings were unjustified and unjustifiable. It found that of all those shot, none were armed and none were posing a serious threat, that no bombs were thrown. Half a century after the incident, no one is punished.

The Israeli Defence Forces

There is a document called *The Spirit of the Israeli Defence Forces*. It lays down in great detail the ethical code for the Israeli defence forces. The code of **purity of arms** is one of the values stated in the Israel Defense Forces' official doctrine of ethics, *The Spirit of the IDF*. It states that:

The soldier shall make use of his weaponry and power only for the fulfilment of the mission and solely to the extent required; he will maintain his humanity even in combat. The soldier shall not employ his weaponry and power to harm non-combatants or prisoners of war and shall do all he can to avoid harming their lives, body, honour and property.

Very impressive on paper. Fully appreciating the complexities of Israeli security challenges, many will not agree that they practice this on the ground. Their use of disproportionate force is universal knowledge. The ratio of people who die on both sides, both combatants and civilians validate the point.

The Pakistan Army

The Pakistan Army does not fit into the framework of ethical soldiering. There have been innumerable incidents of the most inhuman torture of Indian soldiers both by the Pakistan army and the Pakistan-sponsored terrorists, the worst being in the recent Kargil war.

In 1947, the Pakistan army masquerading as the *Razakars* looted, raped and killed Kashmiri women, whom they claim to have gone to liberate. They are infamous for the killing and rape of millions of Bengalis in East Pakistan in 1971, leading to the birth of Bangladesh as a new nation. In the Kargil War in 1999, they refused to accept their dead soldiers who were then buried by the Indian army with full religious rights and military honours, way beyond stipulated by the Geneva Conventions. Pakistan is universally known as the epicentre of global terrorism and the Pakistan army is the fountainhead.

In the 1971 Indo-Pakistan War, India had taken over 94000 Pakistani prisoners of war. A senior Warrant Officer was surprised to see the Indian Army Chief, General Sam Manekshaw inspecting the quality of their food, cookhouses, living quarters, toilets and the arrangements for their families. The Warrant

Officer is reported to have commented, "Now we understand why the Indian Army is what it is."

China

China falls into a category of its own. It is famous for Tiananmen Square where tanks rolled to suppress the unarmed protests and killed an unknown number of people. It is famous for brutal reprisals of Tibetans which unleashed a wave of immolations in protest. There are allegations of committing crimes against humanity and forced re-education camps targeting the Tibetan, Uyghur and other mostly-Muslim ethnic groups in the north-western region of Xinjiang.

https://www-bbc- com.cdn.ampproject.org/v/s/www.bbc.com/news/ world-asia-china-22278037.amp accessed on 20 Aug 22

The Indian Army

Unlike the first three, the Indian army operates in a very different environment. The Indian army fights its wars and battles within its territory, be they conventional wars or foreign-sponsored proxy wars. The government and the people have direct stakes in the success or failure of operations and how it is orchestrated. Army operates in full public view, under media glare and legal scrutiny.

The Indian army has given an excellent account of its ethical conduct barring odd incidents. The complexities of counter-insurgency operations can result in unintended collateral damages, despite all precautions.

This observation from a foreign journalist during the 1971 Indo-Pakistan War in present-day Bangladesh sums up the Indian soldier's ethical standards.

> *'I don't like praising armies. I don't like armies because armies mean wars and I don't like wars. But this (the Indian army) was something... They were great all the way. There was never a black mark...I lived with the officers and I walked and rode with the jawans and they were great. Sure, some of them were scared at first; they wouldn't be human if they were not. But I never saw a man flinch because they were scared. There is a tremendous spirit (in the Indian army) and it did one good to experience it...And they were the most perfect gentlemen, I have never seen them do a wrong thing, not even when they saw how bestial the enemy had been."*

Sydney Schanberg, *New York Times,* quoted by Lt Gen VK Kapoor (Retd) in SP's Land Forces Roundup, Jan 2015.

Author's Notes

Odd incidents should not take away the credit from the majority who put their lives in danger to adhere to the ethical code. These operations are extremely complex and no rules of engagement or training based on any philosophy can equip soldiers for every situation. No two situations are identical. The time to respond is minimal and the human instinct of self-defence takes over.

What goes against the armies is that they sometimes overlook even serious and intentional violations of ethical conduct as we have seen above. That, to my mind, is unacceptable and encourages violations. The justification often stated is that of an isolated incident but the unstated reason is that of the morale of troops.

The behaviour of soldiers is driven by their culture, yet the army's behaviour may not mirror societal values. The US Army's warrior ethos, based on conventional war readiness makes them aggressive and use heavy weapons. The US approach lies in the extensive use of firepower as we saw in Iraq, Afghanistan, Bosnia, Syria and wherever they have been deployed.

The British, based on their experience in Malaya, Northern Ireland and numerous counter-insurgency operations understand the importance of local people and sentiments towards accomplishing the mission in a foreign land. They try to respect the local culture and customs and therefore tend to be minimalist in the use of firepower. They were quick to remove their body armour and helmets in Basra, Iraq, and shed their armoured fighting vehicles after the conventional phase was over in Iraq in 2003. In so doing, they looked less threatening and made it easier to interact with people. You can never inspire confidence amongst the locals or interact with them sitting in a Humvee or an armoured personnel career. The US military continued to operate the same way as before.

Israelis are known to employ overwhelming use of force against terrorists with high collateral damage. Their behaviour is guided by ever-existential threats all around and their past experiences ever since the birth of Israel as a nation. In the end, all actions are condoned in the name of self-defence and the security of the nation; a common sentiment in most armies.

The Indian army has rarely used a weapon in counterinsurgency beyond a Light Machine Gun. In the regimental system, officers serve in the same unit with the same men their entire regimental service. Thus, ethical conduct is intrinsic to the Indian Army. It also has a direct relationship with the Indian culture of respect and deference to elders, women and children, the Indian heritage of righteousness and respect for all faiths and religions and the duty to protect the weak. Operating within their own people, alignment with local culture comes naturally.

Thus, while ethical conduct gets reiterated in units in such environments, it is not institutionalised in the form of a training pamphlet or a structured course. The newly inducted units are put through orientation training in the battle schools in the nuances of counter-insurgency operations in the theatre.

Even while operating beyond its borders in the liberation of Bangladesh in 1971 and Sri Lanka in 1987, where the Indian military landed up fighting the Tamil separatists, their conduct was exemplary. The non-combatants were kept out of harm's way at their own cost.

Ethics is simply not a Code of Conduct for a soldier. It is an Effective Weapon of War.

♦ ♦ ♦

Chapter Five

Soldiers: When Defiance Becomes Duty

It was the defiance of one ordinary soldier in India, which triggered the first war of independence in 1857 and its fructification nine decades later—Mangal Pandey. Many princely states remained loyal and even helped the British to suppress the revolt—for self-preservation. In doing so, they remained glorious slaves to a colonial empire priding themselves on the meaningless fiefs, titles and honours given by their colonial masters to keep them royal slaves.

GOOD SOLDIERS Vs GOOD HUMAN BEINGS

Soldiers live in a soldier box of paradoxes. The box has a rigid boundary of what you can do and what you cannot. These boundaries are established by a combination of rules, traditions, values and some intangibles such as brotherhood and esprit de corps. The value system of the military demands the highest standards of character, integrity, selfless service, sacrifice and a sense of duty. No other institution comes close. The political leadership, under whose control the military operates, in general, is considered among the least ethical. So, some paradox and irony – the most ethical institution is under the control of the least ethical lot of people. Rightly, soldiers across the world see themselves as superior professionals and that they pay a much higher price.

I have often wondered if there is a difference between being a good soldier and being a good human being. Do the two conflict? Because the military is the only organization legally authorized to kill and has immense resources to do so, it brings upon them the greatest responsibility that they use the appropriate means to kill the right man for the right legally justifiable reasons. The critical issue is, who decides the legality of killing. It has to be based on internationally accepted legality and laws of conflict.

So, when a country launches an illegal war on another country like the US-led Iraq War 2003 or the Russia-Ukraine War 2022, that is, a war not supported by the UNO, do the soldiers become culpable of illegal killings and war crimes or do they get covered under the defence of obeying orders of the government?

So, who becomes culpable for war crimes in such illegal wars? Will it be the political leadership of those countries? What is the culpability of the political leadership of the 'coalition of the willing' who joined the illegal US-led war on Iraq? Where does the higher military leadership stand in such a situation? Should they also be held responsible for war crimes as were the Germans in the Nuremberg trials and the Japanese in the Tokyo trials? It is only when the targeted country is weak or surrenders unconditionally that this enforcement is possible as in the case of Germany, Japan or Iraq where Saddam Hussein was hanged. Who amongst the 'coalition of the willing' should be culpable for killing hundreds of thousands of civilians, women and children in Iraq who had nothing to do with WMD?

We have often seen that powerful countries blatantly disregard international norms and human values when it comes to their national interests. They are never held to account for their actions because international institutions are powerless to enforce them.

So, when a soldier violates laws of conflict and human values even in pursuit of legitimate military aims, he ceases to be a good human being. Often this will create a moral conflict.

It isn't hard to define a good soldier, as is generally understood. In my view, there is a lot more to a good soldier that often remains unsaid, and that is the most difficult part of being a good soldier. It is in this part that the paradox of the difference between a good soldier and a good human being resides.

> *A good soldier is a disciplined individual who knows his trade and constantly upgrades his skills to remain relevant with changing times. He has a good attitude to deliver beyond the call of duty and do more than he is mandated to do. He is a good team man and thinks beyond himself and carries his weapon with great responsibility. Most importantly, he is a man of good character and high integrity and lives by military values, even when there is a price to pay.*

Where does disobeying illegal, immoral or unlawful orders fit into the definition of a good soldier above?

A soldier is part of a group and derives his identity and strength from the unit or the regiment he belongs to, which is displayed on his shoulders. The military values include character, integrity, loyalty, camaraderie, selfless service and honesty. These are universal across armies and are sine-qua-non for the effectiveness of the military.

The paradox emerges when we start analyzing the application of character and integrity.

Let us look at the Honour Code of the National Defence Academy, Khadakvasla, India, the **cradle of military leadership:**

> *"I believe that a cadet must be **loyal, truthful,** trustworthy, honest **and forthright under all circumstances. I will not lie, cheat or steal,** nor will **I mislead or deceive** anyone. **I undertake to faithfully live up to this code** and to continuously encourage my comrades to do so."*

In the US West Point Academy, the West Point Leader Development System aims to develop cadets into leaders of character who live honourably, lead honourably, and demonstrate excellence. The Character Program helps cadets understand what it means to live honourably and lead honourably by educating them on the professional standards, organizational values, and personal virtues that comprise "honour" in the Army Profession.

Likewise, the centrality of cadet development in all armies should be character development.

What does living honourably and leading honourably mean for the higher military leadership? It means the same thing as what it means to junior officers in their context. It means selfless value-based living and doing what is right in the interest of the organisation irrespective of the consequences. Integrity is the foundation of living honourably and leading honourably.

THE NATIONAL DEFENCE ACADEMY (NDA) PRAYER—INDIA

Like the honour code mentioned above, the NDA prayer encapsulates all that an officer needs to internalize. There are two aspects that I wish to highlight from this prayer.

The NDA Prayer

> *'O' God, help us to keep ourselves physically strong, mentally awake and* ***morally straight****, that in doing our duty to Thee and our country we may* ***keep the honour of the Services*** *untarnished.*
>
> *Strengthen us to guard our country from external aggression and internal disorders. Awaken our* ***admiration for honest dealing and clean thinking****, and guide us to* ***choose the harder right instead of the easier wrong****.*
>
> *Kindle our hearts with the* ***fellowship for our comrades at arms and with loyalty to the men we command****. Endow us with the courage which is born of the love of* ***what is noble and which knows no compromise or retreat when truth and right are in peril****.*
>
> *Grant us a new opportunity of service to Thee, to our country and* ***to the men we lead, and ever help us to place this service before self****.*

Let us examine the critical aspects of this honour code—**Honest dealing, Be Loyal, Truthful—Will not Lie, Cheat...Mislead or Deceive—undertake to faithfully live up to this code**

What we need to answer are:

- Honest dealing—what does it encompass?
- Loyal to whom—superiors, colleagues, subordinates, the organization, the cause or military values?
- Truthful—what does it really mean and what does it encompass?
- Will not lie—Is it ever okay to lie? How often is it violated?
- Mislead or deceive whom?

Loyalty is a word not so easy to deal with. It comes from the heart and is not based on a contract. It is not a transactional relationship of convenience, coercion or cost. It means commitment and devotion. Normally, it is explained as loyalty to superiors, colleagues, subordinates, the organization and the cause.

Before proceeding further, I wish to highlight **that in the NDA prayer, there is no mention of loyalty to a superior; rather there is mention of loyalty to the men one commands.** There is also no mention of service to the superior; there is an emphasis on service to the men we lead. To me, it is an ingenious, yet, simple thought, for loyalty to a superior would be a function of his credibility as a man of character—it is not a given. Loyalty to men is a given because it is a reverse equation.

A dog is loyal to its master irrespective of the person—good, bad, ugly rich or poor. Humans are intelligent people; they reason, analyse and judge and therefore their loyalty to a man is reflective and not eternal. The loyalty of right-thinking people is value-based. Thus, the NDA prayer has beautifully emphasized—Endow us with the courage which is born of the love of ***what is noble and which knows no compromise or retreat when truth and right are in peril.*** To my mind, this puts loyalty to superiors in the correct perspective.

So, what is the relative importance of the objects of loyalty? In my opinion, the priority lies as follows:

- Loyalty to the cause—assuming it is ethical.
- Loyalty to the organisation—assuming it functions on ethical values.
- The rest can be clubbed together in this order—subordinates, colleagues and superiors. The priority here clearly lies with the subordinates, for, at stake here is the trust between the leader and the led, the most critical aspect of leadership and organisational success.

What is the relationship between loyalty to a superior and loyalty to the mission or the organisation? Can they conflict sometimes? Loyalty to a superior is not dog loyalty, neither is it eternal. It can even be issue-based. Loyalty will have to be earned by demonstration of good character and courage every day. A subordinate can be fully committed to the mission and the organisation despite the superior not commanding his loyalty because of a character deficit.

When one is loyal to the organisation, his sub-unit or unit, what is expected of him and what does loyalty really mean here? Does it mean rationalizing lying, cheating and misleading in the name of the unit? Or, would loyalty mean that one calls out intentional ethical/value violations so that the value system of the organization is not compromised? The value system is the foundation upon which the long-term sustenance of an organization depends – thus loyalty lies here.

Apropos above, what do honest dealing and truthfulness mean to a soldier? Does truthfulness demand that he reports intentional violations or misconduct by his unit or its members? Does it conflict with the loyalty to the unit as is commonly understood? Such people are called whistleblowers and that is not seen positively in the military, which is unfortunate.

Is unethical conduct for the benefit of the organization acceptable? Let us see this example.

In the context of the spirit of the honour code and the NDA prayer, let us get back to My Lai. Out of a company of about 100 all ranks with a few officers, not one prevented or reported the incident when the intent of the company commander appeared decidedly mala fide. No one questioned or clarified what was to be done to the women and children in the village. Only three good men stood up against the massacre, Warrant Officer Hugh Thomson and his helicopter crew. Thomson landed his helicopter between the rampaging American soldiers and the Vietnamese hiding in a bunker and warned them to lay off. As he proceeded to rescue the Vietnamese, he directed his crew to open up on the American soldiers if they shot him or the Vietnamese. He later reported the incident.

No one in the chain of command from the divisional commander downwards took action as was expected of them. President Nixon's act of pardon drove the last nail in the coffin of the concept of ethical soldiering. It drove a nail into the concept of the West Point Honour Code: Duty - Honour - Country for political expediency. The court-martial, as we saw, exonerated all the 29 accused.

So, was Warrant Officer Thomson's concept of loyalty or Duty - Honour - Country flawed? Or, were the others who participated in the massacre, lied under oath, and were involved in the coverup, right under some definition of loyalty? By this code, a whistleblower who brings to light unethical acts is a bad and disloyal soldier.

The soldiers are expected to rise against unethical acts by their comrades and commanders—faithfully living up to the code.

What might seem disloyal to some is preserving the organization from disaster and that is the loyalty that Hugh Thomson demonstrated.

When it was a choice between being a good soldier and a good human being, Hugh Thomson chose to be a good human being. In doing so, he did the US Army a great service. Someone could say, at least there were a few good men at My Lai and they too were American soldiers.

It is this loyalty that the people in positions of authority in ENRON, Manville Corporation and Wells Fargo, the examples cited in this book, failed to demonstrate. As a result, the mighty companies disappeared from the face of the corporate map.

Let us Examine a Few Incidents

As I said earlier, stray incidents of unethical conduct should not take away credit from soldiers in general who risk their lives to conduct themselves ethically despite immense challenges. However, certain incidents are simply incomprehensible and deserve the most severe criticism.

The incident of US soldiers urinating on dead Taliban, while being disgusting is inhuman. These soldiers as we understand have gone through ethical training and are constantly grilled in discipline and soldierly conduct. They wore uniforms of their corps and country and those uniforms represent values that have been raised on the blood and guts of many generations before them. The incident enraged the Afghan government, the Afghanistan people and the US Government. The US paid a heavy price for this most despicable behaviour. Not much later, an Afghan soldier shot down many Allied and American soldiers in the camp called the green-on-blue incident. Eventually, such incidents orchestrated by the Taliban led to the separation of Afghan and US bases and that was the end of cohesion and effectiveness.

These few bad men undid the sacrifice of thousands of their comrades and contributed in some measure to the disgraceful withdrawal of the US from Afghanistan.

Alexander Blackman was a Royal Marines NCO in Afghanistan. In September 2011, he shot dead an injured Taliban and then said, "Obviously, this doesn't go anywhere fellas. I just violated the Geneva Convention." The incident was captured on the helmet-mounted camera, now on Youtube.

Alexander was originally sentenced to serve three life sentences, but the sentence was reduced to seven months leading to his release in April 2017.

Isn't that a big farce?

Source: Pursuing Moral Warfare: Ethics in American, British, and Israeli Counterinsurgency, Marcus Schuzlke.

On Loyalty and Lying. I am not sure, how this incident became public. What does loyalty demand here? Should his buddies who witnessed this have kept silent in the name of the unit's honour and brotherhood, or does the honour code demand that they should have first prevented it if they could and reported it voluntarily? The fact that Alexander was released, exposes the farce of British ethics. Like My Lai, this sends a message, that foreign lives do not matter and that no matter what you do in a foreign country, you will not be punished. I see this as an extension of the colonial mindset. Where does it leave the righteous soldiers who find this disgusting and call out these perpetrators? What happens to the moral values—choose the harder right rather than the easier wrong. This is easier said than done. Right from the training academy, reporting against colleagues, even when offences are serious is seen as un-officer-like and sneaking. During the service too, when a soldier or an officer calls out un-soldierly conduct, it is not seen in the spirit of the honour code but as disloyalty and sneaking.

As we saw in the case of My Lai, the higher authorities so often overlook even serious and deliberate violations of ethics. This makes a mockery of ethical training, the honour code and the legal process.

Let's raise the level. The Iraq War 2003, 'Operation Iraqi Freedom' was an illegal war. From the interviews of Colin Powell, it is evident that he had realised even before the war began that the anthrax powder vial, the evidence he cited in the UN General Assembly was cutting no ice with anyone and was based on falsehood. Yet, he remained an important part of the George Bush decision-making body which was directly responsible for this war, killing hundreds of thousands of innocent people who had nothing to do with the 9/11 attack or terrorism or weapons of mass destruction.

Lots of these unethical acts are rationalized in the name of national interest, maintaining the morale of soldiers and dusting under the carpet in the name of confidentiality, blatantly disregarding international norms.

Now, against this background when conscientious soldiers find themselves facing a moral dilemma—to serve in an illegal war or refuse, what are they expected to do?

THE CONSCIENCE WAR: WHY DO SOME SOLDIERS GET DISILLUSIONED?

Corporal Joe Glenton Takes on the Establishment

It takes as much courage to stand up against the organization as it does to go to war. History is made by people prepared to make that sacrifice.

—Tony Bein, on Joe Glenton

When the War on Terror began, Joe Glenton from Britain voluntarily signed up to serve his nation to make this world a safer place. He served a tenure in

Afghanistan in 2006. What he saw overseas left him disillusioned, and he returned manifesting symptoms of post-traumatic stress disorder. He refused to serve a second tenure, went Absent Without Leave (AWOL), left the country and returned to fight his case, with the military accusing him of desertion.

A corporal in the logistics branch of the British Army, he was not in the heat of combat—relatively safer, more comfortable and with lesser risk of death or disability. Despite being threatened with years in prison, he continued to speak out against the war on terror, and the way it was being orchestrated and won the support of many of his fellow soldiers.

He wrote the book '*Soldier Box, Why I Won't Return to The War on Terror.*

Extracts from the book.

> ... *I had started to question it by then. On the telly and the radio, the same bullshit was being repeated over and over again about how it was going well and about how we were winning, though it was the hardest fighting since Korea; no different from the US. But still, I felt like I had to get back desperately before I had too much time to think about it. At that time the civilian world offended me, with its lack of mortars or helicopters passing overhead...*

By the time I returned to the theatre, the infantrymen were rotating back to Kandahar for their R&R, looking haggard. Many had been ordered to grow a beard which was meant to elicit respect from the locals.

I wondered, if, by growing beards, this would somehow conceal from the Afghans that we were occupying their country by force. The logic seemed to run that an angry Afghan civilian would emerge from his compound to confront a British patrol, only for his venom to disappear at the sight of their facial hair.

I was starting to question the whole thing. It seemed so stupid. I was jaded and pessimistic by that time.

The Hellfire missiles alone cost 100,000 pounds each, and could only be attached to an aircraft for a limited number of hours because of wear and tear, and this included the flight from Britain. They only had eight hours of flight time left once they arrived and then became unstable. So, they would often return to our ammo site useless, scrawled with anti-Islamic graffiti by the loaders. I wondered what ....100,000 pounds could do to win over to our cause or educate children, or what it would look like in medical supplies-simple questions I had no answers for.

There was a trend of officers—young and old-coming out for the qualifying thirty days or so and then heading off home for their medal... (no different from Vietnam).

By then I had started to accept that we had no good reason to be in Afghanistan and my increasing despondency affected my work. It boiled over ...I got into a row with the section second-in-command. I pulled out the rifle, was so pissed off and weighed the idea of putting a bullet into him. One of the guys dissuaded me and I put the rifle away.

The justifications for being there were untrue. It was a case of just acknowledging that we were not helping anyone-certainly not the Afghans. No one on our side seemed to know what they were doing. But what I did know was that millions of dollars were being spent and hundreds of rounds were being fired off, women were being bombed, locals were being alienated and people were dying.

Besides that, serious money was being made in some quarters. Half of our logistics park was filled by the private military companies Kellog, Brown and Root. They had a better kit and pay than we had. War was an enterprise.

We were not wanted there. We just did what we were told. There is no space for questions. This was the soldier box and we were in it.

Joe was promoted and was three years ahead of his career curve. 'I wouldn't trust people who created these wars with my life and I would not trust them with my family—a husband, a daughter, a son. It is a weird world when the man shooting rockets or bullets at you is not your worst enemy. He is just angry you are in his country—he has seen this all before. It is the people behind you that should be your concern-especially the ones a long way behind you. How behind they are is directly proportional to the threat they pose to you. The enemy is all the way back there-probably in the direction from where your plane came from.'

> *I recall all the bad things I have done in life that I should not have done. However, my refusal to return to Afghanistan, and my fight regarding it, would not be among these. In fact, it would be my rightest act... But like my soldier friends, I still have sand in my eyes and it chafes our soul. It recalls that place, those times and those lies.*
>
> *Source: Soldier Box: Why I won't return to the War on Terror, Joe Glenton, 2013.*

That was a corporal's take and all that makes a lot of sense when you read what these Generals said about Afghanistan.

During an interview, Gen David Richards, Commander of NATO forces in Afghanistan said, "We had a lot of tactics but no coherent strategy. Lack of strategy prevented us from the exploitation of early successes and it resulted in corruption and thus a resurgence of the Taliban."

General Danielle Mc Neal said the same thing, "We did not have a strategy."

A US General asked the White House to define, "What was winning in Afghanistan?" No one could tell him anything.

Politicians and Generals all over the world seem to be made from the same clay. Half the time they launch themselves into the cavalry charge first, then go looking for the right windmill to charge.

So, when it seems the ISAF and later NATO was trudging along without a plan, how wrong was Corporal Glenton to defy the authority and fight against it?

The days of a forgotten war in some remote parts of the world like Vietnam are over. All wars in graphic reality and truth are brought to people's mobiles, notwithstanding the information war. The governments cannot get away with any narrative. Ordinary citizens are beginning to question their Presidents and Prime Ministers on the international media on the Iraq and Afghanistan war.

So, when the conscience of soldiers like Captain Jason Wright (US) or Corporal Glenton (UK) question the very basis of the presence of their military in another country and the deaths of hundreds of thousands of civilians, where does it leave the soldier? When a soldier sees that what he is being asked to do is against the very values of the constitution that he has been shown all his life, where does it leave military values and what is he expected to do? Some soldiers are marred by such thoughts and disagree with their government policies but continue to soldier on. And some question the whole thing and refuse to serve. How does it change the military dynamics? Values have no place in politics and in preserving national interests. After Vietnam, the massacres were happening in South and Central America through proxies guided by the unseen hand of the US.

Captain Jason Wright was a military defence counsel in the US Army. He was tasked to work as the support counsel for Khalid Sheikh Mohammed, the self-proclaimed mastermind of 9/11. Khaled Sheikh at that time was detained in Guantanamo Bay prison.

Supposedly a defence counsel for the accused, Jason was expected to do just enough to give a façade of justice and not good enough to get him a fair trial so that he could be punished.

He felt it was against the very concept of the US and human values.

When the US Supreme Court was reviewing the legality of the detention of the 600 Guantanamo Bay detainees and whether what the US was doing with them was legal and justified (the enhanced interrogation techniques or torture etc.) US President George Bush passed the Military Commission Act 2006, legalizing all the things that the US Supreme Court said were illegal. This act made the job of defence counsel difficult.

The Habeas Corpus—that is the right of the accused to appeal to the court against what he feels is illegal treatment was taken away.

Jason resigned from the military. Here is a transcript of the interview with Jason covered in the documentary *Turning Point* on the 9/11 attacks.

Interviewer, "Khalid Sheikh was the mastermind of the attack on WTC that killed almost 3000 Americans. How is your stepping away from the job worth it—essentially leaving the army?"

Jason Wright, "I was not walking away from anything as some people allege, rather, I was standing up for something. I was standing for something much bigger. I was standing for the values and the concept of America. What was being done here in Guantanamo, should be acceptable if it was done to an American on the mainland."

"Guantanamo Bay is not a place; it is a concept. America is a concept too. We have to live by that concept." Jason adds.

He believed in what Anthony Myer said in his book, "**When you have to make a choice between being a good soldier or a good human being, be a good human being.**"

For him, it was a moral decision.

He believed that to deny Habeas Corpus to the Guantanamo Bay detainees, was in essence, to deny the law and justice to the accused. He said, he grew up reading the US Constitution and expected the government to be fair to all human beings. The act made supporting or defending officers' jobs difficult, just good enough to put the shroud of legality. He said, it is unethical to do so and resigned from active military service.

As of 2021, of the 780 detainees, 741 were released under the past three administrations. Doesn't this indicate that most of these people should not have been there in the first place?

A British Navy submarine medic was deputed to Afghanistan. He was disturbed when told that he could only treat Western casualties and not Afghans. This went against ethics as a healer. He refused rifle fire shooting training and refused to serve in Afghanistan having seen WikiLeaks. He was court-martialled.

There is a paradox; terrorism is a tough war and intelligence is the key to success. Captured terrorists and their leaders can be a treasure trove of intelligence that can pre-empt future attacks and save lives. How much is a terrorist likely to share information when treated humanely, fed three good meals and given eight hours of sleep? Torture forces him to speak but he may simply say what you want him to say out of coercion; sometimes it might get you intelligence, and sometimes it will put the other detainees at risk of torture. While the jury will always be out on how to treat terrorists who launch 9/11 types of attacks, some aspects of the treatment of terrorists in Abu Ghraib and Guantanamo may not have helped the cause of securing intelligence. It needs mature oversight for it can prove to be counter-productive as Abu Ghraib did.

Lt Colonel Stuart Scheller Rebels with a Cause

Colonel Scheller was a serving marine battalion commander. He jolted the American defence establishment with his very critical video after the chaotic withdrawal from Afghanistan during which 13 Marines and about 170 Afghans were killed in a suicide attack outside Kabul airport. He sought accountability from the political and military hierarchy for he felt that thousands of American soldiers' sacrifices had gone in vain.

A series of controversial and critical social media posts against hierarchy led to his eventual court-martial and discharge.

'I don't think I've seen an officer consistently in, as we say, the top three blocks of the Christmas tree," Marine Judge Colonel Glen Hines, who oversaw Scheller's court-martial and also handed him a light sentence, said to the court on October 15. "He was on a consistent upward path."

Scheller told *Marine Corps Times* on December 26, "I think there need to be leaders in Congress. Right now, we have a bunch of politicians, and I just don't think that's enough. They've demonstrated that a lot of them don't have the courage that's required to be up there."

Scheller says that he felt in his gut that the "failure" of the withdrawal in Afghanistan was never going to be addressed by senior leadership and that the conduct of the entire war would never be called into question.

"I sat there in my chair and thought, I don't think senior leaders get it," Scheller said. "I don't think they understand the failures. I can't think in military history, at least over the last 30 or 40 years that there has been such a monumental failure, and not one person has acknowledged it."

Scheller felt that "the only way that there would be even an attempt at accountability for the withdrawal would be for him to speak out publicly just one time and demand -accountability -because that's what I think we deserve."

So, what kind of a military leader was Colonel Scheller?

Scheller was an outstanding leader and highly respected by his colleagues and subordinates.

"He would hold us accountable," Matt Underhill, a former platoon commander in his company said. "He would hold himself accountable. I mean, I honestly feel like if the need had arisen, he would have held the company commander accountable."

Underhill added that Scheller was neither a "maverick" nor a "cowboy" when it came to his professional style. Rather, in his opinion, Scheller Jr. was very much "by the book," but with a personal style that built confidence and respect from those around him.

"He was always putting the Marines, and I'd say the junior Marines ahead of him. It was that selfless servanthood leadership." Underhill said. "Commanders wish they had more guys like Stu. I won't say subordinates, but his junior Marines wished they had more leadership like Stu."

Michael Welter, then a corporal under Company Commander Captain Stuart Scheller said the Marine immediately stood out.

"He was a leader. He was fair, and he was emotionally and mentally invested in the success of the human beings below him. Not just as a Marine, but as a human being."

He was always asking if his Marines needed anything for training, logistics or simply improving their quality of life, Welter said.

"That says a lot," Welter said. "Not only about the culture that he was trying to build in his company but also about him as a human being."

Scheller's reputation as a competent officer and leader of Marines resulted in him being selected to train future Marine officers at officer candidate school and The Basic School. As a rule, the Marine Corps invests its best talent into its training programmes.

Sergeant Barbitta, who in 2019 was about to retire from the Marine Corps, spoke bluntly about the type of leader Scheller was.

"If I could have a guarantee that he would have been my battalion commander, or I would have worked in the same command as Stu, I would have stayed in," Barbitta told *Marine Corps Times.*

Barbitta said that leaders in the Marine Corps such as Scheller are few and far between.

One of the things Barbitta most appreciated about Scheller's leadership was his emphasis on communication both up and down the chain of command, which Barbitta said allowed all Marines in the chain of command to feel valued and involved.

Scheller maintained a "first to arrive and last to leave" mindset and dedicated his efforts to enabling his Marines.

"He's just a great f*cking leader," Barbitta said.

While Scheller says that the attack in Kabul, which claimed the lives of 13 service members and 170 Afghans, sparked him to speak out on August 26, 2021, the rationale behind it was more complicated.

Barbitta, who worked with Scheller until mid-2020, a little more than a year before Scheller went viral with his demands for accountability, described Scheller as very deliberate and calculated. Barbitta described Scheller as someone who, when making decisions, would consult multiple opinions before making a decision.

"He was very, he's very conscious of his thoughts and actions," Barbitta said. "He's very, I mean very methodical with his decisions."

Underhill saw Scheller as an officer destined to be a career Marine, possibly rising to general or higher. Further, he described Scheller as a "stone-cold professional" who is very "calm, cool and collected."

"***Stu is not a hothead,***" Underhill said. "***So, if Stu is upset by the current situation and the lack of accountability—America needs to listen.***"

Source: The Making of Lt Col Stuart Scheller, James R Webb
https://www.marinecorpstimes.com/news/your-marine-corps/2022/03/07/the-making-of-lt-col-stuart-scheller/

Author's Notes

The modern-day world is no different from what it was a millennium or two before where might was right and there were no conventions.

In most cases, the so-called rich and advanced countries are doing the same with different tools, much more devastating, and taking it upon themselves to discipline the world and spread their values in the name of the 'White man's burden.' It is they who colonised the world, looted and exploited them, killed them, deprived them of education and progress, and starved them. The cause of most conflicts in the world has been the West or the legacy they left post colonisation, be they countries in Africa, Asia-West Asia, the Middle East or Europe. And today, they sit at the high table of the United Nations to chart the destiny of the nations. How is the West so sure that their values and way of life are any better than countries in Asia?

The things which were glorious had no glory.

—Ernest Hemingway

We have seen how conscientious soldiers get affected by unjust wars, incompetence of their hierarchy or simply by the unethical practices their organisations follow. So, the important question is, should soldiers like Corporal Glenton be forced to serve in a war they are not in agreement with? These are wars in other's lands, which are not threatening their country. These wars kill innocents by tens of thousands and displace millions—women and children who are no threat to anyone. These wars are being fought at the whims of the political leadership, who are among the least trusted lot of people. The wars are big enterprises where big money gets made, the US arms industry being the biggest beneficiary. The price is paid by someone else.

My view is, that no meaningful contribution can be expected from a man whose heart is not in it. If anything, his presence will only detrimentally influence others. They better be allowed to quit without being court-martialled. No soldier will ever refuse to fight a war, where their country is threatened. Was Glenton not proved right by the way the Afghanistan saga wound up leaving Afghans in greater misery than before 9/11? Can one ever forget the sight of hundreds of Afghans running and scrambling on military aircraft to get away? Can one ever forget the sight of a man falling off US military aircraft to his death?

Now, here we have a Corporal, a Captain and a Lt Colonel seeking accountability from their superiors, putting their careers and lives on the line. As Scheller says, we have not heard of one political leader or a General taking responsibility for the fiasco that left the world a worse place than before America attacked Afghanistan or Iraq.

Scheller had a bright career ahead of him and was deeply respected by his men. His commitment to the military values and his men would accept no less and had to speak his mind fearlessly, at a great personal cost. People who defy authority are men of conscience and they see things which go beyond their selfish motives. They leave the organisation better. Those who serve for the next rank will do no good to a man or a beast. The biggest casualty is the value system of the organisation, so critical for its long-term effectiveness. And it is the excellent men and innocent civilians who pay the price.

♦ ♦ ♦

Chapter Six

Vietnam War

A CASE STUDY IN MILITARY ETHICS

Vietnam War is the finest study that brings many lessons home in the context of the theme of this book.

> *GIs joked that "anything that's dead and isn't white is a VC (Viet Cong)" for body count purposes.*

In the combat zone, it is the highest military leadership that sets the stage for military values. In Vietnam, the US military leadership started with what can be described as a perfect antithesis to the operational art of war.

The American General Westmoreland, who was the commander in Vietnam for four crucial years, followed a strategy that was destined to fail. When it was not working, he failed to see the reality and listen to his advisors. He fudged and manipulated statistics to prove that the war was progressing well and was ever ready to abandon truth when it came in the way of his ambitions and personal interest.

Source: Westmoreland. The General Who Lost Vietnam, by Lewis Sorley

> *The true use of history is not to make us clever for the next time but to make us wise forever.*
>
> ***—Sir Michael Howard***

Countries rarely learn from history. The US is a fine example of how the politicians and Generals combined can be detrimental to the country for political expediency and self-serving interests.

After the defeat of the French in the Battle of Dien Bien Phu and their withdrawal in 1954, the US assumed financial and military support for the

South Vietnamese state. The military, which initially came to advise and assist the South Vietnamese government, slowly got sucked into the war. At its peak in 1969, the US had more than 540000 combatants there and had lost 58279 soldiers in Vietnam.

The US fought a decade-long war in Vietnam, ostensibly to check the expansion of communism in South East Asia. The US, which during the Second World War, had supported the rights of colonies to decide their own governance, much to the chagrin of Winston Churchill, landed up financing the colonial French in Vietnam, which at one stage is estimated to have reached eighty per cent. And tragically, Ho Chi Minh, the Vietnamese leader was not a diehard communist. His aim was a united independent Vietnam and believed in the same values as the Americans. It is believed that he wrote a letter to the US President, FD Roosevelt stating so and that he expected support from the US in keeping with their stated position on the rights of colonies. For reasons unknown, that letter was never put up to the President. It cost the Americans dearly and the loss of two million Vietnamese lives.

The character of long military engagements is that both political and military leaders fail to see the reality, hope things will change by doing more of the same, lack the courage to accept it and thus mislead their people with false narratives and statistics. The Vietnam War is one such example. The US War in Afghanistan which terminated in a most unprofessional and chaotic withdrawal in August 21, like Vietnam, was no different.

How is it that five US Presidents in that period promised to draw down in Vietnam and landed up reinforcing it with more and more, till the public opposition to the war would allow no more?

Despite the French experience in exactly the same theatre against the same enemy only a few years earlier, the US military failed to see the nature of warfare in Vietnam and blundered on.

They pursued a mindless strategy of attrition against a guerrilla army that fought an entirely different war, 'everywhere and nowhere' needing very little to survive, never had fixed assets that could be targeted and rarely accepted a pitched battle. Americans were attacking hills, suffering casualties and then vacating them, for the Vietnamese to return unopposed.

They chose peculiar metrics for projecting their progress in that war. Their flawed philosophy was that if they could kill more North Vietnamese soldiers than they could recycle, eventually they will win the war. This is the absolute antithesis of operational art. This led to the number game. People were massacred who had nothing to do with the war. Every North Vietnamese killed—man, woman, child or farmer was added to the statistics and the country fed that victory was near. GIs joked that "anything that's dead and isn't white is a VC" for body count purposes. For every innocent killed, they made ten more enemies. The US engagement in Vietnam lasted two decades, as it did in Afghanistan. Both had similar operational environments, similar approaches and the same catastrophic result—disgraceful withdrawal and a strategic defeat against a much inferior enemy. How was this any less brutal and inhumane than the historic or medieval wars?

Eventually, the public opposition forced the government to end the war in 1973. The North Vietnamese overran South Vietnam and established a communist government. And yes, the American 'domino theory'; the fear that the whole of South Asia will fall under the influence of communism, for which they went to war in Vietnam, did not happen!! A flawed reason to go to war, as was Iraq in 2003.

Why did America, which with others brought down Germany and primarily single-handedly brought down Japan in the Second World War less than two decades earlier, and performed well in Korea a decade earlier, performed poorly in Vietnam?

It is estimated that the Americans dropped between seven and thirteen million tonnes of bombs on Indo-China, the vast majority in Vietnam killing an estimated two million people. Compare that to the estimated 2.25 million tonnes in the entire Second World War and 1.5 million tonnes over German-held territories. A philosophy of attrition against an enemy who negated the conventional superiority of the Americans by their tactics, something that was to be repeated in Afghanistan later.

Why did it become a war that divided a nation, where the war veterans who had immensely suffered physically and emotionally, were ostracised by both the opponents of war for their brutalities and the supporters for losing the war?

Some of the reports published after the war make good lessons for military leadership at all levels. Studies on some armies that engaged in wars highlight what succeeds in war and what does not. (*Source:* excerpts from the book, *'Crisis in Command'* by Richard A Gabriel and Paul L Savage.)

The American army in the Vietnam War gave a poor account of itself. The cases of fragging, desertion, suicide, drug pedalling and other unbecoming conduct by soldiers were higher than ever before, while the stress of combat was not higher than in World War II or for that matter in Korea. The authors in this book bring out some interesting deductions. According to them, the US Army suffered from a lack of cohesion at the sub-unit level. The reasons for this are many.

First, the officers avoided combat service and the risks of the combat soldier. Since military service was compulsory, those who could do so managed softer options in the comfort of headquarters way behind.

To a soldier going through the grind of combat, these headquarters looked like islands of comfort and luxury; officers' clubs with extravagant lifestyles, swimming pools, bowling alleys, tennis courts etc. Infantry, which did the bulk of combat amounted to only twenty per cent of the strength in Vietnam which meant more money was spent on the comforts of the tail than on the cutting-edge teeth. The second major point they bring out was the policy of rotation. While the troops served a tenure of twelve months, officers were turned over after six months.

Careerism came to inflict the officer corps, who used this opportunity to push their careers by what came to be known as 'ticket punching,' i.e., getting all-important endorsements on their CV for promotion. The troops were seeing too many officers of poor commitment and competence made responsible for them.

The next aspect they point out is the unwillingness of officers to face the same hardships and the same risks to life and limb.

> *In essence, they lay the blame for poor performance in Vietnam on the poor quality of officers, obsessed with career obsession and ticket punching, neglecting the basic tenets of soldiering.*

War College Study on Military Professionalism in Vietnam brought out the following:

'Officers of all grades *perceive a significant difference between the ideal values and the actual or operative values of the officer corps.* There is also concern that the army is not taking action to ensure that high ideals are practised as well as preached...that the Army has generated an environment that rewards relatively insignificant, short-term indicators of success, and disregards and discourages the growth of long-term qualities of moral and ethical strength on which the future of the Army depends. *They are frustrated by the seniors who sacrificed integrity on the altar of personal success.* The study found distorted and dishonest reporting of statistics and officer efficiency."

All this created resentment amongst the men. In three years, the Army counted 788 cases of assaults with explosive devices, primarily directed against officers, called 'fragging' in military parlance.

Careerism was the problem in Vietnam for the US military. Career-obsessed and conformist officers are rarely likely to rock the boat.

Vietnam War was a watershed moment for the US Army, from where they have been constantly focussing on developing military ethics to suit the environment in which soldiers operate. How effective they are is a matter of judgment, as the Abu Ghraib and Guantanamo Bay experiences indicate.

Post the Second World War, no other nation got embroiled in wars like the US, of its own choosing. So, the brickbats will come. Very little of consequence can go wrong in a peacetime army. The Generals in other armies have not been put through baptism by fire as the US Generals have. Their stories are unlikely to have been much different if they were in similar circumstances.

Unit cohesion is the secret to success in combat. Unit cohesion directly results from the quality of leadership; officer corps' readiness to share the same hardships and risks as their men, something the Americans in Vietnam were mostly not ready to.

THE MY LAI MASSACRE—JUST A FEW GOOD MEN

The My Lai massacre, 16 March 1968, was one of the lowest points in US history.

Charlie Company under Captain Edina, the company commander and Lieutenant (Lt) William Calley, a platoon commander, operating in My Lai Village, as part of Task Force Barker, killed over 500 unarmed, unresisting, mostly old men, women, children and infants and committed gang rapes.

The world will always be at war somewhere, and the worst hit are the people who get caught between the two sides. In the context of this book, there are useful lessons from the My Lai episode. The incidents of Abu Ghraib prison in

Iraq and Guantanamo Bay, Cuba, five decades later, ring the same bells of unethical soldiering and leadership, as does the My Lai incident.

It will be useful to reconstruct this incident in detail for it has great lessons on leadership, unethical soldiering, positive defiance and moral courage from the lowest rank in the army to the highest position in the country-the president.

As a soldier, it bothers me how any professional army sub-unit with senior NCOs and two officers could do this, never mind which army it was. This was no different in the spirit of brutality and hatred from what the Nazis did to kill the Jews during the Second World War or what Muslim invaders did in India.

The difference between the holocaust and My Lai was mainly in the manner the two parties killed those innocent people. In the case of Germany, it was the Nazi Party policy to exterminate Jews as the 'Final Solution'; while in My Lai, it is fair to assume, as we shall see later, that up to the level of the brigade commander and below, conditions were created by the ambiguity in orders. Many soldiers believe that the ambiguity was by design to set the stage for what happened. At the battalion level, the orders left no doubt that everyone in My Lai is a Viet Cong and must be killed and the village destroyed.

This was not a one-off incident of military brutality. We continue to hear of inhuman brutality in the civil wars in Africa and West Asia where the concept of human values simply does not exist. If there are no consequences for the criminals, little will change and that highlights the importance of positive defiance or constructive disobedience.

Some issues:

- The purported intelligence that the Viet Cong 48 LF battalion was located at My Lai hamlets was false, as it was actually located over 140 miles away. Located within South Vietnam, it is hard to believe that this critical information, based on which such a major operation, supported by artillery and gunships was launched was not confirmed intelligence.
- This has a disturbing similarity with the 29 August 21 drone attack in Kabul post US withdrawal in which ten civilians including seven children were killed. Only, the methodology was different. Like the My Lai incident where everyone was presumed to be the enemy, General Mc Kenzie said that this drone strike was launched with an honest belief that they have prevented an ISIS-K attack by killing the terrorists.

- The majority of those shot point-blank in My Lai were unarmed, unresisting old women, young mothers, children and babies. Many soldiers who were interviewed believed that there were no signs of them being Vietcong or their supporters. They were simply going around their lives; going to the market when they were rounded up and mowed down. The company did not come under fire during the entire carnage from anywhere.
- Years later, some My Lai veterans said in media interviews that after the incident, the company was sent out for operations for two months straight into the mountains. The soldiers believed they were sent there so that they do not speak to anyone and with the hope that no one returns.

In that hour of madness, there were three ethical soldiers including Warrant Officer Hugh Thomson, a helicopter pilot, who deliberately intervened to save and evacuate the injured Vietnamese. He then reported the massacre to his commanding officer. Some veterans believed that this pilot was then sent on dangerous missions, for the same reasons. According to them, he crashed a few times on these missions.

Many factors led to the My Lai massacre, including the flawed strategy of the number game, the frustration of losing men to an unseen enemy who could not be hit back and an accomplice leadership.

The exposure of the My Lai incident shook the conscience of the American public. A stage came when the soldiers marred by their conscience of the brutality they were inflicting on innocent people, protested against the war they were part of. Youths escaped evading the military draft to Vietnam.

THE INVESTIGATION

When the truth of the My Lai massacre became public, and the politicians and the military could not hide it anymore, General William Peers, a blunt and respected General was appointed to hold an investigation. He interviewed over 385 witnesses from the divisional commander Major General Koster, down to the privates and non-combatants in the battle zone.

Peers Report: Summary of Findings

- During the period of 16-19 March 1968, troops of Task Force Barker (three companies) massacred a large number of Vietnamese nationals in the village of Son My (My Lai was one village in that area).

- Knowledge as to the extent of the incident existed at the company level, at least among the key staff officers and commander at the Task Force Barker level and the 11th Brigade command level.
- Efforts at the American Division command level to conceal information, concerning what was probably believed to be the killing of 20-28 civilians, actually resulted in the suppression of a war crime of far greater magnitude.
- The commander of the 11th Brigade, upon learning that a war crime had probably been committed, deliberately set out to conceal the facts from proper authority and to deceive his commander concerning the matter.
- Investigations concerning the incident conducted within the American Division were superficial and misleading and not subjected to substantive review.
- Efforts were made at every level of command from company to division to withhold and suppress information concerning the incident at Son My.
- Failure of American Division headquarters personnel to act on information received from GVN/ARVN (*Vietnamese army/provincial*) officials served to effectively suppress information concerning the Son My incident.
- Efforts of the American Division to suppress and withhold information were assisted by US officers serving in advisory positions with Vietnamese agencies.

The Longest Court-Martial

Lt William Calley, the platoon commander, was found guilty of all the charges arising out of the killing of unarmed civilians in the My Lai village massacre. After a thirteen days deliberation, the longest court-martial in American history, he was given a life sentence.

The Army prosecutor Aubrey Daniel believed that Lt Calley was responsible for most of the murders that took place in My Lai. During the prosecution, Lt Calley replied as follows:

> *"I believed then, as I believe now, that I acted as I was directed. I followed the orders that I was given and I did not feel wrong in doing so."*

He said, "*The only crime that I have committed is that I adjusted my values and valued my soldiers' lives more than the enemies. When my men were being massacred by the enemy whom I could not see, feel or touch, they became my enemy and I valued my soldiers' lives more than the enemies.*"

The Public Outcry. It was the most controversial case and people supported Lt Calley in public rallies on the streets. A survey indicated that people felt that he was the scapegoat in an incident where many of his superiors were more or equally responsible.

The public outcry and the political expediency led President Nixon to order that Lt Calley be released from his stockade and confined to his quarters pending the review of his life sentence for the My Lai massacre.

When asked by a journalist, "Mr President, you said, you have intervened in the Lt Calley case in the national interest. I wonder if you could define for us in greater detail, how it was served by your intervention?"

Nixon replied, "I felt it was proper for me to indicate that I would review the case because there was great concern expressed throughout the country as to whether or not this was a case, that involving as it did, so many complex factors in which Lt Calley was going to get a fair trial."

Ultimately, Calley served only four months in the Stockade of Fort Leavenworth. It was seen as if he had done enough time in prison and was released.

Four months for killing hundred innocent people? Lt Calley was the only My Lai defendant to be convicted. What President Nixon's act did was to tell the military, no matter what, they will not be punished for what they do. The trials of the rest 29 became a sham. They all were either dismissed or acquitted.

The top officer charged General Samuel Koster, who failed to report known civilian casualties and conducted a clearly inadequate investigation was, according to General Peers, the beneficiary of a whitewash, having charges against him dropped and receiving only a letter of censure and reduction in rank. Colonel Henderson, commander of the brigade was found 'not guilty' on all charges after a trial by court-martial.

The My Lai massacre changed the Americans' approach to this war, that if this was the price of this war, it was not worth paying this price.

Forty years later Lt Calley spoke for the first time in Public.

"There is not a day that goes by that I do not feel remorse for what happened that day in My Lai. I feel remorse for the Vietnamese who were killed, for their families, for the American soldiers involved and their families. I am very sorry."

What do you make out of this? I read that he knew all along he was wrong in doing what he did in following that order.

Source: Reconstructed from various documentaries, media reports, summaries of the court-martial proceedings, interviews of veterans, press briefings and other documents on the internet.

Author's Notes

Lt Calley's testimony that the order was to kill everyone in the village seems to be supported by this prelude to the operation.

"On March 14, a small squad from 'C' Company ran into a booby trap, killing a popular sergeant, blinding one GI and wounding several others. The following evening, when a funeral service was held for the killed sergeant, soldiers had revenge on their minds. After the service, Captain Medina rose to give the soldiers a pep talk and discuss the next morning's mission. Medina told them that the VC's crack 48th Battalion was in the vicinity of a hamlet known as My Lai 4, which would be the target of a large-scale assault by the company. The soldiers' mission would be to engage the 48th Battalion and destroy the village of My Lai. By 7 a.m., Medina said, the women and children would be out of the hamlet and all they could expect to encounter would be the enemy. The soldiers were to explode brick homes, set fire to thatch homes, shoot livestock, poison wells, and destroy the enemy. The seventy-five or so American soldiers would be supported in their assault by gunship pilots.

Medina later said that his objective that night was to 'fire them up and get them ready to go in there; I did not give any instructions as to what to do with women and children in the village.' Although some soldiers agreed with that recollection of Medina, **others clearly thought that he had ordered them to kill every person in My Lai 4. Perhaps his orders were intentionally vague. What**

seems likely is that Medina intentionally gave the impression that everyone in My Lai would be their enemy.

Source: Record of My Lai court-martial, https://famous-trials.com/mylaicourts/1656-myl-intro

In the operational environment existing in Vietnam or any counter-insurgency operation for that matter, civilians will invariably be around in the area, and not by choice. There was no way to differentiate a Viet Cong supporter from an innocent civilian. The Vietcong soldiers themselves wore varying kinds of dresses, some similar to what the civilians wore. In such an environment, the orders to deal with women and children have to be explicit. Some men felt that Captain Edina left no doubt that everyone had to be killed and the village destroyed, setting the stage for the carnage.

Given the vagueness of the order about women and children in that environment, no one in that company of 80 soldiers asked that obvious question; or try to stop that carnage when it had started. Lt Calley did neither and was the most active perpetrator.

WHAT SHOULD A SOLDIER DO WITH AN UNLAWFUL/ AWFUL ORDER?

There can only be one deduction—that they were willing accomplices to the premeditated murder of so many.

The other side of the coin is, where does it leave a soldier, who says I won't do it? Chances are he will be hounded, framed, false evidence rigged up and punished to shut him up for a cover-up. There are no reliable safeguards in any military for a whistle-blower that implicates his superiors in the chain.

Because a soldier is authorised to kill, which means a whole family is devastated and thrown to the wolves, he has the greatest responsibility. The responsibility is to make sure that he kills the right man for the right reasons that will stand legal scrutiny. My Lai did not pass any of this audit.

Some veterans of Charlie Company, decades later, stated in an interview that there is no scope for disobeying any order, legal or illegal. A soldier is trained to obey orders and kill and he does what he is told. That conflicts with the basic value of integrity, the laws of conflict and the Geneva Convention.

The answer to that is that a soldier kills his enemies without remorse, but there is a point and circumstances, at which a soldier does not even kill his enemy and treats him according to the laws of conflict. The innocent My Lai victims, living in their own country, going about their harmless daily chores, killed by foreign troops who had no business to be in their country, never received any trials. Many politicians continued to deny that My Lai ever happened, as some people deny that the holocaust ever happened. US President Nixon's act made a mockery of military justice, rubbished the great act of moral courage of a few good men like Warrant Officer Hugh Thompson and set the stage for the perpetuation of brutality that America has come to characterize in the world's perception as seen in Iraq, Afghanistan, Abu Ghraib, Guantanamo etc.

It is a travesty and a tragicomedy that over 500 women, children and babies are massacred and there is no one responsible and no one punished. And this happens in a country that sees itself as the champion of human rights, equality, justice and democracy.

Where do such illegal orders stand? Even the laws of armed conflict protect soldiers who surrender, the medical personnel and assets, prisoners of war and the civilian population. The worst affected are the women and children.

Counter-insurgency, counter-terrorism operations and operations such as Vietnam pose far greater ethical challenges to soldiers. Everyone from the President to the private needs to understand that and be trained in all aspects. In such operations, a leader will so often find himself in a difficult spot. He could continue to suffer casualties without seeing the enemy and the opportunity to get at them in a fight. Where there is no visible distinction between the enemy and the civilians, it is easy for the soldiers to vent their frustration on civilians and rationalise their actions by declaring them as sympathisers, informants, overground workers or fake encounters. Fighting in a foreign land, soldiers get away more easily with the excesses than they would in their own country, as they did in My Lai.

As for the Americans, this is validated by how the 'Black Lives Matter' movement gathered global momentum when a few unarmed black Americans were killed by white policemen without justifiable reasons.

We now need to look at the Vietnam saga from the perspective of the theme of the book—When Defiance Becomes Duty.

From a plethora of pointers such as the revelations in books like *The Crisis in*

Command, media reports of that era, protests by the veterans and the reflections of officers who went on to hold higher ranks, it is very clear now, as it was very clear then that there were serious issues. Now, the bigger question is whether officers or men should defy authority like Warrant Officer Hugh Thomson and his crew did, in such unmistakable circumstances.

That Warrant Officer Thomson and his two brave colleagues were awarded the Soldier's Medal thirty years later, is of little satisfaction. For three decades, a whole new generation of American military men and women must have lived with an uneasy belief that it does not pay to be ethical and that military values in the end count for nothing.

The award of the Soldier's Medal is a vindication that President Nixon was wrong in whitewashing the brutality by a group of men on hapless women, children and babies and Warrant Officer Hugh Thomson was right. Men, who belonged to an organization that prides itself on its values and ethics shot to shreds the same values in those three hours on 16 Mar 1968 at My Lai that will always be cited as a horrible example of soldiering and leadership.

It is also a time to revisit the George Bush order on Guantanamo Bay.

There is something that seems to be in the psyche of the Americans that forms a pattern—the American sense of right and American exceptionalism.

Four decades after the My Lai massacre, the US Administration was struggling with unethical practices, first in Abu Ghraib and then in Guantanamo Bay that detained over 600, nine/ eleven terror suspects for years. There were reports of torture and violation of basic human rights that should have been available to the detainees, given the values that the US Administration keeps priding in their speeches all around the world.

The Military Commission Act 2006, passed by President George Bush legalizing all the things that the US Supreme Court said were illegal in Guantanamo Bay speaks of the US duplicity.

However, that said, the champions of human rights for terrorists need to appreciate that expecting the terrorists to be treated like gentlemen and hoping to prevent terrorist attacks in the present environment is naive. A soldier who is at the wrong end of the barrel and IEDs has a different take from the armchair experts on a TV debate who faces no risks.

These few lines best sum up the sentiments of the American General Peers on My Lai which shows the depth to which the American officers and men at My Lai had fallen.

> *On the ground and in the command chain, people who were in a position to prevent it did not do so, and then those in authority covered it up.*

One commentator best described the sentiments, 'General Peers a well-respected soldier was so distraught with what he found during the investigation on My Lai, that when the few of the likes of Warrant Officer Thomson came forward, he felt a sense of relief, that at least there were a few good Americans.'

My Lai happened because of blind obedience. Constructive dissent and constructive disobedience would have prevented the disaster and saved America many blushes.

♦ ♦ ♦

Chapter Seven

The Dichotomy of Duty and Defiance

What is the military's duty in curbing the power of a reckless commander-in-chief?

'*Theirs not to reason why, theirs but to do and die.*' This 1854 poem '*The Charge of the Light Brigade* ' by Lord Tennyson, in one respect an occasional poem, also offers a timeless reflection on the senselessness that accompanies much of the war, while also praising the unflinching bravery and sense of duty of the soldiers who gave their lives.

Field Marshal Montgomery was a young officer during the First World War. He commanded a platoon, a company and a battalion in that war. Monty participated in the battle of Somme. More than 30000 men died and another 30000 were injured on the first day of the battle alone on the Allies' side. Monty was injured during the battle, and as he spent his time recovering, he realized that the Generals of the First World War, who were called the fighting Generals, were unprofessional and incompetent. They did not care about how many soldiers died and were of the cavalry charge mould in the wrong era of machine guns.

He realized that an army is a place for professionals and not '*Fighting Generals*'. He decided to be one. He cut himself off from all socializing, parties and time wasters. He got down to reading and enhancing his professional threshold and even delayed his marriage till he was forty.

Where does blind obedience stand amidst such incompetence? It is the right of soldiers to demand that they be led by competent officers who care for their lives. And, when they are not, seek accountability, for a soldier's life is not cheap. Generally speaking, and I say this having seen the Indian army for four decades, the military promotion system breeds mediocrity. Incompetence is rarely penalised and that promotes stereotypes and safe play. The armies' challenge is to select leaders based on peacetime assessment who will deliver in battle. In the military, conformist mediocrity will outshine non-conformist brilliance.

Defiance is easily preached but very difficult to practice for the whole system lines up against you. Thus, it is a personal call and very few will have the courage to stand up for what they must, for it is much easier to sail with the wind. This is a duty which must be discharged for the good of the organization and the country. Sometimes, the army and the people must save their country from their own government.

It is generally believed that the military is about '*Theirs is not to reason why...*' That may be the right philosophy to propagate at the lower levels. But that is neither absolute nor applicable without caveats. Why should it be an acceptable philosophy at the lower levels? Simply because it is expected that commanders at the higher level will do what needs to be done. It is meant to nurture a culture of obedience because the military operates in a high-risk environment and there will be a tendency among soldiers to duck life-threatening situations. The military values expect a soldier to stand up for what is right and against what is immoral, illegal or amoral.

How justifiable is the defence that one was simply obeying orders? When should such a defence be valid? What should be done in the case of ambiguous orders or when oral commands contradict written directives? Can a personal belief that the order is lawful or unlawful be tenable? Should different standards apply to privates than to persons higher up the chain of command? What should a soldier do when he is given an order that he thinks is unlawful, immoral or amoral? Is a soldier's personal perception acceptable? Should a subordinate demand that such orders be issued in writing?

After the Second World War, many German SS officers were tried for war crimes during the Nuremberg trials. Their defence was that they were simply obeying orders. This plea was rejected and many were convicted. So, we come to an important deduction that amoral and illegal orders by superiors are expected to be disobeyed. Many American soldiers involved in the My Lai incident regretted what they had done and that realization had come in less than twenty-four hours. Others continued to believe that soldiers are meant to obey orders, whatever they may be.

Officers have a responsibility to question and if necessary, disobey amoral orders. Rommel tore down Hitler's orders to execute the Jewish brigade which was taken prisoner along with allied troops in North Africa. It was against the laws of conflict and against humanity itself once they had ceased to be a threat. Rommel was a true soldier who defied Hitler and would not do such a thing.

General Dietrich von Choltitz, not a saint himself, found a reason to disregard Hitler's orders to burn down Paris. In doing so, he preserved many centuries of art, heritage and history. More importantly, he upheld the honour of the noble profession of soldiering and ethical leadership. However, none of these was the reason why he did it. He did it because by then, he was convinced that Hitler had gone insane and that Paris had lost any military significance, thus, did not serve any purpose to destroy it.

The US experience in Vietnam, Abu Ghraib prison in Iraq and Guantanamo Bay prison are examples where amoral orders or unethical acts by some should have been prevented by others. At the lower level, rationalization of lies, cheating or killing innocents in the name of the unit's honour becomes the excuse, but that is not acceptable at all. Dilution of military values in one field will lead to compromise in others.

Armies are meant to be apolitical. They neither serve any government nor any ideology. They serve to protect the values of the constitution and serve by the ageless values of the military. Anything conflicting with these parameters needs to be questioned and if necessary disobeyed.

These are difficult issues to deal with but must be dealt with.

Your conscience will unambiguously tell you which orders merit disobedience; your character will dictate your response.

THE COMPLEXITY OF DEFIANCE

There are a few episodes in recent times that have important lessons in the context of this book.

Case Study: General Mark Milley

In my opinion, the most complex and sensitive domain concerning positive defiance, even with the noblest intentions, is the civil-military domain. In recent times, General Mark Milley, the chairman of the Joint Chiefs of Staff, United States, stands out as the commander who personifies 'Positive Defiance' and its necessity. He has the character and the courage that is required and often conspicuous by its absence at that level.

Four years of the Trump Presidency were characterized by a fantastical degree of instability: fits of rage, late-night Twitter storms and abrupt dismissals. He had his serious critics and he had his supporters. In the election campaign in Nov 2016, Barak Obama called him “Uniquely unqualified to be President. He is temperamentally unfit to be the commander-in-chief” at a well-attended Democratic rally in Columbus. In the 2020 election that Trump lost, 72 million people voted for him. He accused the Democrats of stealing the election and this was followed by the infamous siege of Capitol Hill, apparently encouraged by Trump, that shook America and shocked the world.

To understand the challenges of positive defiance for a top military commander, we need to understand the environment during the tenure of President Trump and examine the experiences of General Milley with him as the Chairman Joint Chiefs of Staff.

What sums up President Donald Trump’s tenure is that he became the only US President to be impeached twice. The second time for ‘inciting resurrection’ over the deadly mob siege of Capitol Hill on Jan 06 2021 to prevent Congress from certifying Joe Biden’s White House victory.

We begin with the unprovoked death of George Floyd, an African American at the hands of a white policeman, an incident that made international headlines.

Donald Trump wanted ten thousand troops in the streets and the 82nd Airborne called up to quell the ‘Black Lives Matter’ movement after the death of George Floyd. He demanded that Milley take personal charge. When Milley and Defense Secretary Mark Esper resisted and said that the National Guard would be sufficient, Trump shouted, “You are all losers! You are all fucking losers!” Turning to Milley, Trump said, “Can’t you just shoot them? Just shoot them in the legs or something?”

It was in the spirit of keeping the army out of domestic politics that General Milley and the Defense Secretary refused to deploy active-duty troops to quell protests over George Floyd’s death in June 2020.

After Lafayette Square was cleared of the protesters by the authorities using tear gas and rubber bullets, President Trump with his aides took a walk across Lafayette Square for a photo op in front of St John’s Church. General Milley was part of that group, even though he did not join the photo op where Trump stood in front of the Church with a Bible in his hand.

General Milley, in a recorded video, apologized for taking part in President Trump's walk across Lafayette Square for a photo op.

He said, "It Was a Mistake."

"As senior leaders, everything you do will be closely watched, and I am not immune. As many of you saw the result of the photograph of me at Lafayette Square last week, that sparked a national debate about the role of the military in civil society. I should not have been there. My presence at that moment, and in that environment, created a perception of the military involved in domestic politics. As a commissioned uniformed officer, it was a mistake that I have learned from and I sincerely hope we all can learn from it. We who wear the cloth of our nation, come from the people of our nation, and we must hold dear the principle of an apolitical military that is so deeply rooted in the very essence of our republic."

When President Trump declared that the US was ready to strike 50 cultural sites in Iran, this was openly contradicted by General Mark Milley, who clarified, "We will follow the laws of armed conflict".

On another occasion, he reiterated "The Armed Forces of USA take an oath to the constitution of the country—not to any king, queen or any individual, a country, religion or tribe."

It was a crystal-clear message to the political establishment, not to politicise the US Military.

—Gen Mark Milley, speaking at Fort Belvoir, Virginia, November 11, 2020.

Washington Post associate editor Bob Woodward and national political reporter Robert Costa claim in their book *Peril* that General Milley made two phone calls to Chinese officials in fear that Trump would create conflict with the nation, telling the officials that he would forewarn them about an attack if planned by the U.S. on China. The book claims that Milley contacted his Chinese counterpart after he had reviewed intelligence that suggested Chinese officials believed the United States was planning an attack on China amid military exercises in the South China Sea.

It was during this tumultuous period that General Mark Milley spoke twice to his counterpart in China. The second call came two days after the Jan 6 Capitol Hill incident.

General Mark Milley testified about his calls with China over concerns about Donald Trump during a hearing on September 28, 2021. Here is the transcript of his statement.

> *"Mr Chairman, I've served this nation for 42 years. I've spent years in combat and I've buried a lot of my troops who died while defending this country. My loyalty to this nation, its people and the constitution hasn't changed and will never change as long as I have a breath to give. My loyalty is absolute and I will not turn my back on the fallen. With respect to the Chinese calls, I routinely communicated with my counterpart, General Lee, with the knowledge and coordination of civilian oversight. I am specifically directed to communicate with the Chinese by the Department of Defense guidance, the policy dialogue system.*
>
> *My oath is to support the constitution of the United States of America against all enemies, foreign and domestic and I will never turn my back on the oath. I firmly believe in civilian control of the military as a bedrock principle, essential to the health of this Republic and I'm committed to ensuring that the military stays clear of domestic politics."*

Some veterans asked for his resignation as did some lawmakers considering his action somewhere between 'treason and dereliction of duty'.

The challenges facing General Milley and some right-thinking people in Trump Administration are well elucidated in Susan Glasser and Peter Baker's article in the New Yorker – '**Inside the War Between Trump and His Generals—** *How Mark Milley and others in the Pentagon handled the national-security threat posed by their own Commander-in-Chief.*'

Doyle Hodges throws light on important aspects of the dynamics and the predicament of General Milley in his article *A Duty to Disobey?* I have discussed the complexities of positive defiance by military leaders based on these incisive articles.

President Trump's tenure as president was particularly tumultuous, especially in the last days. The author describes the following aspects:

- Trump wanted to deploy regular troops to control the 'Black Lives Matter' protests.
- Attack Iran without a justifiable reason.

- Towards the end, as he alleged stealing of elections by the Democrats, there were efforts and possibilities of preventing the peaceful transition of power by creating situations and using the military. The siege of Capitol Hill was a development that created serious concerns among the military and others.

General Milley resolved to thwart any orders he received from President Donald Trump to deploy troops domestically or to attack Iran without sufficient provocation. A war on Iran did not meet any of the Jus ad Bellum criteria.

As the article details, General Milly settled on four goals: First, make sure Trump did not start an unnecessary war overseas. Second, make sure the military was not used in the streets against the American people for the purpose of keeping Trump in power. Third, maintain the military's integrity. And, fourth, maintain his own integrity."

While the article portrayed Milley sympathetically, his actions to frustrate the policy desires of the president are seen as problematic from a civil-military relations perspective. That isn't to say that the policy goals in question were ethical, legal, moral, or appropriate. Efforts to overturn a free and fair election are none of those things; neither would be orders to start an unprovoked foreign war. **The problem is that the military is not the constitutionally prescribed mechanism to keep these things from happening.** This is interesting yet worth a contest.

Samuel Huntington, in his influential book "*The Soldier and the State*," wrote that "loyalty and obedience are the highest military virtues." In her book, "*On Obedience*," philosopher Pauline Shanks-Kaurin qualifies this somewhat: **"Unreflective obedience is not a virtue and may, in fact, be a vice and counterproductive to the military function."** How ought Milley's efforts to serve as a guardrail against what he perceived as Trump's dangerous impulses be judged in this context?

How far ought the senior military officer go to shape the political executive's policy choices?

What should the officer do if given an unlawful order? How should the officer respond if given an order that is "lawful but awful"? What other options were available to Milley, and what circumstances might have justified his acting on his own authority to stymie the actions of the president?

The author states, the chairman's role is to present his assessment of the merits and wisdom of possible military responses, as well as to convey any dissenting views from other members of the joint chiefs. That responsibility may, at times, extend to advocating with a senior official for or against a particular course of military action, but discussions with NSC members on how to steer the president away from certain military policy choices are different from working with the president's high-level advisers outside of the NSC context on political issues—which Milley was apparently at least prepared to do.

In practical terms, in the US, the guidelines from the military tribunal and related dictates are generally understood globally to mean that members of the military must disobey an order that is "manifestly unlawful." But the standard for manifest unlawfulness is extraordinarily high.

As per law, the head of state clearly has a great deal of discretion in determining when the conditions allowing for the domestic deployment of troops have been met. General Milley could have strongly advised against such an order and would have had a responsibility to craft the mission and rules governing the use of force in such a way that they did not violate domestic or international law, but it's not clear he would have had a legal basis to disobey.

How does this conflict with Nuremberg and Tokyo trials based on the principle that obedience of orders is not an acceptable defence? The trials where the US played a major role and is now demanding action against Russia for their alleged crimes in Ukraine.

"Lawful but Awful": Handling Orders that are Legal but Wrong

A stronger objection to Trump's presumed desire to use the military to prolong his tenure is that such orders—even if carefully tailored to avoid legal pitfalls—would be morally wrong. The question of the moral responsibility of military officers for the effects of orders they carry out is a difficult one.

Philosopher Jeff McMahan has written that soldiers who fight in an unjust war bear full moral responsibility for the killing and harm they do since they commit these acts in the service of an unjust cause. Shanks-Kaurin's concept of "reflective obedience" seems to strike a balance between these two extremes, in that it asks officers not to blindly obey, but to consider the moral implications of obedience and disobedience, including the duty and presumption of obedience.

But what ought soldiers—especially one in a senior position such as the chairman do if given an order they believe to be lawful, but morally wrong?

The options available to soldiers given an order are relatively limited. Boiled down to their essence, a soldier's options are to obey or disobey. If the order is lawful and moral, there is no dilemma. If the order is manifestly unlawful, disobedience is hard but necessary and justified. The more difficult case is when the order is lawful (or the lawfulness is unclear) but morally repugnant. At that point, as Huntington writes, "This comes down to a choice between his own conscience on the one hand, and the good of the state, plus the professional virtue of obedience on the other." If Milley had confronted such a situation, the balance would seem to tip toward disobedience, since in his judgment the moral objection to the order was that it would be dangerous to the state.

But disobedience in the military comes at a price, especially when it involves the military's most senior officer and the elected president. The author says, it is impossible to have a military subservient to civilian authority if the most senior military officer refuses to follow the orders of the most senior civilian, *no matter the reason* (emphasis added). As a consequence, many civil-military scholars argue that an officer confronted with this choice must resign. Unlike a civilian official who may consider "civil disobedience," so long as they are ready to accept any punishment that results, disobedience by the person who controls the military—which has the means to violently enforce its will if it chooses to—is not an acceptable option.

Going by their views, one would infer that there is never a case for disobedience for the top military leader. Their views may be guided by the subconscious fear of a coup and the civilians' paranoic concern for unquestioned civil supremacy over the military. No one is questioning the supremacy of civilian control over the military. What is in question is, when the supreme authority goes rogue and the civil institutional mechanisms fail or are unable to exercise prudence and judgment in the interest of the nation, as in this case, should someone step up and prevent a disaster or not?

I have a serious disagreement with this view. Suppose, the president had ordered to launch an unprovoked and unnecessary war on Iran as he was threatening to, what was General Milley expected to do—obey and launch another misadventure like Iraq 2003 with its serious consequences? This takes us to the Iraq War 2003; not supported by the UN, launched by President

George Bush on the false premise of weapons of mass destruction and plunged the entire region into chaos. What about Vietnam; five presidents in a row, till the defiance by the veterans and the public brought the war to an end? This would be no different.

General Milley was in an unprecedented predicament, and it's easy to condemn his actions once the crisis has been averted. It is condemnation by theorists from the comforts of their drawing room who had no responsibility or accountability for what they say or for implementing anything.

According to the article, Milley considered resignation and went so far as to draft a strong resignation letter that can be done only by a man of courage and character. However, he eventually decided that he had a responsibility to try to thwart Trump's actions rather than resign. "He would not quit. "Fuck that shit," [Milley] told his staff. "I'll just fight him." The challenge, as he saw it, was to stop Trump from doing any more damage, while also acting in a way that was consistent with his obligation to carry out the orders of his Commander-in-Chief. Yet, the Constitution offered no practical guide for a General faced with a rogue President.

Never before since the position had been created in 1949 or at least since Richard Nixon's final days in 1974, had a chairman of the Joint Chiefs encountered such a situation. "If they want to court-martial me, or put me in prison, have it," Milley told his staff. "But I will fight from the inside."

Ensuring a peaceful transfer of power between Donald Trump and Joe Biden was called landing the plane. "Our job is to land this plane safely and to do a peaceful transfer of power on the twentieth of January," Milley told his staff. "This is our obligation to this nation." There was a problem, however. "Both engines are out, the landing gears are stuck. We're in an emergency situation."

Thus, the situation with Milley is complicated further by the fact that he didn't clearly receive unlawful or immoral orders and was acting in anticipation to prevent a situation. Isn't that the job of a military commander to anticipate and be prepared for the crisis rather than react?

There was a similar situation in India when General Sinha, the Army Commander represented against the Prime Minister's orders to arrest the Sikh militant leader Bhindranwale. This incident is covered in detail ahead. Here I wish to highlight the merits of acting in anticipation. Anticipating the developments, he had written a standard operating procedure (SOP) for the army to clear the Golden Temple of militants if they had to in future. More importantly, having seen the gathering storm, perpetuated by political expediency, the military leadership should have advised, urged or implored the government to act before it turned from a law and order to a serious national security situation that had serious consequences. It would have avoided the traumatic military operation in the Golden Temple, Amritsar which had disastrous consequences for the country. So much for the merit of acting in anticipation, contested by the American observers in the case of Mark Milley.

An argument might be made regarding Milley's deliberate choice to undermine the norms of civilian control by choosing to "fight" the elected president. The circumstances were extraordinary. The stakes were high. His choice, at least on the account provided by the New Yorker article, appears to have been made from honourable motives.

The article quotes this very interesting conversation between Donald Trump and John Kelly, a retired US Marine Corps General and Chief of Staff for President Trump. This demonstrates the predicament of a conscientious and righteous General like Milley.

Donal Trump expected of his Generals—unfettered blind loyalty. It turned out that the Generals had rules, standards, and expertise, not blind loyalty.

The President's loud complaint to John Kelly, one day was typical: "You fucking Generals, why can't you be like the German Generals?"

"Which Generals?" Kelly asked.

"The German Generals in World War II," Trump responded.

"You do know that they tried to kill Hitler three times and almost pulled it off?" Kelly said.

But, of course, Trump did not know that. "No, no, no, they were totally loyal to him," the President replied. In his version of history, the Generals of the Third Reich had been completely subservient to Hitler; this was the model he wanted for his military. Kelly told Trump that there were no such American Generals, but the President was determined to test the proposition.

The German Generals teach us a lesson. When Hitler's policies were leading the country to disaster, they were working for the good of Germany by trying to assassinate him. If they had succeeded, Germany would have averted this disaster and humiliation. It would have saved millions of lives on both sides.

This brings me back to the issue of loyalty. What does loyalty mean and what do the superiors expect in the form of loyalty?

The varied opinions by theorists on General Milley remind me of an incident that took place in the Kashmir Valley, J&K in India.

Damned if you Do, Damned if you Don't

Indian Army's Major Leetul Gogoi had stirred up a controversy by tying a local youth in front of a jeep in April 2017 in Kashmir Valley to avoid being attacked by stone-pelters.

Stone pelting has been a major nuisance in the Valley. Terrorists and their supporters would resort to stone pelting by large crowds to disrupt the army's operations and provide cover to enable the holed-up terrorist to escape.

During the Srinagar by-polls in April 2017, a stone-pelting mob of over 1200 tried to disrupt the polling and set fire to a polling booth with 12 polling staff inside, a mix of civilians and police personnel.

Major Gogoi, a company commander of a Rashtriya Rifles Battalion, received a distress call from the police personnel at the polling booth that a large mob has gheraoed the pooling booth and are trying to burn them down. Major Gogoi reached the spot with his quick reaction team, despite roadblocks. In trying to extricate this polling team, he was confronted by a large mob pelting stones and petrol bombs and preventing his exit. Appeals on megaphones to clear a passage to allow them to leave made no headway. He quickly came up with a bright idea. He grabbed the leader of the mob and tied him to the bonnet of the military jeep. That stunned the crowd and halted the stone pelting, allowing him to extricate his charge safely without firing a shot.

As he explained later, his out-of-the-box solution was meant to save the lives of the locals pelting stones. If he had fired to force his way out, a dozen would have been killed.

The Aftermath

This raged a debate in the media on the ethics of his action. The human rights activists fired scathing criticism on the officer, demanding punishment for violating the human rights of the instigator. The out-of-the-box idea of the officer saved the lives of many stone pelters themselves and the polling staff. None of these armchair human rights activists had a solution for what he should have done. That is the problem of people who have not been at the wrong end of the barrel and have no responsibility.

Befittingly, the Chief of the Army Staff in India decorated him with the Chief of the Army Staff commendation card.

The issue in both cases i.e., General Milley and Major Gogoi are the same. The officers in the hot seat are being judged by people with no experience, accountability or responsibility after the crisis is over. At their respective levels, there was a huge price to pay. Maj Gogoi was the commander of a small team of a dozen soldiers charged with a critical mission, surrounded by a murderous crowd. He had no time to seek the advice of human rights experts. He did what I see as the best solution under the circumstances. I applaud him for his leadership and decision-making, as much as I applaud General Milley. The Indian Army Chief General Bipin Rawat did well to reward him.

I bet, if he had fired and some people had died in the process, he and the army would have had more questions to answer, starting with human rights experts, possibly his own bosses and the self-serving politicians. Such a situation had already occurred earlier after which the chief minister of Jammu &Kashmir and the defence minister conferred to file an FIR against a young Major. That is a soldier's curse in counter-insurgency operations—damned if he does and damned if he doesn't.

Lt Gen SK Sinha: When Courage Saved Many Blushes

While we examine Gen Milley's predicament, here is another incident by an Indian Army Commander that needs to be studied by all military leaders. I have referred to this earlier in the chapter.

Lt General Sinha was a brilliant Indian Army officer, the kind you need at the helm. He was superseded to appoint someone else as the Chief of the Indian Army. He was the Western Army Commander in 1981 and Vice Chief before he resigned on supersession. Post-retirement, he was the ambassador to Nepal and governor of two states.

During the period that he was the army commander, Jarnail Singh Bhindranwale was an emerging Sikh militant leader of the prominent orthodox Sikh religious institution Damdami Taksal. He was also the leader of the separatist Khalistan movement that was gaining traction during that time. In all, a messy political situation was developing with a dangerous potential for national security.

One day, General Sinha was approached by the Chief Secretary of Punjab. He said that Bhindranwale was at Mehta Chowk Gurudwara near Amritsar with 40-odd armed followers and he has to be arrested for alleged murder. For this, he asked for a few tanks. General Sinha replied, "This is a strange request. The army does not give weapons to the police and uses them itself. When we are called in aid of the police, we use our weapons and do not hand over weapons like this. The police are not trained to use tanks and even if they used them through ex-servicemen of armoured corps in the police force, what would be the repercussions?"

Not much later, General Sinha got a message from Chief Minister Darbara Singh. The army commander met him and explained his rationale. Chief Minster agreed with his reasons for not giving tanks but asked him to send the army and arrest Bhindranwale and clear up the place. He said the army has no power to arrest anyone, only the police can arrest, you should use the police. Darbara said Bhindranwale has 30-40 rifles. Gen Sinha replied, so has the police. The Chief Minister said in Punjabi, you are not helping us. The meeting ended.

Two days later, Headquarters Western Command got orders from the Prime Minister that Bhindranwale has to be arrested by the army. In the absence of the army commander, the Chief of Staff detailed a Gurkha battalion to carry out the task. When Gen Sinha landed back at the headquarters, he was informed of this. He directed that the order be cancelled and the battalion stopped. The Chief of Staff reminded him that it was the Prime Minister's order. General Sinha told his Chief of Staff, that as far as he was concerned, he will obey the Army Commander's order and the Army Commander will deal with the Prime Minister himself.

He then called up the Defence Minister Venkataraman and apprised him of the Prime Minister's order. He said he has asked his officer not to take any action till he had his views presented to the Prime Minister. Taken aback, the defence minister said, "Are you not going to carry out the Prime Minister's order?"

General Sinha replied, "No Sir. I am going to carry out the prime minister's orders. But my submission is that I am an Army Commander and I should be allowed to present my views to the Prime Minister before she makes a decision. And then if I am ordered to go, I will go."

Venkataraman, reluctantly said that he will speak to the Prime Minster.

Two hours later, there was a call from the Prime Minister's office cancelling that order. The task was then done by the police which was messed up. It resulted in the deaths of several people, further compounding the problem. Another travesty- Bhindranwale was released after a few days for lack of evidence in the murder case! In all a needless exercise that could have been avoided with due diligence. Later, Bhindranwale took over the Golden Temple, the most sacred Sikh shrine and over time, converted it into a fortress with the expertise of Maj General Shubeg Singh, a renegade army veteran of Mukti Bahini fame of the Indo-Pak War of 71.

General Sinha had the vision to foresee that one day the army will have to go into the Golden Temple to clear it of Bhindranwale's militants. He formulated a guideline (SOP) for that eventuality; doing it in a manner that created the least political and emotional turmoil, both for the army and the Sikhs in general as the Western Command had over 80,000 Sikh soldiers on its strength.

It happened three years later in 1984. Under the code name 'Operation Blue Star', the army was ordered to enter Golden Temple and clear the place of Bhindranwale and his militants. By then the temple complex had been strongly fortified under Shubeg Singh.

General Sinha's SOP had been filed safely somewhere and forgotten for good. Given the challenges and the opposition, the army had to use tanks to overcome the opposition and clear the place of the militants. The army suffered 83 fatal casualties and 249 injured.

Later, this led to the assassination of Prime Minister Mrs Indira Gandhi by her Sikh guards and the retired Army Chief, General Vaidya, who oversaw 'Operation Blue Star'. The Prime Minister's assassination then led to riots that resulted in the estimated killing of over two thousand five hundred Sikhs in different parts of the country. A national tragedy that left deep scars.

Source: General SK Sinha interview. www.daysandnightnews.com

The Captain Chooses to Sink to Save His Sailors

In March 2020, Captain Brett Crozier the commander of the USS Theodore Roosevelt, a nuclear-powered aircraft carrier, was relieved of his command after warning superiors about the danger of COVID-19 spreading among his crew – a message that got leaked to the *San Francisco Chronicle* because of the unclassified method he chose, addressing 30 recipients.

He faced an ethical dilemma that he had to resolve by either waiting for his superiors to act on his requests or choosing his people's loyalty and their lives. He prioritised his sailors' lives over his career and possible disciplinary action.

At the peak of the Covid pandemic, when 100 to 200 of his sailors had tested positive for Covid, he wrote: "We are not at war. Sailors do not need to die. If we do not act now, we are failing to properly take care of our most trusted asset – our Sailors."

He added: "Decisive action is required. Removing the majority of personnel from a deployed US nuclear aircraft carrier and isolating them for two weeks may seem like an extraordinary measure.

This is a necessary risk. It will enable the carrier and air wing to get back underway as quickly as possible while ensuring the health and safety of our Sailors. Keeping over 4,000 young men and women on board the TR is an unnecessary risk and breaks faith with those Sailors entrusted to our care."

While this became a controversy, it is worth considering that this commander would not have taken this decision if it was not necessary. The last line reveals the essence of military leadership '*Faith with those sailors entrusted to our care.*' His persuasive language made his superiors take notice and take action.

This decision must not have been easy and he would have known the consequences. This is moral courage in leadership. This is positive defiance that no leadership manual talks of while touting moral courage as a leadership quality. This has dividends no money can buy—trust between the leader and his men—the ultimate battle-winning factor.

Such decisions will invariably bring you head-to-head with the authority. This is a price worth paying to build, retain or restore the trust of the men in their commanders. Even when one man has the spine to do it, it strengthens the system as men develop trust in the system. Yet, it can only be sustained when this 'strong spine behaviour' becomes a culture amongst the officers.

Author's Notes

Academic observers are looking at General Milley's episode from the narrow prism of civil-military relations saying that the damage to norms of civilian control is real and serious. If the norms of civilian control of the military and military professionalism are to survive, such damage demands condemnation in some form. (Doyle Hodges—A Duty to Disobey?)

This argument is missing the woods for the trees. This is a situation where the civilian institutional oversight mechanism seems to have become dysfunctional, allowing the president to run riot, as the Capitol Hill incident demonstrates. This highlights the challenges of military leadership. He is facing a dangerous situation with an erratic president which has serious repercussions for America and the world—an unnecessary war with Iran or China, or a kind of coup to extend his tenure with the use of the army on some pretext.

This brings me to another point. Some observers accusingly point out that no illegal orders were given to General Milley and he was acting in anticipation. General Sinha was given an illegal order which he rightly protested against, and he anticipated a disaster in the making in Punjab which happened three years later. For politicians, all such things are politics and they allow things to drift till the dangerous genie gets out of the bottle and becomes a national security issue. Then they look at the army to pull their chestnuts out of the fire. In India, the military is effectively not a part of any decision-making body on security. Bhindranwale could roam around with forty armed men and the government does nothing about it and is scared to use the police, the well-armed and trained law enforcement agency. In such cases which have serious repercussions for the nation, why should the military, who ultimately have to shed blood, not take it up with the government, in anticipation, to prevent a looming disaster as we saw in Punjab? Where was the civilian institutional oversight that academicians talk of?

The long and short of it is, that when a military leader faces such a situation, he is on his own—left to act by his conscience and values and be prepared to face the consequences. Most choose the easier path. When the institutional system becomes paralysed, it becomes the duty of the top military commander to act in the interest of the nation, never mind the business of civil-military relations. The armchair experts will fire their academic criticism from the narrow prism of their own fields and biases without giving a workable solution. They have no implementation responsibility or accountability for anything.

After the Afghanistan withdrawal fiasco, during the Senate hearing, General Milley was specifically asked, "Why he did not resign when President Joe Biden did not heed his advice that led to the disgraceful withdrawal from Afghanistan?" Here we are; damned if you do and damned if you don't.

That explains my perspective on positive defiance and highlights a military leader's predicament in such situations. Civil-military relations, while important cannot override national honour.

General Sinha's episode highlights important aspects of the military psyche. The Chief of Staff of Western Command immediately implemented the order of the Prime Minster to arrest Bhindranwale, assuming, that given the high office from where the order came, the Army Commander would do the same.

General Sinha, on the other hand, analysed the order and directly spoke to the defence minister that his views be presented to the Prime Minister before she takes the decision. The decision was reversed preventing the undesirable sucking of the army into domestic politics and unforeseen developments.

This highlights the need for 'reflective obedience'. Blind obedience is dangerous to every organization including the military. Eventually, the army had to use tanks to overpower the same group at a great national cost. That breed of military leaders who could question the directions of a powerful prime minister like Indira Gandhi is long extinct.

History has proved that War is too serious a business to be left to the Generals alone. History also proves that it cannot be left to the politicians alone. Generals must keep abreast of politics while remaining apolitical and prevent undesirable developments because of political expediency through appropriate intervention.

What is required is an institutional oversight that brings multiple perspectives and prevents one-man sinking the ship as happened with Germany during the Second World War and other places. While such institutions exist, sometimes they are either rendered redundant by the man at the helm or fail to ensure oversight and seek accountability, as happened in the run-up to the Indo-China war of 1962.

Sources: 1. Inside the War Between Trump and His Generals: How Mark Milley and others in the Pentagon handled the national-security threat posed by their own Commander-in-Chief. *Susan B. Glasser and Peter Baker https://www.newyorker.com/magazine/2022/08/15/inside-the-war-between-trump-and-his-generals*
2. A Duty to Disobey? Doyle Hodges, August 19, 2022, https://www.lawfareblog.com/duty-disobey

In the case of Captain Crozier, as expected, the Naval and the Pentagon hierarchy's response was as predictable and despicable as it was. They focussed on the damage to their reputation and loss of trust in the military caused by his leaked email. A case of shooting the messenger and missing the woods for the trees. Captain Crozier was removed from command post haste.

How would this play out in the corporate? The consequences of such an action are unlikely to be any different, for this would tarnish the reputation of a company and thus its capacity to earn revenue. But, in the corporate, the whistleblower could sue the company for vengeance when acting against unethical business practices. For sure, it would do larger good.

♦ ♦ ♦

Chapter Eight

The White Man's Burden

The White Man's Burden

Image: Credit Internet

OPERATION IRAQI FREEDOM—2003

It was a routine chilly day in Ankara, Turkey, in the second week of March 2003. I loved that place and being a defence attaché meant, I was in familiar territory. Had lots of like-minded friends wearing a uniform from eighty different countries. As an Indian, the US or Israeli military attaché was as much at ease with me as were the Iranian or Iraqi.

I often drove over to some defence attaché for coffee and routine business.

It was the 18th of March 2003. I got a call from the defence attaché of Iraq.

In his heavy Arabic accent, he said, "As-Salam Walaikum, Anil if it is fine, I want to come over for coffee with you."

I said I will love it, come at your convenience.

When he walked into my office, I could see a worried colonel.

We discussed the developments in the region and then he asked me, "Do you think America will attack Iraq?"

I said, "No."

"Why do you think so?" he queried.

I said, "To date, no weapons of mass destruction have been found by the UNOMOVIC. Iraq is mostly cooperating with the UN investigation. The UN is against this war. The majority of countries, including France and Russia oppose this war. I do not see one justifiable reason why America should attack Iraq."

I don't think my assurance seemed to comfort him. He had an intuition and he was not voicing it.

"Where is your family?" I asked him.

"They are in Baghdad." He replied.

I then understood the reason for his great concern. I was wrong, the US attacked Iraq not much later. Years later, reading the book *Wargaming for Leaders,* I learnt that regime change and attack on Iraq had been war-gamed in the US years earlier.

Turkey's parliament had voted against allowing the passage of US troops through Turkey for attacking Iraq from the North. The US 4th Infantry Division which had already disembarked at the Incirlik port in Southern Turkey was on its way to the Northern Iraqi border. It had to recoil and head for Southern Iraq all the way around through the Mediterranean and Suez Canal.

UN General Assembly.

General Colin Powell, the US Secretary of State was a respected General of the US Army. I clearly remember, even today, Colin Powell justifying the case for invading Iraq in 2003, with a small vial of white powder in his hand, which he called dry anthrax that shut down the Senate in 2001, hoping to convince the world that Iraq was preparing to destroy the world.

Vladimir Putin called it washing powder.

Colin Powell said Iraq has violated all the UNSC resolutions. What an Irony, the US violated all the UN resolutions to attack Iraq on the 20th of March on false information.

The US was attacked on 9/11. Out of 19 men affiliated with 9/11, fifteen were citizens of Saudi Arabia, two from UAE and one each from Lebanon and Egypt. There was no Iraqi or Afghani involved. Isn't that ironic that the countries that the US chose to attack had nothing to do with the 9/11 attack or was it just a fabricated excuse?

Everyone that President Bush spoke to advised against the attack, including the Saudi Ambassador who said that Saddam and Osama were bitter adversaries. UK Prime Minister Tony Blair sought evidence against Saddam, there was none, and yet the UK went on to be the major ally of the US in the Iraq War. The US administration had misled the gullible, utterly ill-informed US public. So did Tony Blair in the UK.

A *Washington Post* poll conducted two years after the 9/11 terrorist attack dramatically illustrated the story: 69 per cent of Americans at the time believed Saddam Hussein was "personally" involved in the 9/11 attack. Even more staggering, 82 per cent believed that Saddam provided assistance to Osama Bin Laden. Both were utterly wrong.

Source: Bruce Riedel. September 17, 2021https://www-brookings- edu.cdn.ampproject.org/v/s/www.brookings.edu/blog/order-from-chaos/2021/09/17/9-11-and-iraq-the-making-of-a-tragedy/

Iraq is a case study which demonstrates how an individual obsession (President George Bush) with a person can inflict a human tragedy of monumental proportions. George Bush disregarded all sane counsel resulting in the deaths of millions of people in the West Asia region as a result.

Author's Notes

Speaking in an interview, Colin Powell acknowledged being embarrassed because he made the presentation at the UN General Assembly based on false information certified by the CIA. The same information was used by the President, Congress and others.

The sad part is that American politicians involved in supporting and planning the attacks on Iraq justify the attack on the grounds that Saddam is gone and there is some kind of democracy. They express hope that Iraqis will somehow solve their sectarian problems, having created all these problems themselves. How many civilians were killed in the process is never mentioned.

In my book *The Be-Know-Do of Generalship,* I have written about a major folly that afflicts politicians and Generals alike—failure to appreciate the possible consequences of their actions or failure. Colin Powell also mentions in one of his interviews that they made three major blunders in Iraq. One, dismantling the Bath Party, two dismantling the military structure that deprived them of the institutions necessary to provide security, and three, failure to win the population, which resulted in terrorism that needed a surge of troops to control the situation and it was too late.

Isn't it tragic, that such experienced politicians and war veteran Generals who carry on their shoulders the self-proclaimed 'white man's burden' to civilise the world repeatedly blunder in these very fundamental issues? And they are back again, this time ensuring that nothing is left of Ukraine. History teaches us that it will repeat itself in the hope that people will learn next time. The world failed to learn after the First World War which sowed the seeds of the Second. The US learnt the lessons and applied them in Japan to nurture a progressive and peaceful country. They forgot those lessons in Iraq to plunge the whole region into chaos. The same lessons were highlighted in the wargame on the attack on Iraq, and the same were forgotten on the ground at a great cost to humanity.

AFGHANISTAN

Image: Compiled from Internet

Why did the US Invade Afghanistan?

We know that the World Trade Towers and the Pentagon were attacked on 9/11 in 2001 in New York. That incident changed the world forever, as did the Covid pandemic.

So, over the next two years, the US attacked two countries that had nothing to do with 9/11, Afghanistan in September 2001 and Iraq in Mar 2003. In both countries, hundreds of thousands of people died as a consequence of American unilateralism and exceptionalism.

Why did the US invade Afghanistan? Well, the most powerful superpower had to hit back at someone after being hit in the guts with almost 3000 people dead, the first time on its mainland. The question is if America was at war with terrorism, who was the enemy and what was the best strategy to defeat it? How was the US certain at the time that it was Osama Bin Laden when their intelligence establishment had missed glaring clues of the build-up to these attacks? At one point, they also blamed Saddam Hussein for his role in the 9/11 attack.

It is important to reflect on an article written ten years after 9/11.

Why Did the United States Invade Afghanistan? Tim Kelly, 12 October 2011

...the one question I believe to be the most fundamental regarding the war probably won't be discussed: Was the US invasion of Afghanistan necessary?

President Obama, who had campaigned as an opponent of the US invasion of Iraq as a war of choice said of US military operations in Afghanistan, "This is not a war of choice. This is a war of necessity."

Obama's words might have made for a good sound bite, but the evidence shows that, like the war in Iraq, the war in Afghanistan is, indeed, a war of choice.

Many supporters of the US invasion of Afghanistan argue that even if the military campaign has turned into a quagmire, the initial attack was a just and necessary response to 9/11. Perhaps President Obama provided the best summary of this position in a speech at West Point. He said:

> *"We did not ask for this fight. On September 11, 2001, nineteen men hijacked four aeroplanes and used them to murder nearly 3,000 people. They struck at our military and economic nerve centers. They took the lives of innocent men, women and children without regard to their faith or race or station… As we know, these men belonged to Al Qaeda, a group of extremists who have distorted and defiled Islam.… After the Taliban refused to turn over Osama bin Laden—we sent our troops into Afghanistan."*

Here we have the conventional view: The 9/11 attacks were carried out by 19 fanatical Muslims acting on the orders of Osama bin Laden, the founder and leader of Al-Qaeda, who was being given sanctuary by the Taliban regime in Afghanistan; and the invasion became necessary when they stubbornly refused to turn him over to the US authorities.

The Bush administration then commenced a bombing campaign and invasion of Afghanistan, asserting the need to capture or kill bin Laden and crush his terrorist organization so that they could not launch another deadly attack on the American homeland.

The problem with this narrative is that the claim that the Taliban had stubbornly refused to turn over bin Laden is not true.

CNN reported on September 21, 2001,

The Taliban … refused to hand over bin Laden *without proof or evidence* that he was involved in last week's attacks on the United States. … The Taliban ambassador to Pakistan said that deporting him *without proof* would amount to an "insult to Islam." (Emphasis added)

CNN also provided an explanation for the Taliban's "refusal," reporting:

"Bin Laden himself has already denied he had anything to do with the attacks, and Taliban officials repeatedly said he could not have been involved in the attacks."

So, the Taliban were not really refusing to turn him over but rather were demanding certain conditions be satisfied before they did so. That is not unusual. Governments routinely have evidentiary standards that must be met before they grant an extradition request. Bush, however, was not in a diplomatic mood, and he told the Taliban "The demands were not open to negotiation or discussion."

The refusal by the Bush administration to put any evidence on the table made it extremely difficult, if not impossible, for the Taliban to turn bin Laden over. *The Washington Post* ran a story in October 2001 that quoted Milton Bearden, a former CIA official, who said the Taliban needed a "face-saving formula." While the Bush administration was saying, "Give up bin Laden," the Taliban were saying, "Do something to help us give him up."

Even after the US bombs began falling in October, the Taliban tried to negotiate by offering to turn bin Laden over to a third country if the United States would cease hostilities and provide evidence of his guilt. But Bush remained adamant, saying, "There's no need to discuss innocence or guilt. We know he's guilty." London's *Guardian*, reporting on this story, printed an article titled *"Bush Rejects Taliban Offer to Hand Bin Laden Over."*

Why was the Bush administration so stubbornly opposed to meeting the Taliban's reasonable demand that they release at least some of the copious evidence they claimed to have gathered against bin Laden? After all, such a gesture might have spared the United States and her NATO allies, and the people of Afghanistan, the costs and consequences of a war that is now entering its eleventh year.

Well, the answer to that question could be that US officials might well have lacked solid evidence of bin Laden's complicity, notwithstanding their certainty that he was behind the attacks. Certainly, the US government has never shown such evidence to the American people.

Let's review how the Bush administration presented its case against Osama bin Laden after 9/11.

Here is what the Secretary of State Colin Powell said during a September 23, 2001, appearance on *Meet the Press*:

Question: Are you absolutely convinced that Osama bin Laden was responsible for this attack?

Secretary Powell: I am absolutely convinced that the al-Qaeda network, which he heads, was responsible for this attack. You know, it's sort of al-Qaeda —the Arab name for it is "the base"—it's something like a holding company of terrorist organizations that are located in dozens of countries around the world, sometimes tightly controlled, sometimes loosely controlled. And at the head of that organization is Osama bin Laden. So, what we have to do in the first phase of this campaign is to go after al-Qaeda and go after Osama bin Laden. But it is not just a problem in Afghanistan; it's a problem throughout the world. That's why we are attacking it with a worldwide coalition.

Question: Will you release publicly a white paper, which links him and his organization to this attack, to put people at ease?

Secretary Powell: We are hard at work bringing all the information together, intelligence information, law enforcement information. And I think, in the near future, we will be able to put out a paper, a document, that will describe quite clearly the evidence that we have linking him to this attack. And also, remember, he has been linked to earlier attacks against US interests and he was already indicted for earlier attacks against the United States.

The next day banner headlines were appearing in newspapers across the country telling Americans of the Bush administration's imminent report on bin Laden's guilt. *The New York Times* ran a story citing a government official who claimed evidence "reaches from the southern tip of Manhattan to the foothills of the Hindu Kush mountains of Afghanistan."

But by the following day, the Bush administration was backpedalling. The White House press secretary, Ari Fleischer, said there were no plans to produce a report and that Powell's remarks had been "misinterpreted." At a joint press conference with President Bush, Secretary Powell withdrew his pledge, saying that "most of the evidence" is classified.

Within days, all mention of the promised "white paper" had disappeared from the news media, which continued to credulously repeat the US government's narrative of events.

Investigative journalist Seymour Hersh, citing officials from the Department of Justice and the CIA, said the real reason the Bush administration reneged on its pledge to release the evidence was a "lack of solid information."

Further questions were raised regarding the US government's charges against Osama bin Laden by the FBI's Most Wanted Terrorists webpage. While the page mentioned bombings in Kenya and Tanzania as terrorist acts for which bin Laden was wanted, it made no mention of the 9/11 attacks. When the FBI was asked about this conspicuous omission, Rex Tomb, the Bureau's chief of investigative publicity replied: "The reason why 9/11 is not mentioned on Osama bin Laden's Most Wanted page is because the FBI has no hard evidence connecting bin Laden to 9/11."

So, the US government's case against Osama bin Laden was not good enough to take to court, but it was good enough to take the country to war, a war that killed or maimed countless people who had absolutely nothing to do with the 9/11 attacks. The anger arising from the invasion and occupation of the country has created a perpetual supply of terrorist recruits, enabling the US officials to use the never-ending "war on terror" to eviscerate the Bill of Rights. And we now have a president who asserts the authority to kill off any person he deems a "threat." **I submit that this claim of unaccountable power represents a far greater threat to the peace and security of the country than any terrorist or group of terrorists could ever pose.**

Surveying the evidence, it is clear the Bush administration did not even come close to exhausting its diplomatic options in the fall of 2001 and that some other route could have been chosen to respond to the 9/11 attacks. Moreover, the invasion of Afghanistan did not even succeed in its principal goal: the capturing or killing of Osama bin Laden.

Source: https://www.fff.org/explore-freedom/article/united-states-invade-afghanistan/

According to the US government, that mission was accomplished almost ten years later by a team of Navy Seals in an operation lasting only a few hours … in neighbouring Pakistan.

The US Withdrawal from Afghanistan.

As we have seen before, the US withdrawal from Afghanistan was a disaster that hurt the US pride, its international image and the allies' trust immensely. After two decades, trillions of dollars, thousands of American and NATO soldiers and countless Afghans dead, the Taliban are back in the saddle with billion-dollar US military equipment and the people of Afghanistan are worse off than they were before the US attack.

Lt Col Stuart Scheller, a US Marine Corps officer called out senior military leaders on social media over the US military withdrawal from Afghanistan and resigned his commission.

In his original video, posted after the deaths of 13 service members, he said, "I want to say this very strongly. I have been fighting for 17 years. I am willing to throw it all away to say to my senior leaders I demand accountability. All I ask for is the accountability of my senior leaders when clear and obvious mistakes were made."

*Source: Marine Lieutenant Colonel Resigns Commission over Afghanistan, Vows to Bring the Whole F*cking System Down*

https://www.breitbart.com/politics/2021/08/29/marine-lieutenant-colonel-resigns-commission-over-afghanistan-vows-to-bring-the-whole-fcking-system-down/ accessed on 12 May 2022

The issue in question is the widely perceived incompetence of President Biden in deciding the timing and manner of the catastrophic withdrawal.

US President Joe Biden called it a success. "We achieved what we had gone there to achieve," he said:

- To get the Taliban who attacked them on 9/11.
- Deliver justice to Osama bin Laden.
- To degrade the Taliban threat and keep Afghanistan from becoming a base from which attacks could be continued against the US. He said we did not go to Afghanistan to build Afghanistan. It is the responsibility of the Afghanistan people to decide how to run their country.

It took them 20 years to realise this and how much they achieved in other aspects is there to see.

One does not have to be a smart General or lawmaker to appreciate that this modus operandi had only one consequence and that happened.

THE DILEMMA FOR THE STRATEGIC LEADERSHIP

There is a great dilemma when fighting terrorism anywhere. It is for this reason that politico-military leadership should be cautious when opting for war. In all counter-terrorism operations such as Afghanistan, reduced footprints lead to acceding control to the Taliban. Reduced footprints lead to more reliance on aerial attacks to beat back the Taliban. This leads to more civilian casualties and pushes innocent fence-sitters into the lap of the Taliban. The terrorists control what the security forces do not hold around the clock, and in a country like Afghanistan, you can't hold, sustain and protect everything of importance. Isolated posts become vulnerable and difficult to sustain. How long are you prepared to be there? Eventually, the war fatigue will set in at all levels. The people are at the mercy of the terrorists by night. This is not a discovery. This has been the character of the counter-insurgency and terrorism war. How did the US factor this into its plans? What did they learn from the Russian experience in Afghanistan? Should they have asked themselves these basic questions?

It was the same in Iraq. What lessons did the US learn from Afghanistan that it went into Iraq all guns blazing in the much-publicized 'shock and awe' offensive? Did they not appreciate the challenges of the post-war stabilization in Iraq? How different were the end results in Vietnam, Iraq and Afghanistan? When US President George Bush declared mission accomplished aboard the aircraft carrier USS Abraham Lincoln on May 1, 2003, the war had just begun which continues to rage in West Asia and the Middle-East even today.

Gen Milley and others had advised the US Administration that 2500 troops be retained in Afghanistan even after the withdrawal, advice that was heard but not heeded by President Biden. He was also advised that the withdrawal be condition-based and not time-based.

When Senator Tom Cotton (R-Ark.) asked General Milley why he didn't resign when his advice on the Afghanistan withdrawal wasn't heeded, General Milley replied.

> *"As a senior military officer, resigning is a really serious thing. It's a political act if I'm resigning in protest. My job is to provide advice, my statutory responsibility is to provide legal advice or the best military advice to the president. And that's my legal requirement. That's what the law is."*
>
> *"The president doesn't have to agree with that advice, he doesn't have to make those decisions just because we're Generals. And it would be an incredible act of political defiance, for a commissioned officer to just resign because my advice is not taken."*
>
> *"This country doesn't want Generals figuring out what orders we are going to accept and do or not. That's not our job. The principle of civilian control over the military is absolute and it's critical to this republic," Milley said, adding on a personal note that soldiers, like his father in Iwo Jima and the*

13 soldiers killed at the Kabul airport — "those kids at Abbey Gate" as he referred to them—did not have the option of resigning.

"They can't resign so I'm not going to resign. There's no way," said Milley.

Source: Live coverage: Senators press military leaders on Afghanistan By the hill staff - 09/28/21 8:27 am, https://thehill.com/policy/defense/574218-live-coverage-senators-set-to-grill-milley/

Throughout history, ambitious kings, dictators, autocrats and democratic governments have pushed their countries into avoidable wars leading to the deaths of millions of people including their own.

So, in the modern-day, on whom does the responsibility lie to prevent such human tragedy because of incompetent, ambitious, indifferent or simply arrogant political or military leadership? The US Congressional approval to authorise the President to use military force against Iraq as deemed necessary, essentially made it a one-man decision. We saw that the basis on which the war was waged proved to be false. If the political safeguards fail to prevent this catastrophe, it falls upon the military hierarchy to step up and prevent the country from wading into an unjustified disaster.

Author's Notes

What General Milley has said is true. Generals cannot be resigning every time their advice is not heeded. The military advises and the decision is taken by the political authority. Here, it is important to emphasise one aspect. When the issue at hand is so critical and the disastrous consequences so apparent, as in the case of the hasty Afghanistan withdrawal or India in the 1962 Indo-China War, I believe Generals would serve the country's cause well by preventing the disaster through constructive dissent, constructive disobedience or even resignation rather than acquiescence in the name of civil supremacy. When the naiveté of the political leadership is driving the country to a certain embarrassment, someone must save the country from their incompetent government. General Milley did set a good example on certain issues relating to President Trump.

Later, an investigative report by *The Washington Post* quoted sworn testimony by military commanders saying that the White House and State Department left evacuation planning too late, ignored Taliban gains, were too late in responding to the Taliban's final offensive and resisted efforts to prepare an evacuation of US Embassy staffers and Afghan allies in the weeks before Kabul fell. That they were overtaken by events, leading to the frantic final days of mass evacuations from Kabul.

President Joe Biden flatly rejected the US military's criticism of his administration's handling of the Afghan withdrawal. Asked in an interview by NBC's Lester Holt if he rejected the accounts in the army report, he said: "I'm rejecting them."

So, it was as simple as that for the President—end of the story—dusted and done—no accountability. The rejection does nothing to assuage the catastrophe or the sufferings of the Afghan people. Who will demand accountability from these people who hold the reins of human destiny? There was just one crusader, Lt Col Scheller, who sought accountability; he was court-martialled.

I always have a question to ask the military. Stating what went wrong when the damage is done and the country disgraced is of no consequence. The military is expected to foresee the consequences, which in this case were clear and needed no sixth sense. They either measure up to the task or if it is unimplementable, take up a stand against it, as did General Sam Manekshaw in India in 1971.

Source: https://nypost.com/2022/02/11/white-house-defends-biden-rejection-of-army-report-critical-of-afghan-withdrawal/ accessed on 22 Jul 2022.

When a military officer resigns in the hope of preventing a disaster, it is not political defiance. It is the exercise of moral courage and a reflection of a sense of responsibility. There is always a possibility that the events may not turn out as the military leadership appreciated. That does not take credit away from the good intention. The politicians are wary of senior officers' resignations because of the political fallout. Resigning is not disobedience, neither is it defiance nor is it a coup. When it achieves something credible for the organization, it is well worth it. Admiral DK Joshi, the Indian Naval Chief did so in protest against the lackadaisical attitude of the defence minister and the ministry of defence.

The German army, once convinced of the insanity of Hitler's destructive path tried to eliminate him on numerous occasions. It was not treachery on their part, it was for the good of the nation that would have saved them from disaster and loss of countless lives, more on the German side.

Did the US political and military leadership not realise?

- That Pakistan, supposedly an ally of the US in its war on terror in Afghanistan, would be a part of the problem rather than a part of the solution. If they did and still went ahead, they chose the wrong battlefield and the wrong ally. It was a fatal political decision. If they did not, it was a fatal politico-diplomatic-intelligence failure.

- The challenges of Afghanistan; a landlocked country with Iran, a sworn enemy on the west, and the most unreliable ally Pakistan on the east with its internal security challenges.
- How did it assume that Russia will not return the favour which was dished out by the US to them by arming the Taliban to fight them when they were in Afghanistan?
- The history of the graveyard of empires.

How was this any different from Vietnam? Doing more of the same at the tactical level and hoping things will turn around at the strategic level. More money was spent on reconstruction in Afghanistan than on Europe under the Marshal plan after World War 2.

According to senior officials who were responsible for various aspects of Afghanistan, mismanagement was rampant.

- 36 million dollars building that the military did not want and never used was constructed. Thirty per cent of the budget was lost in corruption, waste and mismanagement e.g. Italian goats for the cashmere wool industry were brought to Afghanistan. The Afghan woman in charge quit in disgust at the mismanagement saying, "You can't do in two years what takes ten." After, two years, no goats were left; they were either eaten or died because of unsuitable environments and conditions.
- Camouflage uniform—the disruptive pattern selected for the Afghan army was not owned by the US, thus paying 30 to 40 per cent more. The pattern selected was 'forest green' suitable for only 4 to 5 per cent of Afghanistan's terrain.

The common acronym in Afghanistan was VICE – VERTICAL - INTEGRATED - CORRUPT - ENTERPRISE and Afghanistan President Karzai was believed to be heading that enterprise.

Ten years into the war, the political and military leadership would have seen the writing on the wall, as evident from the comments of the NATO Force commanders.

So, the big question is when the political leadership failed to define what was winning in Afghanistan, on what basis was the military continuing to operate?

It appears the military continued to do more of the same without a clear objective or direction, no different than Vietnam.

Apropos above, what was expected of the commanders for the larger good of the country? What would have been better—muted compliance of the political authority and feeding a false narrative to the country or well-informed constructive dissent and demanding critical answers when the tipping point had been crossed? Should they have not been seeking answers to the basic questions:

- What was the desired end state in Afghanistan based on which the US would withdraw from there?
- What were the political objectives? What were the benchmarks to assess progress?
- What were the military objectives that would enable the accomplishment of the political objectives? What were the benchmarks to assess progress?
- What were the contours that defined the exit strategy and the complete withdrawal of the military? Are they achievable?
- What was required to empower the Afghan Forces to manage their security in the long run? Were they doing the needful?
- Did they do a regular politico-military audit of their progress and draw lessons? If so, why were they there for two decades with the outcome that we saw?

Let us draw a parallel. Less than two years after the invasion of Afghanistan, in March 2003, Colin Powell waved a vial of white powder in the UN General Assembly, calling it dry anthrax. He showed pictures of a mobile biological van and recorded phone conversations as proof of Iraq developing weapons of mass destruction. All the CIA intelligence proved to be false and fabricated. Hundreds of thousands of Iraqis and Afghanis including women and children who had nothing to do with US allegations are dead and the world has been in turmoil since. How could they be so sure in less than a fortnight that it was Osama Bin Laden directly responsible for 9/11 when all their hard evidence against Iraq fell apart on falsehood?

Both Afghanistan and Iraq are classic episodes that sum up human history. It has great lessons that highlight the concept of *confirmation bias* on the part of the American administration, digging up fabricated evidence to prove what they wanted to believe and hoodwink the world. Colin Powell stated in an interview that as the secretary of state, he had discussed with President Bush that if Iraq proved it did not have weapons of mass destruction, would he be prepared to give up the war option, even if Saddam remained in power as 'changed regime,' as against the 'regime change.' According to him, President Bush said yes, he would. But what happened was entirely different. Till a day before the American coalition launched a devastating shock and awe bombings of Iraq, there was no evidence of weapons of mass destruction, nor did they find any during their entire deployment. I have no doubts the Americans would have turned Iraq upside down in their endeavour to find one.

Afghanistan was no different. George Bush had effectively closed the possibility of extradition of Osama by refusing to discuss and giving an ultimatum that no self-respecting government could accept, and Afghans are very proud people. The Taliban were reportedly ready to repatriate Osama to a third country if evidence of his involvement was furnished.

So, Bush became the judge, the jury and the executioner. He did the same in Iraq, only to become an object of ridicule because of false evidence by the most powerful and disruptive intelligence agency in the world. Taliban refused to buckle down, as did Saddam Hussein to leave the country. Even in insignificant cases of money laundering and corruption, countries demand due legal process and evidence before effecting the extradition of individuals. Julian Assange and Edward Snowden are still not extradited, a decade after the information leak despite the best efforts of the US. Rather ironic, the UK, seen more as the US sidekick, which supported the false cause of the US in Iraq, refused to extradite the corrupt Indian liquor baron Vijay Mallya, a member of parliament, who defrauded the banks of 9000 crores and fled to the UK. They expressed concerns over the state of jails in India in this regard. Indian PM Modi is understood to have told the British PM Theresa May that their raising concern over the Indian prisons was unjustified as Vijay Mallya would be put in the same prisons in which the British had put great Indian leaders like Mahatma Gandhi. What an irony, the British who had shot dead 400 and injured 1200 unarmed peaceful Indians including women and children in Jallianwala Bagh, Amritsar in 1919, was concerned about the state of prison for Indian criminal absconding in the UK.

George Bush expected implicit compliance without a word from a country that had nothing to do with 9/11. The US behaved like a bully in both cases.

Before NATO took charge in Afghanistan, the International Security

Assistance Force (ISAF) was in charge of operations there as part of the collective security arrangement.

From June 2002 to February 2003, Turkey was the leader of ISAF II in Afghanistan. I was posted as the defence attaché in Turkey at the time. During a briefing to the defence attaches on Afghanistan, I asked the Turkish General, what would your sentry at the gate do if two armed Taliban men walked past your headquarters gate? The General said, nothing, they would do nothing. To me, the future of Afghanistan was clear and my prognosis was not encouraging. His reply also was an indicator of the challenges the military faced. So, most of the countries of ISAF, it seemed to me, were simply passing time without a clear direction and purpose. No surprise that the force commanders said, there was no strategy in Afghanistan.

On the twentieth anniversary, the US made a disgraceful exit from Afghanistan. The manner of withdrawal shocked and surprised its NATO allies amidst scenes of anarchy and people falling off military aircraft. They left millions of Iraqis at the mercy of the Taliban and a large number of Americans behind. As of today, the Taliban is back to its brutal Sharia ways of executing people and denying women basic rights to education and dignity.

This excerpt from an article sums it up succinctly.

> *"President Biden's withdrawal from Afghanistan is a foreign-policy humiliation. It has brought shame to our country as our allies doubt America's dependability and our enemies exploit the administration's signs of weakness. It has dishonoured the memory of the courageous American servicemen and women who have made the ultimate sacrifice to serve in Afghanistan over the last two decades, delivering justice and ensuring our nation's safety. Biden's incompetence and continuous lack of honesty and empathy are disgraceful to our nation as his administration's faults have now welcomed the spread of evil throughout the world."*

Source: Opinion - Biden's Disgraceful Withdrawal From Afghanistan, Chloe Choi, Aug 31, 2021, https://www.bipartisanhighschoolpoliticaldigest.com/post/opinion-biden-s-disgraceful-withdrawal-from-afghanistan, accessed on 07 May 2022

So, after two decades, the US handed over the country back to the Taliban, whom they had invaded arrogantly to destroy. They handed them a grand victory, a shot in the arms of terrorist organizations all over the globe and left behind billions of dollars worth of military equipment.

Was Corporal Glenton wrong when he summarised his view to say that the West's pattern of logic seems to run like this:

> *"We must be right because if we are wrong then that means you are right and that cannot be allowed. That is virtually impossible, we could not even consider it. It's just not possible, is it?"*
>
> *Source: Why I Won't Return to the War on Terror, Corporal Glenton.*

World War 1 lasted four years and the World War 2 lasted six. Fighting the ill-equipped rag-tag Taliban, ten years into the invasion, the US had achieved little to show, except the false narrative that they were winning. In 2011, the US Navy Seals killed Osama, a stone's throw distance away from the military academy in Abbottabad, inside Pakistan, their major ally in that war. Why did it take them ten more years to realise that they needed to get out? Clearly, the military leadership would have known the end game having seen the past.

I think no better advice can be given to Generals than by this young German Lieutenant:

> *"The soldier must say 'Yes' when he thinks 'Yes,' but when many say 'Yes' and think 'No', or when they feel forced to say 'Yes' though they think 'No', or when they say 'Yes' for the sake of their career, their comfort or self-interest, while their conscience tells them 'No', the point has been reached where true soldiering dies out altogether."*
>
> ***—Lt Karl Krafft, Officer Factory, Hans Helmut Kirst***

♦ ♦ ♦

Chapter Nine

The Indian Experience

India has been a peace-loving country. Throughout its 5000 years of recorded history, it has never crossed its borders to loot any other country's wealth, annex anyone's territory, or spread its religion and culture by force.

The British colonized India for two centuries starting from the Battle of Plassey in 1757, having come to India as traders, till India's independence in 1947. They turned the richest country in the world into one of the poorest. It was the defiance of one soldier in India's First War of Independence in 1857 - Mangal Pandey that laid the foundation of freedom that came a century later. It was the obedience and compliance of kings and millions of Indians that made colonization successful. While many contributed in different ways to the freedom struggle, the tipping point was the Indian National Army and their court martial after World War II, and the often-forgotten Indian Naval Mutiny of 1946 by 20,000 sailors that galvanized the nation. It terrified the British that they could not rule India anymore with Indian troops, which was the basis of their continued subjugation. They realised that they had to go. The charming smile and the personal bonhomie of leaders like Nehru and Ambedkar with British rulers would not have got India freedom.

In World War I, 1.5 million Indian soldiers fought for the British on battle fronts spanning Europe, Africa, and the Middle East. By the end of the War, India had suffered 1,20,000 casualties - killed, wounded or missing.

At the height of World War II, 2.5 million Indian soldiers served under the British. Approximately 87,000 Indian troops died in this War.

Field Marshal Claude Auchinleck, former Commander-in-Chief, India had stated that Britain Couldn't have come through both wars (World Wars I and II if they hadn't had the Indian Army.

While the dynamics of India during that period were complex with 565 independent princely states, it is hard to digest that the political leadership of the Indian Freedom Movement agreed to fight for the British, who, in 1919 at Jallianwala Bagh, Punjab, had most brutally used Indian troops to kill unarmed men, women and children—estimated between 379 to 1500 killed, 379 being the British official figures. Another 1200 were injured, 192 of them seriously. In 1943, it was Prime Minister Churchill's policies that led to the deaths of 3 million in the Bengal famine. Tragic that we were still fighting for and not against the British colonialists.

India would have attained independence with a fraction of the casualties suffered in those wars by fighting the British at home. They were the invaders on our land. It was the perfect time for defiance for the right cause. It was possible to galvanise the nation, unfortunately, the Indian National Congress was made up of Indian elites and loyalists. If the Britishers could get Indians to kill Indians, and they exploited every form of wile, guile, cunning and brutality, there is no reason why the leadership of the time should not have attempted to bring Indians together for independence and throw the colonialists out, when they were weakest and most vulnerable.

The fact that just 77000 British soldiers subjugated 300 million Indians is the story of too much obedience, too quietly by too many, led by kings and politicians for their own interests.

General Nathu Singh Rathore, an Indian General post-independence is famous for this stunning episode. One cannot but tip his hat to this fine breed of a soldier, regretfully long extinct. This episode should serve as an example to present-day Generals around the globe that there are things that are more important than you and your next rank. This supports my postulate in this book that positive defiance is an important part of higher leadership in every organisation.

It was post-independence days when the Indian constitution was being written, had its own Government and India was planning to lay out a defence strategy for the country. Many in the government and the Army wanted to select the best Indian commander and the most experienced person as the Army Chief.

The powerful Prime Minister Jawahar Lal Nehru had different plans. Immediately after India got independence, Nehru, without consulting anyone appointed General Rob Lockhart, a British officer as the Commander in Chief of the Indian Army. Most people were shocked to know that Nehru selected a British officer after fighting for independence for over 200 years!

One day Lockhart met Nehru with a strategic plan and proposed many government directives for the defence policies of the country.

He placed it on the table and explained to Nehru. After a while, a shell-shocked and stunned Lockhart walked out of the room and met Maj General Jick Rudra.

When asked what happened? He said "**The PM took one look at my paper and blew his top. Rubbish! Total rubbish! We don't need a defence plan. Our policy is ahimsa (non-violence). We foresee no military threats. Scrap the army!**"

One year after the incident, the Kashmir crisis had erupted and General Lockhart used to exchange notes with Gen Douglas Gracie who was Commander in Chief of the Pakistan Army! There were infiltrations taking place all along the border which Lockhart knew but took no action. It was Maj General Cariappa who responded to the crisis and with his bold decisions saved Kashmir. This issue was later raised with the government, with many people questioning the integrity of Lockhart. Finding no excuses, Nehru had to question his pet chief. He asked Lockhart whether he knew about the crisis in Kashmir and what measures were taken?

Lockhart replied "Aghast, Mr Prime Minister if you have to ask me that question, I have no business being the commander-in-chief of your forces. I know that there is a boat leaving Bombay in a few days, carrying British officers and their families to England. I shall be on that and leaving India soon!"

The next day emergency meeting was called to select the new Army Chief. Prime Minister Nehru chaired the meeting which was attended by the then Defence Minister Baldev Singh, who had earned the reputation of being Nehru's yes-man. Maj General Nathu Singh Rathore, Maj General Cariappa and a few defence experts were present too. Everyone knew that General Cariappa was the most deserving and wanted him to lead the army.

In the meeting, Nehru stated, "We should appoint a new Army Chief, as General Lockhart had resigned from the post. I consider that it is better to appoint a British man as the Army Chief since we do not have a capable and experienced Army man in our country."

Everybody in the meeting was silent. The army officers felt very humiliated by Nehru's words. Baldev Singh immediately endorsed Nehru's suggestion saying, "Yes, we do not have any capable Army man!"

There was one man who stood up and said "Sir, I have a point. You see Sir, we don't have a man with enough experience to lead the nation too, so shouldn't we appoint someone from Britain as the first PM of India? It was none other than General Nathu Singh Rathore.

Suddenly there was pin-drop silence in the room!

Annoyed, Nehru interrupted and said, "Are you saying that you are ready to be the first General of the Indian Army?"

Even though the officer got a golden opportunity, he replied, "Sir, why me? We have a very capable army officer, my senior General Cariappà, who is the most deserving among us. Do we need a better person than General Cariappa to guard our country? How could you say that our country does not have capable leaders?"

Nehru was then forced to appoint General Cariappa as the commander in Chief.

Source: https://postcard.news/how-general-cariappaslammed-nehru-in-public/

Moral courage is the most precious quality of a senior military leader and defiance becomes necessary sometimes. He must say what must be said and do what must be done. Courage means many things to a man in a position of responsibility.

Since Generals deal with important issues that have serious long-term implications, it becomes one of their most important leadership traits. Constructive disobedience is a natural extension of true loyalty and integrity. Acquiescence and failure to speak up on your convictions for personal gains or lack of courage is poor character.

In combat, covering up mistakes and failures can cost men their lives. In peacetime, it destroys the fabric of the military values woven over centuries.

In the Indian context, there is no better example than the India-China 1962 War, of how the lack of moral courage on the part of the senior military leadership can bring untold embarrassment to a nation.

Despite the glaring battle indicators and their convictions, the senior military leadership failed to prevent the political leadership led by Pundit Nehru, Defence Minister VK Krishna Menon and an incompetent army General from plunging the Indian Army into a misadventure that they had not been prepared for in any manner. We have already seen the attitude of Nehru towards the army.

The senior army leadership failed to stand up on many counts. General Thapar, the Army Chief then seemed to have become an inconsequential bystander.

The Indo-Pakistan 1971 War, on the other hand, is a glorious example of how the exercise of positive defiance by General Manekshaw, the Army Chief then, prevented a possible embarrassment and brought the nation glory.

♦ ♦ ♦

WHEN DEFIANCE DID THE INDIAN NATION A FAVOUR

India and China fought, what some call a 'short war' in 1967 on the desolate watershed of the strategic Nathu La and Cho La passes in Sikkim, on the India-China border. The defiance of one Indian General against superior authority resulted in a small but critical victory for India, which exorcised the ghosts of the India-China War of 1962 and shaped the behaviour of the Chinese leadership for the future. To appreciate this, it is important to briefly recapitulate the events of the War of 1962.

The India-China War 1962

In Oct-Nov 1962, India and China fought a month-long war. It was a national humiliation and a military debacle for India. The primary reason for the war was the dispute over the border; a legacy of colonial British India. The Mc Mohan Line which demarcated the border on the map along the watershed principle was the legally accepted border between British India and Tibet, based on the Shimla Convention of March 1914. In 1950, the Chinese forcefully occupied the whole of Tibet. This resulted in the Tibetan spiritual head Dalai Lama, with many of his followers fleeing to India where they were given refuge. This soured the harmonious relations that existed between India and China till then. The Shimla Convention demarcating the border between India and Tibet was refuted by the Chinese. In the Eastern Sector, China claimed the whole of present-day Arunachal Pradesh as Southern Tibet and in the Western Sector, the whole of Aksai Chin. Despite these dangerous indicators, the Indian government remained indifferent to this threat.

Jairam Ramesh, the author of the book *A Chequered Brilliance...* a book on VK Krishna Menon, the infamous defence minister of India during the Indo-China War of 1962, brings out the deplorable state of civil-military relations and relations within the military when the war clouds had begun to gather.

General Thimayya, the then Chief of the Army Staff had tendered his resignation over disputes with Defense Minister Krishna Menon. Later, he withdrew his resignation at the urging of Prime Minister Nehru.

Before the 1962 War, Lt General Thorat, the Eastern Army Commander had accurately predicted the fault lines in the 'Forward Policy' advocated by Prime Minister Nehru and the defence minister. He had unequivocally stated that with our state of all-around preparedness, the Chinese attack could not be contained. He also provided a timetable of how the defences will fall day by day if the Chinese attacked. He advocated the use of the Air Force to counter China.

His forthrightness and criticism did not find favour with the defence minister. Shortly before his retirement, Menon ordered an investigation into flimsy allegations against Thorat through the Chief, General Thapar.

General Thorat wrote to the Prime Minister.

> *"Should the PM not be satisfied with my explanation, I request that I may be given an opportunity to clear myself in person, in the presence of those who have made these allegations."*
>
> *Source: Conspiracy of Silence by Claude Arpi, Mail Today, 05 July 2018.*

During the late 50s and early 60s, tension began to rise on the border as both sides tried to consolidate their claims with troops on the ground in what was termed by the government as the 'Forward Policy'. Both countries claimed the territory while accusing the other of transgression. The flashpoint came when Indian troops occupied a post that China claimed was on its territory.

It was amidst such an environment, internal and external, that, on 20 October 1962, China launched a violent attack on Indian posts preceded by heavy artillery fire. Unknown to Indian intelligence, China had been preparing for this offensive for the last two years.

Prime Minister Jawahar Lal Nehru had always believed that China will never attack India because of good relations and Panchsheel, the five principles of peaceful co-existence mentioned in the Sino-India Agreement of 1954. Thus, the Indian army's basic modernization needs were outrightly ignored and it remained ill-prepared in every aspect to fight the Chinese in the rugged high-altitude terrain due to political apathy. During the war, they were denied the use of air force by the political authorities where the Indians had a great advantage and would have turned the fortunes of war. They were not equipped for the mission they were given and were constantly pushed to the brink.

Despite the best efforts and sacrifices of the battalions, the Indian Army was routed and suffered heavy casualties. It was a major body blow to the psyche of the nation and the international standing of Prime Minister Nehru. Two years later, he died; the 1962 setback had taken its toll.

It is important to understand the following aspects, in the context of the theme of this book.

- That the political leadership was criminally indifferent to the national security needs is one thing. The military leadership too failed here on every count. The genesis of India's partition, the experiences of the violence of the partition, the deceitful Pakistani attack in Kashmir, 1947-48, by violating the 'Standstill Agreement' where Pakistan annexed one-third of Jammu and Kashmir, insurgencies in the North-Eastern states since the early 1950s, the Chinese annexation of Tibet, the existential Indo-Chinese border dispute, and the open belligerence of Pakistan left no doubts on the trajectory the future would follow. The military leadership failed to impress upon the political leadership by convincing, urging, cajoling or simply 'positive defiance' on the need for a strong national defence, and later, to prevent a devastating war whose outcome was clear to them, is a major leadership failure. This was a serious situation that needed positive defiance by the military authority of the time. What shape this positive defiance should have taken place would be the call of the leadership of the time.
- In the Kargil War 1999, the government ordered the army and the air force not to cross the Line of Control (LC), when Pakistan had entered miles into India across the LC. In the 1962 War, the government prevented the use of air force which would have changed the course of

> the war. The military did not stand up against this order, even though the army was in retreat and the Chinese were threatening the plains of Assam. In such a critical situation, when the District Magistrate, Superintendent of Police and government functionaries had fled from Tezpur in Assam and the exodus of people had begun, would the chiefs have been justified to defy the government orders and employ the air force? My take—a bold **YES.**

During World War II, the German army attempted to save the country by trying to eliminate Hitler. In Italy, Mussolini was shot. In the UK, Churchill was voted to office during the war and voted out of it after the war. In India, the larger-than-life political leadership, on the other hand, was risking a military gamble over false assumptions, with an army that had been neglected ever since independence. It was a recipe for disaster; a dysfunctional military leadership and militarily ignorant and interfering political leadership far detached from reality.

It serves the government to have pliable officers as service chiefs, for they sing their tune. That is detrimental to the army and the country. Barring General Thimayya and Lt General Thorat who retired before the war, the rest including General Thapar, the Chief during the 62 War, became irrelevant onlookers. Pursuing a risky policy without preparing for it militarily led to national humiliation.

The Watershed War 1967

The developments of the Watershed War 1967 with China must be read against the background of the Indo-China 1962 War explained above. A militarily ignorant but arrogant political leadership, a pliable and incompetent military leadership, and in the end, a psychologically bruised and humiliated nation.

Pakistan, perceiving the Indian weaknesses in the Indo-China 1962 War, launched an offensive in August 1965 to annex Kashmir. At the height of the Indo-Pak War in 1965, China issued an ultimatum to India to vacate the posts at Jelep La and Nathu La passes in Sikkim and started troop build-up along the Line of Actual Control (LAC), especially opposite Sikkim to release pressure on Pakistan. Sikkim was then a protectorate state of India. It formally became a state of India on 15 May 1975.

The India-China relations deteriorated on every count during this period.

Indian 33 Corps was responsible for the defence of Sikkim. Its 17 Mountain Division had in its area of responsibility (AOR) two strategic passes on the India-China border, the Nathu La Pass at an altitude of 4310 meters (14150 feet) and the Cho La Pass at 4783 meters (15,692 feet. The other formation, the 27 Mountain Division had the Jelep La Pass at 4386 metres (14,390 feet) in its AOR. These passes provided the approaches to the heartland of Sikkim and thence to the strategic Siliguri Corridor, between Sikkim and then East Pakistan (now Bangladesh). Siliguri Corridor is a thin strip of land, about 25 kilometres at the narrowest section that connects the Eastern part of India with the mainland and Bhutan. Thus, because of its vulnerability, it is also called a Chicken's Neck.

Major Gen Sagat Singh was the commander of the 17 Mountain Division.

The border passes of Nathu La, Cho La and Jelep La, between Sikkim and China, were long and narrow watersheds. The Chinese had never accepted the McMahon Line as the border. Going by the history of the 1962 War, they implicitly expected India to avoid a tense stand-off and retreat from the two passes on the watershed line—Nathu La and Jelep La.

The Indian army had decided to fight the battle from defensive positions deeper inside its territory if the Chinese forces came in from Nathu La and Jelep La. The Indian decision-makers had overlooked the possibility that the Chinese may simply occupy these passes and advance no further. This would give them a strategic advantage in any future conflict as they would have control over dominating military heights and be able to look deep into Sikkim.

General Sagat, not comfortable with the idea, acquainted himself with every inch of his AOR and understood the lay of the land better. He interacted with junior leaders, post commanders and soldiers at the forward posts.

In the India-China War of 1962, some senior military leaders had ignored the feedback from ground commanders leaving them bereft of a realistic understanding of the evolving Chinese attack. This had led to disastrous decisions.

By the time Chinese forces built up their troop strength opposite Sikkim in September, Sagat had gained enough understanding of the terrain and had grown confident about the ability of his division to repulse a Chinese attack.

The divisional commander of the 27 Mountain Division, responsible for Jelep La, followed the directives of the 33 Corps headquarters, vacated Jelep La and retreated. Sagat, on the other hand, disagreed with his superior commanders and argued that if India were to vacate the Nathu La pass and retreat behind the watershed, the Chinese would be well placed to occupy the pass and simply control the watershed.

This would give them a decisive advantage in dominating the lower region of Gangtok and the entire state of Sikkim. It would also make the Siliguri Corridor extremely vulnerable to being cut off by advancing Chinese troops.

Given this criticality, the decision of the corps headquarters to withdraw from Nathu La was baffling. General Sagat remained steadfastly defiant and refused to withdraw his troops from the forward post at Nathu La. He believed that regardless of any provocation by the Chinese, not an inch of ground was to be surrendered. From the increased presence of troops on the Chinese side, it appeared that their plan may have been twofold: one, to make India commit its troops on two fronts, and two, to push India down the watershed and occupy the heights. Sagat was known to make decisions that often irked his seniors.

As soon as India decided to withdraw from Jelep La, China promptly occupied the vacated pass. The Chinese had managed to evict the Indian army from Jelep La without firing a shot! The decision on Nathu La thus became an even more critical one—both from a point of view of strategy as well as the morale of the troops. General Sagat refused to withdraw his troops from Nathu La even at the cost of confronting the corps commander. He stressed that as a division commander, he was authorized to take a call pertaining to a forward post in his jurisdiction. Finally, everyone reluctantly came around to his proposition.

The Indian decision to hold Nathu La, especially after the quick withdrawal from Jelep La, left the Chinese dumbfounded. This irked the Chinese who increased the frequency of firing exchanges along the sector, much to the concern of the Indian side. One evening when heavy firing lit up the hills, the corps commander was terribly concerned that a conflict might break out and indecision got the better of him.

Anticipating that tensions in the corps headquarters could result in a reversal of his decision and he may again be asked to withdraw from Nathu La, General Sagat walked out of his headquarters to avoid a confrontation, thus making himself unavailable on the phone. As expected, an anxious corps commander called up the division headquarters that evening. General Sagat's staff officer had to bear the brunt of the corps commander's fury when he informed him that Sagat was not in the office. Despite the onset of winter and the India-Pakistan ceasefire of late September 1965, China persevered with a low-scale war of attrition.

General Sagat dug his heels, he knew that he had to stake a claim to the watershed, come what may. His troops continued to mark the watershed with barbed wire fencing and minefields amidst recurring tense face-offs, scuffles and skirmishes. On the morning of 11 September 67, the Chinese Commissar got roughed up in a scuffle during fencing when soldiers on both sides got injured. Then all of a sudden, the Chinese soldiers disengaged and withdrew into their bunkers. The tension exploded. On a pre-determined signal of a long whistle, they opened heavy fire at a point-blank range from the protection of their bunkers on the wire obstacles laying party. The Indians caught in the open, took many casualties, including their commanding officer. The Chinese opened up artillery fire, for the first time since the 62 War. General Sagat ordered the artillery to respond in kind without waiting for political clearance, which was the norm. As the Indians reorganised themselves after the initial setback, they returned heavy fire and launched a close-quarter assault to silence the Chinese automatic weapons. The battle lasted three days when the guns went silent. The Chinese were given a bloody nose having lost 340 soldiers dead and unknown injured. Indians had lost 88 dead and 150 injured. It was the Chinese who threw in the towel.

Nathu La having fallen silent after the indirect Chinese truce, the battle spilt over to Cho La pass, where sharp exchanges took place. Smarting under the defeat at Nathu La, the Chinese raked up trouble at Cho La pass on 28 September opening fire first. Intense close combat and heavy small arms fire raged for the full day and night. Chinese attacks were beaten back. The sheer raw courage of Indian soldiers wielding khukris (Gurkhas' traditional personal weapon) unnerved the Chinese, inflicting heavy casualties. The Chinese sought a truce by firing a very light signal as the uneasy silence returned in an eerie night.

Chinese suffered heavy casualties, having lost close to 400 soldiers dead in the two battles at Nathu La and Cho La. India too lost about a hundred soldiers in the two battles. The setback was severe for the Chinese as the deadly close combat skills of Indian soldiers had resulted in pushing back the Chinese post way inside their territory. The small but critical redemption at Nathu La and

Cho La exorcized the ghosts of 1962. The two battles didn't result in the gain of any territory. Both sides went back to where they had been before the conflict began. But these battles would turn out to be a watershed in the region's history, events that heralded an era of peace between India and China.

By showing China that the 1962 War was an aberration and that the Indian army would defend India's borders fiercely, these battles ironically were the harbingers of peace and demonstrated to the Chinese the resolve of the Indian Army. It ensured that Peking would never embark on such a misadventure again. For China, psychological warfare was a crucial way to dominate an entire army's strategic mind space. Nathu La and Cho La would become the inflexion points of the turnaround in psychological ascendancy. Nathu La and Cho La had set the template for the next half a century and more.

The loss of around a hundred lives at Nathu La and Cho La became a political issue and the prime minister had to face a barrage of criticism in the Parliament from the opposition leaders. After the battles, General Sagat was posted out to a fringe appointment in some remote part of the country and was considered a blow to his career prospects.

Author's Notes

Disobedience and defiance of authority have no place in the military—legally. Does that make sense after reading what General Sagat Singh did? Does that philosophy need a review? Thankfully, some wise men saw the merit in his defiance and he was promoted to Lt General. He then commanded 4 Corps in the liberation of Bangladesh in 1971, where, he yet again challenged the established wisdom and practised manoeuvre warfare in an obstacle-ridden terrain. He set a glowing example of operational leadership, greatly contributing to the surrender of Daca, the capital of East Pakistan.

When a commander chooses the path of defiance based on his strong convictions, he is putting his career on the line. It could even result in disciplinary action. It is a tough call. In the case of watershed war, the line was very thin. If the Chinese had prevailed, Gen Sagat would have been sacked for sure and maybe a lot more.

Loss of soldiers' lives is a very painful thing, particularly for the immediate commanders, for they give their lives on their orders in the belief that he knows what he is doing. There are times when such sacrifices are worth the cause. In my opinion, the watershed war of 1967 and what it achieved was a cause worth that sacrifice. Sagat's actions did not go down too well with a section of the leadership in Delhi 2000 kilometres away. However, his foresight to appreciate the strategic implications of withdrawal and the body blow to national pride that it would have inflicted, as the 62 War debacle did, would have been devastating. It was his stubbornness and defiance that restored national pride.

Some paradox that the Chinese political commissar with the battalion decided to initiate this bloody battle including artillery fire, while the Indian army, on the other hand, was seeking permission from the prime minister to open up artillery guns when they were being pounded by the enemy. General Sagat waited for no permission and retaliated in kind.

Today, the nation should be grateful for his defiance, or else, the Chinese would be breathing down on Gangtok, with all three strategic passes under their control. A nation that was demoralised and humiliated in the 62 War, had redeemed its honour and had something to cheer about. History would go on to judge Sagat Singh as the man who rightly defied authority to restore national honour and teach the Chinese a long-term lesson.

These defiant battles by our battalions determined the military template for India's resolute and aggressive posture in stand-offs such as Sumdorong Chu in 1986, Doklam in 2017, Galwan in 2020 and Tawang in 2022. That India and China have not fought a war in fifty years has a lot to do with the watershed saga—defiance of their own authority and the Chinese belligerence, the steadfastness of our men and one man's defiant leadership.

Similar positive defiance by some military leaders would have prevented some blunders that I have narrated above.

♦ ♦ ♦

The Sri Lanka Fiasco 1987

The Indian army went to Sri Lanka to implement a peace accord in 1987 between the separatist Tamils, the Liberation Tigers of Tamil Eelam (LTTE), also called the Tamil Tigers and the government of Sri Lanka in the Island nation. Interestingly, the accord was signed between India and Sri Lanka. The LTTE, the main party to the conflict was not a party to the accord!

Sri Lanka had seen decades of discontent and years of brutal conflict with

LTTE who were fighting for greater autonomy and freedom for the Tamil-dominated North and East Sri Lanka. Indian Army landed up fighting the Tamil separatists in a third country with no preparations when the peace accord failed due to some developments. The Indian government failed to factor in or overlooked the historical linkages between the Sri Lankan Tamils and the Indian Tamils. The Tamil Nadu government was not favourably disposed to the Indian Army's operations across the narrow strait. Tamil Nadu became a safe haven for the LTTE cadres.

Switching from the sedate implementation of a peace accord to fighting the most vicious militant group of the time, the army did not ask the government or itself some basic questions.

- Did it occur to the political and military authorities that they have not been able to end India's own insurgencies in the North Eastern States for four decades? So, how did they assume that they will do so in another country in a quick time given the history of the conflict?
- Were they operationally prepared for the drastic change of mission in a foreign land? What was needed before launching into the unknown?
- What did winning mean in Sri Lanka and what was the minimum desirable to achieve the political and military objectives?
- Was the forced disarmament or destruction of LTTE, as is understood to be the stated objective, attainable in a reasonable time frame in a foreign land?

Disappointingly, the Indian troops operated in densely forested terrain with tourist maps throughout the deployment. The Sri Lankan Army which had immense experience and knowledge of the local environment was not coopted suitably. In the end, despite the gallant show by the battalions against immense odds, India came out with little to show, having lost more than 1157 officers and men and 3000 injured. Even though they had compressed the LTTE around the jungles of Vayunia, the LTTE leadership was intact. It took Sri Lanka another two decades with massive civilian casualties to subdue LTTE, with allegations of war crimes against the civil population.

To add insult to injury, the Chief Minister of Tamil Nadu MG Ramachandran refused to receive the Indian Army at Chennai when they returned. Indian Army had the enemy in front and their supporters back home—some of our own countrymen.

The worst was yet to come. In May 1991, Prime Minister Rajiv Gandhi was assassinated by a LTTE suicide bomber, changing the political equation forever.

Source: India's Battlefields, From Kurukshetra to Balakot, Ajay Singh

The story repeated itself. The Indian Army was ordered to mobilise under 'Operation Parakram' in December 2001 after the Pakistan-sponsored terrorist attack on the Indian parliament. Prime Minister Vajpayee was asked by the then-defence secretary, "What is the political objective of this mobilization?"

The Prime Minister looked at his National Security Advisor and said, "They are asking for the political objective." And went on to add, "We will tell you that later." This was never stated.

So, the army mobilized for war without knowing the political objective, what to fight for, and what military objectives to frame which would dictate a favourable conflict termination. The army remained deployed for a year without knowing the political objectives of the mobilization, losing hundreds of men without fighting. In the end, Pakistan claimed victory and continued its proxy war killing service members' families in the cantonment while the army was deployed on the border.

Importance of Vibrant Politico-Military Interface

National security is a whole of nation approach, today more than ever before. Different organs of the state have different expertise and role to play. The military brings to the table its own, no one else can. Yet, every organisation suffers from turf parochialism, nepotism and tunnel vision disregarding others' perspectives.

It is important that the politico-bureaucratic machinery understands the nuances of national security and heed the advice of the military. The civil-military interface has to allow for the institution to function without fear or favour. It is not a question of them and us. The nation is in it together, more so in the present international security environment.

Political leadership should not be left alone to decide on matters that impact the military, for that impacts national security. Neither can they be left to the military hierarchy alone, for the military is comfortable in the status quo and averse to change. Since independence, India has had a history where the military has been kept out of the decision-making process even on matters that have severe military implications, and issues that they understand best. Prime Minister Nehru, with all his experience, believed that India did not need an army. We saw what happened in 1962. Their future is being decided by politicians and bureaucrats who are ignorant of military nuances or even paranoid about the military. In India, the office of the defence minister is often the musical chair. This office has been occupied by some of the most ignorant and ineffective politicians. It takes more than three decades of institutional training, yearly assessment in a three-tier reporting system and an extremely steep promotion pyramid to make it to a General. A bureaucrat who could be the secretary of the animal husbandry department one day could be the defence secretary the next day, with no domain experience or expertise. A politician who has no expertise could be the defence minister today and the finance minister tomorrow. They have all the authority with no accountability.

For the military, the end is always military victory. In the larger scheme of things—military victory is only the means to a political end. Thus, sometimes military gains may have to be sacrificed for larger political objectives.

However, the Indian experience highlights that it is in the interest of the country that the political leadership heed military advice and the military must be co-opted in the security planning and decision-making where necessary. The political leadership may unwittingly give away strategic gains through military ignorance. India has experienced this on more than one occasion. And when that is happening, the military must not remain a mute spectator where the national interest is being jeopardised out of ignorance.

Immediately after the partition, Pakistan invaded Jammu & Kashmir in 1947-48 to forcibly annex it, violating the Stand Still Agreement. This agreement required both India and Pakistan not to interfere in Kashmir, allowing them to decide to join either India or Pakistan. When India responded and the Pakistani raiders supported and led by their army were on the run, the then-Indian Prime Minister Nehru took the issue to the UN, which led to a ceasefire. This resulted in Pakistan illegally occupying one-third of Jammu and Kashmir, which it still occupies as Pakistan Occupied Kashmir (POK), violating the UN ceasefire terms. At that time, the military momentum was on India's side and a lot more could have been achieved. We continue to pay for that folly even today.

The next great political folly was the return of the strategic Hazipir pass in J&K to Pakistan, which India had captured in the Indo-Pak war of 1965. This again was an unprovoked war where Pakistan violated the 'Line of Control' to annex Kashmir. This strategic pass would have given India an immense advantage and its retention would have been perfectly justified for Pakistan's repeated violation of bilateral and international agreements. This was done by a very respected Prime Minister, Lal Bahadur Shastri in the Tashkent Agreement after the war. I guess, a case of military ignorance in the absence of professional military advice. Yet again, post the Indo-Pak War of 1971, Indian political leadership failed to exploit 94000 Pakistani prisoners of war – this time under a very shrewd Prime Minister Indira Gandhi.

During the Kargil War in 1999, the Pakistan military, masquerading as terrorists, crossed deep inside Indian territory and occupied commanding heights over a frontage of 130 kilometres in the Kargil Sector. This threatened the Srinagar-Leh Highway, the lone lifeline to Ladakh. Worse, this was happening when the Indian prime minister was in Pakistan to discuss peace with their prime minister. The Indian political leadership prevented its military from crossing the Line of Control in support of its operations in Kargil to project a good international image! We lost over 500 soldiers in that war as a consequence.

These are not realisations in hindsight; these were as clear then as they are now. Given the consistent deceitful nature of Pakistan, as much experienced by the US in Afghanistan, such follies are hard to fathom. The military should not sit quietly when national interests are at stake.

Author's Notes

In a democracy, the paranoia of civilian control over the military tends to marginalise the military to the detriment of the nation. The government has the prerogative to select the chief. Something seriously goes wrong when supersession disregards the merit to place a favoured officer at the helm. This wrong is the 'sense of obligation' to the political establishment which the individual feels obliged to repay in different ways. Indian military faced the consequences when General Bipin Rawat was elevated over two very competent Generals to the post of the Army Chief and later made the first Chief of Defence Staff. What followed during his tenure was unprecedented, and it started with the dilution of the apolitical nature of the highest military office. On one occasion, he skipped the Navy Day Wreath Laying Ceremony at the National War Memorial to attend a politico-religious ceremony presided over by the chief minister of the ruling political party. His approach to most of the issues demonstrated a lack of due diligence and defied conventional military wisdom and norms. The personal staff officers and the army commanders seemed to have lost their voice, as the carrot dangled for everyone. When the criticism of his approach and attitude reached a feverish pitch amongst the veterans, he contemplated slapping a veterans' code of conduct, which threatened their pension if the code was violated.

The Indian army may be the only army in the world where Brigadiers draw more pension than Major Generals and it has been so for a decade. Bipin Rawat and his team of Generals, and others later, either did not care or were simply incompetent to address this open and shut case that was acknowledged by the then finance minister on national TV. That left the veterans no choice but to go to court, something that should not have been necessary: a case that deserves positive defiance against the government of the day and the military hierarchy.

It was during his stewardship that the unprecedented incident of positive defiance by junior officers recounted below happened.

AFSPA is a special provision that comes into effect once a state or parts of it are declared disturbed areas by a government notification. This allows for the deployment of security forces including the military. AFSPA gives special powers to the army in disturbed areas against those who violate the law, arrest anybody even without a warrant, and carry out searches without consent. Once a person is taken into custody, he/she has to be handed over to the nearest police station as soon as possible.

Prosecution of the security forces officer on duty for alleged violation of human rights requires the prior permission of the Central Government.

AFSPA powers notwithstanding, the Indian army has been very ethical in conduct and responsible in the use of force. Less than three per cent of alleged cases of human rights violations have been found to be true. The clamour of human rights activists, chair-bound experts and vested political interests started demanding that AFSPA be withdrawn and FIRs be filed against army officers for every death, which meant even when the person is a confirmed terrorist. That is a serious situation and the protection of AFSPA is necessary to operate in counterinsurgency from false allegations and collateral deaths that may take place due to operational circumstances.

Around 2018, this issue became serious. Organised stone-pelting and disruption of security forces operations had become a serious nuisance in Kashmir. In one incident an army column had to fire to disrupt a stone-pelting mob interfering in their operations. Two persons in that mob died as a result. An FIR was filed against a company commander. Apparently, the army did little and it was his father who ran around the Supreme Court to obtain a stay. This reportedly happened with the collusion of the chief minister of Jammu and Kashmir and the defence minister of the time.

When it appeared to the rank and file that the military hierarchy was not addressing their concerns, almost 700 hundred Indian army officers and men directly knocked on the doors of the Supreme Court and appealed against the dilution of AFSPA, bypassing the command chain. This is a serious commentary on the credibility of the army leadership to safeguard the interests of its officers and men who operate in exceedingly difficult circumstances in the counter-insurgency areas.

When this happened, I asked a serving army commander what was going on that hundreds of officers disregard the command chain and choose to go direct to the Supreme Court on the AFSPA issue. His reply was, "It did not happen in my command." A disappointing reply from an army commander in my perspective!

It is a blistering statement on the failure of the senior army leadership. An army commander cannot feel happy and sit back that it did not happen in his command. This would be an acceptable answer from a commanding officer of a unit. This blazing arrow of distrust must pierce the soul of every army commander and give him sleepless nights. They must act and get the hierarchy to introspect and set things right. This is no mean issue—the trust deficit in the senior army leadership.

Do I blame the officers for bypassing the chain of command? I do not. Constructive disobedience/defiance is sometimes necessary to bring the focus back on critical issues that have been forgotten or neglected by the hierarchy, sitting far from where the shit flies.

Army's mission in Sri Lanka was to implement the peace accord which had fatal flaws—LTTE was not a signatory to the accord. Quite incredible, no wonder that the accord fell apart at the first tremor. How many political problems have been resolved militarily?

When the role changed, it needed an entire reset of mind, material and strategy to fight a professional and ruthless militant organization like LTTE in their own backyard and an unknown environment. Fighting in another country when the people (Tamils) were bound to be against you, makes the challenge that much more formidable. When some sections of the same ethnic group across the narrow strait, in your own country support them, it gets much worse.

The army jumped into the mission without appreciating the challenges and without due diligence. They underestimated the adversary and the environment. When we had not succeeded in controlling our own insurgency in the North East for decades, it is incomprehensible how the military authority can take on a mission with such a high degree of unpreparedness. The political leadership will often not appreciate the challenges in accomplishing military missions as Iraq, Afghanistan, Vietnam, India-China War 62 etc. demonstrate.

It is an important function of the military hierarchy to fully comprehend the complexities and the consequences of the mission thrust upon them by the political authority. General Manekshaw had set a glowing example of this during the 1971 War.

One cannot blame the young officers for bypassing the command chain on the issue of AFSPA. It is they who are at the wrong end of the terrorist's gun and the wrong end of the law? Clearly, from their perspective, they lacked trust in the higher leadership to secure their genuine interests in counterinsurgency operations.

That India chose not to use the air force against the Chinese in 1962 even when the army was routed and the Chinese were threatening the plains of Assam is incomprehensible. That the military leadership failed to get the political leadership to sanction the use of the air force even at this stage is grotesque. That they chose not to defy the government orders to employ the air force when national sovereignty and honour were being hammered is a criminal offence.

Blind obedience to political authority under such circumstances is disloyalty to the nation.

Let me ask this question. If the military leadership had decided to use the air force in defiance of the government orders, in defence of national sovereignty and honour under those circumstances, what action could the government have taken against the Chiefs? Nothing at all; on the contrary, they would be looking for cover and the country would have applauded that decision.

These were just the circumstances that demanded defiance of political directives on the use of the air force for national honour. This act of defiance, by any parameters of the laws of conflict or judicial prudence, would be justified, as was the action of Azad Hind Fauz (INA) to fight the British colonialist during the Second World War when Gandhi and Nehru were following the path of non-violence. The nation acknowledged the role of Subhash Chandra Bose by installing his statute at India Gate. The British with all the authority as the colonialist power could not punish the defiant INA soldiers because of people's support.

Pakistan has been toying with India and pushing the envelope on the proxy war under the threat of nuclear ambiguity. We continued to demonstrate weak leadership in the name of a mature nation, yielding nothing. Choosing not to cross the Line of Control (LC) during the Kargil war to demonstrate restraint and maturity, after seeing the blatant Pakistani defiance of the LC was misplaced restraint and maturity. When India presented irrefutable evidence of the involvement of the Pakistani army masquerading as terrorists, it was time to up the ante, politically and militarily. We still did not cross the LC either by ground troops or by the air force in support of ground operations. It was the soldiers who paid the price and it is my view that we came across as a soft state. Often, the justification given is that we earned the reputation of a responsible country in the international fraternity and the support of the US. It is my bet; India's image would not have suffered one bit and the US would have acted no differently if India had crossed the LC. In any case, we did not need the US support as the Pakistan army was on the run and Pakistan was in political turmoil. The case was open and shut in India's favour given Pakistan's reputation in the world as a terror state. It was an opportunity to hammer Pakistan militarily and diplomatically. Despite the Kargil intrusion and the military coup by General Musharraf and Pakistan's state policy on terrorism, the Pakistani army remained the trusted ally of the US. At the end of the day, nations across the globe have a short memory and their national interests override everything else. India's nuclear explosions are long forgotten, the world is lining up for Indian markets. China's support to Russia in Ukraine has taken a back seat and European leaders made a beeline to visit China in 2023. With all the hatred and animosity against Israel, Muslim nations are lining up to re-engineer their ties with Israel.

The Indian government thankfully changed the paradigm in 2016. India struck terrorist camps in Pakistan across the LC by Special Forces in 2016 and then by an airstrike deep inside Pakistan in 2019 in Balakot. Earlier it did the same in Burma. If Pulwama terrorist attack that killed 40 security personnel was a justification for crossing the LC, the Kargil aggression by Pakistan was a monumental trespass that would have justified any Indian action, both within the laws of conflict and international laws of self-defence. Despite those cross-border strikes, India is the toast of the international community because of various factors. Its reputation as a responsible state, I am sure has not been dented one bit.

Now, just imagine what would have been the state of Israel, if they also had political leaders seeking to project an image of maturity and restraint, instead of going for the jugular of their enemies and securing their national interests. In the six-day war in 1967, the Israelis launched pre-emptive air strikes against the Arab adversaries and won a convincing victory, occupying Sinai and Golan Heights and more. In the Yom Kippur War of 1973, despite having confirmed intelligence of the pending Egyptian attack 24 hours in advance, Israeli Prime Minister Golda Meir, under pressure from the US failed to do this, despite the advice of the military. Israel paid a very heavy price for this folly in every way, only to be resurrected by a defiant Ariel Sharon and gallant fighting by the military. The PM had to resign later. That none of its enemies all around dare challenge it, is the result of its no-nonsense, defiant character.

Remember the Machiavellian principle—Evil often wins. There is little space in this world for good. The evil of the few needs to be challenged by the good majority.

Regarding the civil-military interface, I would like to compare three famous personalities of the Second World War. Churchill, Hitler and Stalin. In the earlier phase of the war, Hitler sacked those who questioned or disagreed with him as defeatists; in the later stages of the war, he sacked or executed Generals who would not blindly obey his directions. Hitler's personal view became the German World view without the benefit of multiple perspectives and wargaming. German Generals brushed off very valid objections of officers. When asked if Germany had the economic resources to fight a long war or a war in Russian winters. They were summarily dismissed by a simple reply, 'The war will be over much before that.' History lessons had been disregarded at the altar of misplaced confidence and assumptions.

In the earlier phase of the war, Stalin purged or executed Generals who were inconvenient or lost battles and thus lost the benefit of experienced military leadership. An introspective cognitive General who loses a battle has many advantages over the one leading in battle the first time. In sacking those Generals, Stalin disregarded the environmental factors and the momentum of the German Wehrmacht at that stage of the war. Russia won the war, albeit with a prohibitive loss of lives as a consequence. Germany was devastated.

Churchill on the other hand had been the First Lord of the Admiralty during the First World War. He was part of the group that had orchestrated the disastrous Dardanelles campaign and the landings at Gallipoli in 1915. He had experienced personal failure and was pragmatic. An experienced politician in a democracy, he was tolerant of and understood the value of dissent and multiple perspectives. In the war room, they had heated debates with Generals free to thump the table. He had serious differences of opinion with the chief of the Imperial General Staff, General Alan Brooke. He would walk away in a huff, think it over, take the points on merit and change his decisions for the better. It was business as usual the next day. No one was sacked for their dissent, criticism and disagreements with him. The results were there to see.

It is difficult to imagine that Hitler or Stalin would have created a lighter moment or appreciated a joke. Churchill was a man with a great sense of humour. Once a man was arrested in London for calling Churchill a fool. There was an uproar in the parliament on what kind of democracy was there that a person could not criticise the prime minister. Churchill replied, "The man was not arrested for calling me a fool. He was arrested for letting out a national secret during the war." In Germany and Russia, he would have been executed summarily.

So, in such an environment of constructive dissent, there would rarely be a necessity for positive defiance. The institutional mechanism, the interactive personality of leaders and the culture of free expression prevent that stage to arrive.

In India, civil-military relations are mostly seen as dysfunctional in the name of civilian authority over the military. In an environment of political ignorance and indifference to the military, the bureaucracy has occupied that space and squeezed the military out. There is a lack of confidence and suspicion in the bureaucracy. They are seen as stumbling blocks rather than enablers.

Admiral Joshi, former Naval Chief said on his resignation, "Where there is authority, there is no accountability. Where there is the responsibility, there is no authority."

Hopefully, the transformation and restructuring taking place in the Indian military should improve functionality.

♦ ♦ ♦

Chapter Ten

Defiance in Combat

In combat, there are times when superior commanders issue orders that do not factor in the local situation or are simply out of touch with ground reality. We saw that with the 'Fighting Generals' of the First World War and Hitler in the Second. The commanders on the ground need to use their discretion in disobeying for a purpose; never an easy proposition.

Friedrich Wilhelm Ernst Paulus was a German Field Marshal during World War II who commanded the 6th Army during the Battle of Stalingrad (August 1942 to February 1943). He was cut off and surrounded in the subsequent Soviet counter-offensive. Adolf Hitler prohibited attempts to break out or capitulate, and German defence was gradually worn down. He was known as a theoretical 'yes' man General. Even when he knew his army was in no position to fight, he never told Hitler what he should have or did what he needed to.

Hitler continued with his no breakout—no surrender orders. Finally, Paulus surrendered in Stalingrad on 31 January 1943, the same day on which he was informed of his promotion to Field Marshal by Hitler. This led to the death of more than 200,000 soldiers in battle or due to starvation and cold. Ninety thousand prisoners surrendered, of which only 5000 returned to Germany after a long period of captivity.

Source: Friedrich Paulus https://en.wikipedia.org/wiki/Friedrich_Paulus

While they will have a reason of their own for their decision, the ground criticality makes it difficult for the local commander. Sometimes, it is the personality of the commander and his proximity to ground zero that shapes the decision. There are many examples when the commanders have defied higher authority and saved the day for the country.

In the Indian context, I have mentioned the Watershed War of 1967 where

General Sagat Singh defied his superiors for a tactical victory that had strategic implications.

Let us look at two battlefield commanders with similar personalities who defied the higher authority to pull their country out of a deep hole.

Hermann Karl Bruno von François

Hermann Karl Bruno von François (31 January 1856 – 15 May 1933) was a German General der Infanterie during World War I and is best known for his key role in several German victories on the Eastern Front in 1914.

When war broke out in August 1914, François' 1 corps, the 8th Army faced the right wing of a two-pronged Russian invasion of East Prussia, led by Paul von Rennenkampf's Russian First Army. On 17 August the overall German theatre commander, General Maximilian von Prittwitz, nervously eying the advance of the Russian left wing far to the south, ordered Von François to retreat while under heavy attack from Rennenkampf.

François, reluctant to surrender any of his beloved Prussia, and naturally pugnacious, also felt breaking off while engaged would be deadly, and so he ignored Prittwitz's order, responding with the famous reply "General von François will withdraw when he has defeated the Russians!" He counterattacked Rennenkampf's massive army, bringing on the Battle of Stalluponen, and won a surprising victory while inflicting 5,000 casualties and taking 3,000 prisoners.

After winning the battle, François obeyed Prittwitz's order and withdrew 15 miles to the west, where three days later he fought Rennenkampf to a draw at the Battle of Gumbinnen. Von François' aggressiveness resulted in the cautious Rennenkampf halting his advance westward.

Following that battle and a change of overall commanders (Prittwitz was judged to have lost his nerve by the German High Command), François' corps was transferred by rail to the southwest, to confront the Russian Second Army advancing into southern East Prussia under the command of General Alexander Samsonov. Although not trusted by the new German commanders Paul von Hindenburg and Erich Ludendorff due to his previous disobedience, François played a decisive role in the upcoming Battle of Tannenberg. On 27 August François attacked the lead elements of Samsonov's army and began to make steady advances into their rear. Ludendorff, fearing a Russian counterattack by Rennenkampf, now ordered him to break off the advance. However, François twice ignored his direct orders and played a decisive role in the following encirclement and defeat of Samsonov's army.

When Hindenburg and Ludendorff went south to lead the 9th Army in Russian Poland, François remained with his corps in East Prussia and led it with much success in the First Battle of the Masurian Lakes the following month. When General Richard von Schubert, the new commander of the 8th Army, ordered him to retreat, he dispatched a telegram to the OHL describing his success and stating "The Commander is badly counselled." The telegram impressed Kaiser so much that he immediately relieved Schubert and, on 3 October, gave von François the command of the 8th Army. He did not hold it for long. When Hindenburg and Ludendorff prepared their counter-attack from Thorn in the direction of Lodz, François was reluctant to send the requested I Corps, sending the badly trained and ill-equipped XXV Reserve Corps instead. That was too much for his superiors. In early November 1914, von François was removed and replaced by General Otto von Below.

He continued to distinguish himself. He won the Pour le Mérite, Germany's highest military decoration for his performance in the breakthrough at Gorlice, and had the Oak Leaves attached to it in July 1917, for outstanding performance during the Battle of Verdun.

However, he never received any further promotion or serious commands under Ludendorff and gave up his command in July 1918 and soon retired.

Source: Hermann von Francois https://en.wikipedia.org/wiki/Hermann_von_Fran%C3%A7ois

♦ ♦ ♦

Field Marshal Claude Auchinleck Defies Churchill

General Auchinleck was an outstanding British General. He rose rapidly, serving in Egypt and Mesopotamia during World War I. In the last 18 months of the war, he was awarded the Order of the British Empire, the Distinguished Service Order and the French Croix de Guerre.

During World War II, he was appointed the Commander-in-Chief of the Middle East Theatre in 1941. His troops forced Field Marshal Rommel's forces to retreat from Egypt along the North African coast but the Germans fought back to defeat the British at Tobruk.

General Auchinleck took personal command of the British forces after Field Marshal Rommel had pushed the British troops back to the Egyptian frontier. A biography of the British military commander credits him with having ended "the dreary catalogue of reverses and retreats, tactical follies and ham-fisted Generalship."

Churchill dismissed General Auchinleck in August 1942 after the commander refused to launch an immediate counterattack when Field Marshal Rommel halted outside Cairo.

General Auchinleck argued that his men had not regrouped and needed reinforcing and that a hasty counter-attack without adequate preparation will cause needless heavy casualties. Several military analysts accused Churchill of misunderstanding desert warfare tactics, saying he placed too much emphasis on territorial occupation.

Field Marshal Auchinleck was promoted to the army's highest rank in 1946 and was appointed Commander in Chief in the Indian subcontinent in 1947 during the partition between India and Pakistan. During the serious Hindu-Moslem riots, he advocated using British troops to suppress the violence. The British viceroy in India, Admiral Louis Mountbatten, disagreed and Field Marshal Auchinleck withdrew from active duty the next year. The riots resulted in the deaths of hundreds of thousands of people including women and children.

https://www.nytimes.com/1981/03/25/obituaries/field-marshal-auschinleck-desert-commander-dies.html

(Print on 25 March 1981, Section B, Page 10 of the National edition with the headline: FIELD MARSHAL AUSCHINLECK, DESERT COMMANDER, DIES.)

Ariel Sharon Saves the Day in Yom Kippur War

Maj General Ariel Sharon, a controversial personality has been called the greatest field commander of the Israeli Defence Forces. He has also been called the Israeli Caesar. His superiors described him as reckless, unbalanced, undisciplined and too independent. Sharon is widely regarded as the Hero of the Yom Kippur War.

He was part of every Israeli war, right from its independence in 1948 to the Yom Kippur War in 1973 where he was the commander of the Armoured Division tasked to establish the bridgehead on the Suez Canal. Relying on his judgment, intuition and strategic sense, he exploited the capability of his formation to establish the bridgehead west of the Suez Canal, which extended just 62 miles short of Cairo. This isolated the Egyptian 3rd Army, making it vulnerable to destruction and threatening the supply routes of the Egyptian 2nd Army. In doing so, he disobeyed the orders of his higher headquarters, the Southern Army and the Chief, borne out of a defensive approach. He bypassed the command chain to reach out directly to Defense Minister Moshe Dayan to proceed with his offensive west of Suez into the Egyptian mainland.

Later, when Defense Minister Moshe Dayan wanted him to halt his offensive, he disregarded his orders and followed the orders of his superior headquarters to continue the offensive creating a situation for the US-brokered peace agreement to bring the war to an end and lay the foundation for a long-term peace with Egypt.

Obedience and discipline have their place in the military. It is not sacrosanct and if followed blindly, it could spell disaster as we saw in the case of the India-China War in 1962. People may have different opinions on Ariel Sharon, but the 73 War was a close thing. The Israeli defeat at one point threatened the state of Israel in a manner that Prime Minister Golda Meir on the advice of Moshe Dayan is known to have ordered the assembly of its nuclear weapons. It was the audacity and defiance of Ariel Sharon that saved the day for Israel.

Defence Minister Moshe Dayan famously said of his Generals that he preferred to restrain war horses rather than "prod oxen who refuse to move." Sharon, though, proved difficult to contain.

In the aftermath of the Suez War, then-prime minister David Ben-Gurion wrote of Sharon in his journal: "The lad is a thinker, an original. Were he to be weaned of his fault of not speaking the truth in his reports he would make an exemplary military leader."

Well, this is interesting. One wonders at the context of his statement on truth. Ben Gurion emphasised speaking truth by Generals; today most political leaders will not be amused if a General spoke truth to the powers. I guess, sometimes military leaders may need to hold back the truth at a time when the larger good is at stake – context and consequentialism.

Source: Israel's indomitable protector, Ariel Sharon emblemized military audacity, evolving politics. Mitch Ginsburg, 11 January 2014. https://www.timesofisrael.com/israels-indomitable-protector-ariel-sharon-emblemized-military-audacity-evolving-politics/ accessed on 17 June 2022.

WHEN COMMANDING OFFICERS STOOD TALL

As a battalion commander, I have personally felt the heat and weight of responsibility in combat. That is the most critical level of 'Contact Leadership' as I call it. It is here that there is a direct responsibility for the honour of the unit, the mission and the well-being of the men under your command. It is here the commanding officer will have to face the direct stare of the men when he fails to measure up to their expectations. In combat, this responsibility is immense and needs a mature head over broad shoulders and a lion's heart with the courage to kick the enemy's butt, as much as stare back at the higher commanders when their unsound orders demand so and get them rectified or simply disobey when warranted.

Commander, You Will Crash Land in My Estimate

2nd Battalion, Brigade of the Guards has a stellar history. It has had commanding officers who have set glowing examples in leadership.

In the 70s, this battalion was deployed in the high-altitude area and was maintained by animal transport. Colonel Freddie Muthanna, a no-nonsense man of values and principles was the commanding officer. During a maintenance trip to his company posts, two mules collapsed and died. The death of a mule in the Indian army kicks up more dust than the death of a soldier. The commander, Brigadier Rodrigues, who later became the Indian Army Chief was furious and spoke to the commanding officer. The commanding officer explained that the mules seem to have died because of some medical condition, possibly heart failure. The commander wanted to ascertain the cause, as he had been informed that the mules had been given rum which resulted in their deaths.

A day later, the commander quietly sent a low-profile officer posted as the Ground Liaison Officer (GLO), an insignificant appointment in peacetime, to quietly investigate the death of two mules.

Col Muthanna, much annoyed wrote to the commander, "The case of the death of mules was discussed between the commander and self. And now, I learn that the commander has sent a 'Jasoos' (spy) to quietly investigate the same matter. I would suggest the commander believe the commanding officer's word and not send spies. I may also mention, sir, that, actions such as these will result in you crash landing in my estimate." (The commander was an army aviator.)

The commander wrote back, "I know whom to believe."

Col Muthanna replied, "As I mentioned, you have crash-landed in my estimate."

The issue here is, that the commanding officer is the tallest giant of any army and he has to have very high self-worth. It must hurt their pride when their word is doubted, and therefore, they must always speak the truth no matter the consequences. In this instance, the commanding officer had no reason to cover up and the commander should have realised that.

♦ ♦ ♦

Lt Colonel Cariappa (Later Brigadier), an outstanding officer known for his values was commanding 4 GUARDS. He was out on short leave. An accident took place in the unit during his absence. On his return, the brigade commander mentioned the accident, saying that he was not informed of the accident by the second-in-command and he does not think highly of him.

Now that annual confidential reports are due, he should take note of this.

Colonel Kipper, as he was known, asked the commander, "How much do you know my second-in-command, sir?"

"I have seen him for two weeks when you were away," replied the commander.

Kipper replied, "I have known him for sixteen long years and knew him well. I will do justice to the officer as he deserves. The commander had his own column in the confidential report and he can do what he felt appropriate." And Kipper stuck to his words.

I had one of the finest officers serving under me, Colonel Sudhir Bugalia, armoured corps. As the commanding officer, based on his assessment, he graded some officers outstanding. On directions from the corps commander, his brigade commander asked him to change these reports to a lesser grade. Colonel Bugalia declined to do it because the officers deserved that, and the reports have already been communicated to the officers and could not be changed at this stage. He paid for his moral courage and the Indian Army lost an outstanding officer in higher ranks. A tragedy, not so rare in the Indian Army.

♦ ♦ ♦

General Himmeth was another outstanding commanding officer of 4 GUARDS. The divisional commander visited the battalion when he was on leave due to the death of his mother. He commented that this commanding officer is always on leave. When Colonel Himmeth returned, his second-in-command, amongst other things, mentioned what the divisional commander had said about him being on leave.

Colonel Himmeth promptly called up the divisional commander and told him that it was inappropriate of him to discuss the commanding officer with his officers. If he has any issues, he could tell him now. General Himmeth was one of the outstanding Generals of the Indian Army. In questioning the divisional commander, he was not being defiant. He placed value on the institution of the commanding officer and himself as one and felt the divisional commander had to be conveyed his displeasure.

♦ ♦ ♦

During the Indo-Pakistan War of 1965, the Indian army faced reverses in the Chhamb Sector in J&K. When the commanding officer of a Dogra battalion, which was brought in as reinforcement, was being rushed into the attack without preparation, which he knew will get his troops butchered (as he termed it), he refused. He demanded minimum reconnaissance and preparation time.

When the commander continued to insist, he told him bluntly, "I am not prepared to get my men killed foolishly. If you still insist, you will have to find another commanding officer. Till then, you will find me in the battalion B Echelon area."

(Above episodes contributed by Lt Gen HRS Mann, 5 GUARDS)

Author's Notes

These were great military commanders who knew what they were doing. Such defiance to be pulled through successfully needs to fulfil the following criteria.

- Professional competence and confidence in own ability.
- Moral courage to withstand the pressures and tensions that this will generate. The courage to face the consequences if the effort of defiance fails and the superior is proved right.
- Such characters have special genetic engineering. Whatever the genetic engineering, defiance brings mental stresses that are not easy to deal with. It is hard to inculcate a defiant attitude unless a person is made that way.

- No matter how positively successful such a person is, he will come up against organisational friction and is likely to be targeted.

It needs conviction, very fine judgment and courage to do what Sagat, Francois or Sharon did. It needs a good understanding of the environment and confidence in your subordinates and troops to pull it off. As they say, nothing succeeds like success, yet, despite the success, such brilliant commanders get side-lined. Most superiors are uncomfortable with non-conformist brilliance like the Generals above. They are happy to have conforming mediocrity around them which makes them feel taller.

A competent and selfless Commanding Officer of character will have no quarrel with 'Reflective Obedience/constructive dissent/constructive disobedience /positive defiance.' He will himself not obey blindly, and they should not, because on their judgment and character depends the safety of 800 men and the lives of thousands who are dependent on them.

♦ ♦ ♦

Chapter Eleven

When Saints Humbled the Mighty Crowns

"Hind Di Chader"
When all has been tried, yet Justice is not in sight,
It is then right to pick up the sword, it is then right to fight.

—Guru Gobind Singh (Zafarnama)

Guru Tegh Bahadur

The Mughal Empire ruled over India for over 300 years. Twenty Mughal emperors ruled India from the 16th to 18th century. For the Mughals, power and pelf was the prime motive. As Audrey Truschke writes, "For the Mughals, power was often about the rulers first and foremost rather than the ruled" (*Culture of Encounters, Sanskrit and the Mughal Court*). This addiction to power made a disputed succession a tradition in the Mughal family. As Stanley Lane Poole writes, "It was a tradition in the Mughal monarchy that the dying eyes of the father witness the rebellion of the son." (*Rulers of India: Aurangzeb, Emperor of Hindustan, 1620-1707*). Following this trend, Akbar had forgiven his undutiful heir Jahangir on his deathbed. Shah Jahan was himself in revolt when his father died and it was now Shah Jahan's turn to suffer the like fate. The eldest brother of Aurangzeb, Dara Shikoh was a secular intellectual, he was loved by his people and was the favourite son of King Shah Jahan. He was also the preferred choice of his father to succeed him on the throne. Unhappy with his father's decision, Aurangzeb, a fundamentalist Muslim, the third son, imprisoned his father in Red Fort in Agra. In the cruel war of succession that followed, Aurangzeb killed his two brothers. In the battle with his eldest brother Dara Shikoh, he initially defeated him followed by his humiliation amongst his people and then finally beheaded him. His cruelty saw no bounds when he sent his severed head to his father, an act which utterly devastated him.

The pages of history are testimony to the fact that the reign of Aurangzeb unleashed a wave of horror and death across the country. Under the tutelage of Mir Hasham, Aurangzeb had never, as N.S. Inamdar writes, "displayed a weak mind or heart" (*Shahenshah*: *The Life of Aurangzeb*). This indomitable mind set out to conquer the entire India and establish a strong fanatic Muslim rule. To substantiate his thought, ruthless destruction of temples, forcible conversions and discrimination became the order of the day.

It was in 1679 that Mughal Emperor Aurangzeb ordered the division of Hindus into rich, middle and poor classes to impose the Islamic 'Jaziya tax' on non-Muslims. (SAA Rizvi, *The Wonder that Was India-Part II).* This was part of a deliberate act of enforcing humiliating conditions so that the Hindus and other non-Muslim castes may give up their religion. The barbaric nature of Aurangzeb can be gauged by his brutal command to his officers to bring one maund (approximately 37 kgs) of *Janeu* (a sacred cotton thread worn across the neck by Hindus) and weigh it every day by killing or converting Hindus. This led to mass killings, however many succumbed to fear. Audrey writes, in 1669 Aurangzeb issued orders to all his governors of provinces to "destroy with a willing hand the schools and temples of the Hindus, and that they were strictly enjoined to put an entire stop to the teaching and practice of idolatrous forms of worship". (*Introduction, You Aurangzeb So Noble*)

Some temples were destroyed entirely; in other cases, mosques were built on their foundations, sometimes using the same stones. Idols were smashed, and the city of Mathura was temporarily named Islamabad in local official documents. This was not enough to break the will of Hindus as the majority of Hindus chose death over conversion.

This led Aurangzeb to devise another clever plan and he aimed at the conversion of all the Kashmir Pundits into Islam. The reason was that Kashmir was the seat of Hinduism and he strongly believed that if Kashmir pundits were subdued into conversion, then the entire country will follow. Thereafter he passed the brutal order for the forcible conversion of Kashmiri Pundits into Islam. Resistance to this order would end in a forcible torturous killing. In those grievous times, when the fear of death gripped around, a prominent Kashmiri Pundit—Pundit Kirpa Ram along with 500 Pundits approached the then-ninth Sikh Guru, Guru Tegh Bahadur at Anandpur Sahib to seek his help.

Guru Tegh Bahadur was born in Amritsar, Punjab, India in 1621 and was the youngest son of Guru Hargobind, the sixth Sikh guru. A principled and fearless warrior, he was also a learned spiritual scholar and a poet. Guru Tegh Bahadur was acknowledged throughout as the protector of the weak. He assured them of their safety and that he would oppose the forced conversions being undertaken at Aurangzeb's behest. Guru had gone into deep thought after Pundit Kirpa Ram's request.

At this point, it is said that Guru Ji's son, Gobind Rai walked into the *Sangat* and saw Guruji deep in thought. Gobind Rai was merely nine years old when he, after listening to the entire problem, gave his father the reply "Pitaji, there is an easy answer to this problem. You are the most spiritually aware person in the whole Hind. You can make the sacrifice" (Dr Satveer Gill, *Guru Tegh Bahadur's Sacrifice as The Crusader of Religious Practices, Journal*). So, it was decided that to break Aurangzeb's myth of religiosity and to save the Kashmiri Pundits, Guruji would risk laying down his life. The commitment by Guru Tegh Bahadur to protect and support the liberty of all the people of the country is unprecedented.

The Guru then told the congregation of Kashmiri Pundits to return and tell their governor, Iftikhar Khan, that he should send this message to Aurangzeb, "If you can convert the Guru to Islam then the whole of India will convert, but if you can't, you have to give up your dream of making India an Islamic Country," (Dr Satveer Gill). On hearing this, Aurangzeb was jubilant as he felt that converting and subduing a single person would be an easy task.

Guru Tegh Bahadur was arrested on orders of Aurangzeb at village Mallikpur Rangran on 12 July 1675 with his three companions, Dewan Mati Das, Sati Das and Dayal Das. They were persuaded to convert to Islam during their four-month imprisonment at Sirhind. When they refused to accept this proposal, they were taken to Delhi in iron cages.

Guru Tegh Bahadur held three meetings with Emperor Aurangzeb and during discussions and arguments that ensued in these meetings, Aurangzeb told Guru that it was his uttermost desire to see all Hindustan embrace Islam and that it was with this intention that he had imposed Jaziya on his non-Muslim subjects; had ordered the demolition of their temples and destruction of their scriptures (Vedas), and had ordered them to embrace Islam or face death. As Prithi Pal Singh writes," The emperor believed in the superiority and existence of one religion and that was Islam. He believed that he would please his Allah, the prophet Mohammad and the Khalifa at Baghdad (the Islamic head) by his act of making India an Islamic State" (*The History of Sikh Gurus*). The emperor then tried to persuade the Guru to embrace Islam, for he knew that Guru Nanak's House was equally against idol worship.

The Guru told Aurangzeb, that he was committing these crimes and atrocities to satisfy his own selfish ends and that he was covering them up under the cloak of religion. The Guru told him that conversion could not be carried out by force, threats or bribes. Conversion depends on a change of heart. Why did not the uncle of the prophet Mohammed become a convert to the faith of Islam? "You say your religion does not allow idol worship in any form. Then where is the justification to enjoin the kind of worship to be offered to the black stone of Kaaba?"

At the end of these discussions, the emperor gave the Guru three options:

- To embrace Islam as his religion and receive the highest honours in his court.
- To show Karamaat (miracles) which the Muslims regard as the fundamental characteristic of a true prophet.
- To accept death.

Unhesitatingly, the Guru replied that if those were the only choices before him, then he willingly accepted the third choice. The Guru declined to accept Islam or to show any miracles.

The next day Aurangzeb ordered Guru's three disciples Matidas, Bhai Sati Das and Bhai Dayal Das should either embrace Islam or be executed. They all refused to accept Islam. Matidas was ordered to be sawn alive.

At the place where Bhai Matidas was executed, now stands in his memory the famous Fountain of Chandni Chowk, Delhi. The fountain symbolises the blood of Bhai Matidas which once oozed out from his pliant body.

Bhai Dayal Das and Bhai Sati Das were executed next. Bhai Dayal Das's hands and feet were tied firmly and he was thrown into a cauldron of boiling water. Not a sign of grief was uttered by this beloved disciple of the Guru. Bhai Sati Das, who was the younger brother of Mati Das, was ordered to be torn into pieces, and this cruel order was complied with by the authorities.

Guru Tegh Bahadur was made to watch the martyrdom of his beloved disciples in the hope that this would scare him into embracing Islam. The Guru, on the other hand, remained unmoved and unconcerned. He was happy that three of his dearest disciples had played their part to fulfil the great mission of Guru Nanak and paved the way for hundreds of the Khalsa martyrs who later followed in their footsteps.

The tyrant emperor then issued his final orders that Guru Tegh Bahadur should be beheaded in Chandni Chowk which was the central marketplace of Delhi, then as it is now.

The Guru performed this "supremely heroic act to uphold righteousness" on Thursday, the eleventh day of November 1675 A.D. a few minutes after the clock had struck nine.

At the place where Guru Tegh Bahadur was martyred, there now stands the magnificent shrine Gurdwara Sis Ganj Sahib.

Lakhi Shah—a Sikh of the "Vanjarah" was an intimate devotee of Guru Tegh Bahadur. He lifted the holy body and then rushed towards his residence at Rakabganj. Lakhi Shah reached there at about midnight. He asked his family and neighbours to move out of their huts quickly. He then set fire to the whole village so that it appeared as if the whole place was on fire and not as though one body was being cremated. The next morning Lakhi Shah had the ashes of Guru Tegh Bahadur put into two urns and buried at the same place where his body had been cremated. At this place now stands the historic shrine of Rakabganj Sahib, not too far from the Houses of Parliament of the Republic of India.

The holy head of the Guru was carried to Anandpur Sahib. At the place where the head of Guru Tegh Bahadur was cremated, stands the historic shrine of Gurdwara Sis Ganj Sahib.

Aurangzeb became very unsettled ever since the day of the martyrdom of Guru Tegh Bahadur; his soul having been shaken by this heinous sin.

Source: Compiled from different sources.

Guru Tegh Bahadur (1621-1675): The True Story, Gurmukh Singh OBE, UK

https://www.sikhnet.com/news/book-review-guru-tegh-bahadur-1621-1675-true-story.

After the martyrdom of Guru Tegh Bahadur, his son Guru Gobind Singh, the tenth guru carried forward his struggle against oppression. Out of his four biological sons, two died fighting on the battlefield and two were executed by a Mughal governor Wazir Khan of Sirhind at a very young age. When he arrested the two younger sons of Guru Gobind Singh, he tried to force them to embrace Islam. When they refused, he ordered them to be bricked alive.

Guru Gobind Singh, one of the all-time great kings formed the Khalsa Panth or the Sikh warriors who formed the Sikh Empire to carry forward the legacy of their gurus.

Source: Dr Harjinder Singh, 'Sikh History in 10 Volumes', Sikh University Press, https://en.wikipedia.org/wiki/Wazir_Khan_(Sirhind) accessed on 10 Jul 2022

The Sacred Flames of Defiance – Self-Immolation by Vietnamese Monk

Monk Thich Quang Duc
(Image: Credit Internet, Malcome Brown)

In the spring of 1963, when Vietnam was undergoing conflict with the US in thick of it, the US-backed South Vietnamese forces suppressed Buddhist religious leaders and followers, which led to a political crisis for the government of President Ngo Dinh Diem, a Roman Catholic himself.

Thich Quang Duc was a Vietnamese Mahayana Buddhist monk who immolated himself on 11 June 1963. He was protesting against the persecution of Buddhists by the South Vietnamese government led by Ngo Dinh Diem. The immolation was considered to be an act of political defiance against a corrupt government.

President Ngo Dinh Diem, supported largely by the United States, alienated his countrymen by openly discriminating against Buddhists and favouring his fellow Roman Catholics in every aspect of Vietnamese life, from government and military promotions to land grants and tax breaks. The problem with Diem's pro-Catholic policies was that South Vietnam was overwhelmingly Buddhist, with about 70% of the population.

The last straw for Buddhists was Diem's prohibition of public celebrations of Buddhist festivals.

The trigger for this silent political defiance came on May 8, 1963. Thousands gathered in the city of Hue to celebrate Buddha's 2,527th birthday. Normally, there were floats and lantern parades, but this celebration had a sharp political edge, with marchers demonstrating with Buddhist flags, which had been specifically banned by Diem. The national police and army (ARVN) ordered the demonstrators to disperse. Then, the government forces attacked. Within minutes, nine Buddhists were dead, including two children, who had been crushed under armoured personnel carriers.

Diem denied ARVN and police involvement, casting blame on the Vietcong. The disavowal only fuelled further protests. ARVN forces used tear gas to quell the rising demonstrations around the country.

This precipitated the shocking incident on 11 June 1963.

The Buddhists were media savvy and politically astute. They knew the best way to get President Diem to agree to their demands for religious equality was through US public opinion. By creating a crisis in Vietnam, they could make President John F. Kennedy pay attention and pressure Diem, who was supported by large amounts of American aid, to ease up on the Buddhists.

Thich Quang Duc's associates contacted American journalists like the Associated Press's Malcolm Browne, letting them know that "something important" would take place on the streets of Saigon on June 11.

Malcolm Browne's award-winning photographs of Thich Quang Duc's self-immolation affected US President JFK who exclaimed, "Jesus Christ" when he saw it in the papers. He is known to have said, "No news picture in history has generated so much emotion around the world as that one."

Ngo Dinh Diem remained intransigent despite this. The South Vietnamese leader resisted the Kennedy Administration's appeals for calm and a semblance of democratic reforms and power sharing. Diem's sister-in-law and South Vietnam's effective 'First Lady,' Madame Nhu, made her own headlines by declaring: "If the Buddhists want to have another barbecue, I will be glad to supply the gasoline."

As the Buddhist Crisis escalated, the Kennedy Administration lost faith in Diem's ability to hold South Vietnam together as a non-Communist American ally.

In November 1963, Diem was overthrown in a military coup with the approval of the US and eventually killed by ARVN.

Self-immolation was not an impulsive act of desperation. It was a well-deliberated act of defiance to get their voice heard across the world. Journalist Malcolm Browne was informed of the planned big event. In another civilization, it might have taken the form of some violent act.

The monks well understood the impact that immolation was likely to have. The monks and nuns were chanting a type of chant that's very common at funerals and so forth. At a signal from the leader, they all headed towards the central part of Saigon on foot. There, they quickly formed a circle around a precise intersection of two main streets in Saigon. A car drove up. Two young monks got out of it. An older monk, leaning a little bit on one of the younger ones, also got out. He headed right for the centre of the intersection. The two young monks brought up a plastic jerry can, which proved to be gasoline. As soon as he seated himself, they poured the liquid all over him. He took out a matchbook, lighted it, dropped it in his lap and was immediately engulfed in flames. The monk died in ten minutes without a single cry of pain as he burned to death. Everybody who witnessed this was horrified. The incident had the intended effect on JF Kennedy.

Source: Malcolm Browne: The Story Behind the Burning Monk, https://time.com/3791176/malcolm-browne-the-story-behind-the-burning-monk/ accessed on 6 June 2022.

Thich Quang Duc wrote a letter to President Diem before his self-immolation which is reproduced below.

> *"Before closing my eyes and moving towards the vision of Buddha, I respectfully plead to President Ngo Dinh Diem to take a mind of compassion towards the people of the nation and implement religious equality to maintain*

the strength of the homeland eternally. I call the venerable, reverends, members of the Sangha and the lay Buddhists to organise in solidarity to make the sacrifices to protect Buddhism."

The Tibetan Monks' Defiance of Chinese Occupation

Tibet is a country of Buddhists—holy and peace-loving people. Without going into the details of history, the Chinese forcibly occupied Tibet in 1950. They proclaimed it as its sovereign territory on the logic that it had always been part of China and on the Seventeen Point Agreement that they claimed was reached in 1951 with Tibetan leaders. The Tibetans refute this assertion as do many scholars of history. They question the very basic rationale of China.

The 1959 Tibetan uprising began on 10 March 1959 when a revolt erupted in Lhasa, the capital of Tibet, which had been under the effective control of the People's Republic of China since 1951. The initial uprising occurred amid general Chinese-Tibetan tensions and in a context of confusion, as Tibetan protestors feared that the Chinese government might arrest the 14th Dalai Lama. The protests were also fuelled by anti-Chinese sentiment and separatism. At first, the uprising consisted of mostly peaceful protests, but clashes quickly erupted and the Chinese People's Liberation Army (PLA) eventually used force to put down the protestors. The last stages of the uprising included heavy fighting, with high civilian and military losses. On the night of March 17, 1959, the Dalai Lama escaped from Lhasa under cover of night. On 28 March, while still on Tibetan soil, he formally repudiated China's infamous "17 Point Agreement for the Peaceful Liberation of Tibet," upon which consenting Tibetan seals had been forged in 1951. On March 31, exhausted and seriously ill, the Dalai Lama set foot on Indian soil. Lhasa city was fully retaken by the Chinese security forces on 23 March 1959.

After the flight of the Dalai Lama, Mao crushed Tibet with vengeance. Institutions of government and education were systematically destroyed. The Buddhist religion was labelled a "disease to be eradicated"; nearly 1.2 million out of about 6 million reportedly died through armed conflict and famine; large numbers of Tibetan children were forcibly taken from their families and sent to Chinese orphanages for "re-education." Research suggests that close to 1 million Tibetans tried to escape to India, Nepal, Bhutan or other regions of their country, but given the vast distances, lack of food in mountainous terrain and military invasion, most either surrendered to the Chinese or died in flight.

In the end, only 110,000 Tibetans survived the journey over the Himalayas to join the Dalai Lama in India.

The testimony of many of these refugees was gathered by the International Commission of Jurists (ICJ) and presented in its 1959 report "The Question of Tibet and the Rule of Law."

The third report by the ICJ titled: "*Tibet: Human Rights and the Rule of Law*" documented and verified the full extent of the biological and cultural genocide inflicted upon the Tibetan people by Mao's armies and brought it to the attention of the United Nations.

Source: Genocide in Tibet, Maura Moynihan, 25 January 1998 https://www.washingtonpost.com/archive/opinions/1998/01/25/genocide-in-tibet/27c0891c-57f1-4a7c-b873-a1071d93cbfd

In 1994, for the first time in 15 years, China began a ban on the worship of the Dalai Lama, a ban on his photograph and a ban on any kind of religious worship or religious practice at all for anyone who worked in the government, even if they were persons who cleaned the floor in a government office. Since then, China has strictly regulated religious institutions and practices all across the country.

Source: Tibet's Uprising - 50 Years Later World, 10 Mar 2009, Robert Barnett, https://www.pbs.org/newshour/world/tibets-uprising-50-years-later

China is infamous not just for the Tibetan cause but also for the systematic atrocities and mass indoctrination—"Re-education" of Uyghur Muslims in the Xinjiang province in Western China that has caught the world's attention.

Cases of self-immolations have gone up in Tibet in recent times. Since 2009, a total of 159 Tibetans have self-immolated to protest China's takeover of their homeland. Earlier, the social, cultural, political, and ethnic grievances that led to the protests of 2008 included, severe restrictions on religious practices, forced denunciations of the Dalai Lama in the monasteries and throughout society and attempts to reshape Tibetan beliefs. These restrictions were imposed upon Tibetans in the name of "harmony", "stability", and "patriotism", reshaping society and people's lifestyles were enforced through more stringent laws and restrictions.

Tapey, a 24-year-old Kirti monk, was the first monk to self-immolate on 27 February 2009.

Since then, many cases of self-immolation have resurfaced including a 25-year-old popular Tibetan singer, Tsewang Norbu chose self-immolation in Lhasa on 25 February 2022.

Recently, bans were imposed on the study of the Tibetan language in favour of Mandarin Chinese as the primary language of instruction; an attempt to reshape the Tibetan linguistic and educational environment.

The Chinese government is also trying to reshape the region's demographics as it organized an influx of Han Chinese migrant workers into Tibet.

Self-immolation is an extreme act but also a means to highlight the opposition when no other peaceful means are available.

Self-immolations have become central to the Tibetan protest movement as an act to draw global attention to Chinese policies in Tibet, more so in the complete absence of 'freedom of speech and protest in Tibet'.

Source: Tibetans take to self-immolation to protest against China, 9 April 2022. https://theprint.in/world/tibetans-take-to-self-immolation-to-protest-against-china/909565/

Author's Notes

Immolations are extreme acts of non-violent defiance that delegitimise the state's violence. These deaths are sacrificial gestures that paradoxically strengthen the Tibetans against Chinese aggression. Immolations are acts of desperation when there is no other recourse available to make your voice heard. A powerful and repressive communist state like China seems powerless to deal with it. It inspires others to defy the authorities and that is the reason the Chinese fear such acts and take away the bodies to prevent them from becoming inspirational martyrs. While Dalai Lama has condemned immolations, he holds China responsible for such violent acts of protests against their brutal policies.

There are two important issues here relating to the method of defiance by holy men. Religious gurus and Buddhist monks are peaceful people with a non-violent code of living. The monks in Vietnam and Tibet chose a personally violent, yet publicly non-violent means of protest that harmed no one and nothing else. That non-violent act rendered the mighty military machine of the state toothless. Monk Thic's letter to the President is polite, courteous and devoid of hatred which can only come from a spiritually evolved person. This divine-like gesture of tolerance by a man who was ending his life made the President look pedestrian and powerless. Through his painful sacrifice, he sets the stage for positive defiance by the right-thinking people to stand together for the larger cause.

The protests and sacrifice of Guru Tegh Bahadur and monks in Vietnam and Tibet have many things in common. They were all voluntary and peaceful as they did not take recourse to violence and did so to defend religions against oppression by brutal rulers. The acts had the desired impact, far greater than a violent response to oppression would have and brought the attention of the world to the issues.

My take is, that while the holy men have their peaceful ways of defiance, such brutal regimes and their inhuman practices need to be confronted by all means. Guru Tegh Bahadur's son, Guru Gobind Singh having exhausted all peaceful means to seek justice, adopted all means and that is justified.

Thus, when we talk of positive defiance, there is a lesson here. While positive defiance is done for a worthwhile cause, the oppressor will see it as defiance of authority. Further, while the end is important, the ways and means of defiance are important too. The biggest impact of positive defiance is likely to be achieved by the least hostile means for that renders the state machinery powerless. Yet, as we see in the case of China, while it has exposed Chinese brutality to the international community, it has not appreciably changed Chinese behaviour. The world has the power to make it happen, for no country can prosper in isolation in this interdependent world. Various restrictions have been imposed on China in response to its human rights violations. The Chinese and the Iranians continue to protest despite extreme state oppressive violence. In the final analysis, all the power of a state fails and a tank, the destructive weapon of war becomes utterly useless against peaceful non-violent defiance.

The principle of defiance is applicable in every aspect of life where brutality, unethical practices, nepotism, corruption, and incompetence prevail and where evil rules over good. Those who suffer injustice and do not raise their voice and sword against it are as much to blame as those who perpetrate injustice.

♦ ♦ ♦

Chapter Twelve

CEOs – Ethics Trumps Money and Moolah

One thing that comes to mind when talking business is the bottom line or profits—every quarter. That is the metrics of success of a business as is commonly understood. The trouble with quarterly assessment is that it places a skewed focus on the short term, ignoring the more important long-term aspects. Since the CEOs and managers are assessed by quarterly profits, they are inclined to ignore the long-term good of the company and try to look good by showing short-term profits, whichever way. This can easily lead to unethical practices of extreme kinds.

Well, profit is not a bad word and at the end of the day, 99 per cent of people in this world are looking to make more money. Money is a necessity for the survival of an individual, a family and a business.

The question is, what responsibility does a business have to its employees who rake in the moolah for them and other stakeholders? Those stakeholders today are not only its employees or shareholders, it is the entire society. The universe is suffering the onslaught of indiscreet industrialization and young people like Greta are shaking the political leaders by the scruff of their collars and demanding accountability.

> *If you remove all the insects from the earth, the earth will be devastated in one decade. If you remove all human beings from the earth, the earth will boom in six months.*

It is an extremely competitive world for everyone, even the beggars on the street. Some businesses have defied all ethics and yet failed and there are businesses which are a hallmark of values and they have survived successfully for over a century. They have defied the gravitational pull of easy money by taking the value-based harder right rather than the easier wrong in pursuit of profits. It is the focus on values and not on profits that have kept them relevant a century later.

We will look at a few of them and draw some useful lessons.

THE ENRON SAGA

The Enron scandal is likely the largest, most complicated, and most notorious accounting scandal of all time. Through deceptive accounting tricks, Enron Corporation—the US-based energy, commodities, and services company was able to trick its investors into thinking that the firm was doing much better than it actually was till one day it all collapsed. Enron was also the biggest donor to the American Republican party during the times of Presidents George HW Bush and his son George W Bush and that came in handy.

It was all one big scam, a fraud filled with lies and political manipulation. It was the biggest scam of corporate greed in US history.

Business Background

In 1985, Enron was incorporated as Houston Natural Gas Company and Internorth Inc. merged with it. In 1995, the business was recognized as the most innovative business by Fortune, and it made a successful run for the next six years. In 1998, Andrew Fastow became the CFO of the business, and he created Special Purpose Vehicles to conceal the financial losses of Enron. During the period 2000, the shares of Enron traded at the price level of $90.56.

On 12 February 2001, Jeffrey Skilling came in place of Kenneth as the chief executing officer (CEO). On August 14, 2001, Skilling abruptly resigned, and Kenneth took over the role again. In the same period, the broadband division of the business reported a massive loss of $137 million, and the market price of the stock fell to $39.05 per share. In October, the CFO's legal counsel instructed auditors to destroy the files of Enron and asked to maintain only the utility or necessary information. The business reported a further loss of $618 million and a write-off of $1.2 billion. The price of the stock deteriorated to $33.84.

Fall of the Giant

On 22 October, the business got under probe by the Securities and Exchange Commission. With this news, the stock of Enron further deteriorated and was reported at $20.75. In November 2001, the business, for the first time admitted and made the revelation that it had inflated its income levels by $586 million. Also, that it has been doing so since 1997. On December 2, 2001, the business filed for bankruptcy, and the stock prices ended up flat at $0.26 per share.

On 9 January 2002, the justice department ordered a criminal proceeding against the business. On 15 January 2002, the NYSE suspended Enron, and the accounting firm along with Arthur Andersen was convicted for obstruction of justice.

Enron Hiding their Debt

The Enron corporation and its management resorted to an evil scheme and malpractice of the off-balance-sheet mechanism. It created a special economic vehicle to hide the massive debt from its external stakeholders, namely creditors and investors. The special purpose vehicle was utilized to conceal the realities of accounting rather than focus on the operating results.

The CEO of Enron Corporation Jeffrey Skilling transitioned the accounting practice of Enron Corporation from a historical cost accounting method to a mark-to-market accounting method.

The 'Mark-to-Market' gives insights into an institution and is regarded as a legitimate practice. The method, however, is also exposed to some form of manipulation. The mark-to-market is based on fair value rather than taking up the actual value. It caused the business to fail miserably as they reported the expected profits as the actual profits.

The scandal tells us why strong corporate governance is the key to success for any business to sustain and drive profitable business.

Due to the bankruptcy, employees lost several perks and pension benefits. Many came on the verge of a financial crisis. The crisis was so deep that the business shareholders lost an estimated value of $74 billion.

ENRON, which became a 60-billion-dollar company in 16 years, became bankrupt in one month. Twenty-nine thousand people lost their jobs and medical insurance. America's oldest Accounting Firm Arthur Anderson collapsed due to a loss of reputation for destroying tons of documents. Andy Fastow, former CEO pleaded guilty to committing wild fraud and cut a deal to testify against other executives. He was sentenced to ten years but served only six. Ken Lay, the CEO and a consistent character in Enron earned 300 million dollars and was sentenced to 45 years. He died of a heart attack a month before his sentencing. Executives were paid 55 million dollars during bankruptcy and encashed another over 774 million dollars in the year before the collapse. Jeffrey Skilling, the fraud mastermind was sentenced to 24 years and 180 million dollars in fines. While in jail, his son and his father died.

Enron's motto was 'Ask Why', but no one ever asked why, how or from where the big money was coming. In the end, the high flyers ruined their lives, some died and one committed suicide.

Money without values and ethics is a source of trouble. None of them could use the money they earned by fraud.

Source: Compiled from multiple sources, Enron Case Studies and Senate hearing on Enron.

MANVILLE CORPORATION

How could top-level executives at the Manville Corporation have suppressed evidence for decades that proved that asbestos inhalation was killing their own employees?

Johns Manville Corporation (JM) operated as a leading manufacturer and marketer of insulation products for buildings and equipment, roofing systems, various engineered products including fibres, fabric and nonwoven mats, and filtration media. The company had 55 manufacturing facilities in North America, Europe, and China. Until the mid-1980s, JM mined and sold asbestos for use in insulation, building, aerospace, automotive, and other industries. The company divested itself of its interests in all asbestos-related businesses but remained involved in substantial litigation brought by asbestos workers with claims based on the effects of working with the material.

At one point in time, Manville Corporation (then Johns Manville) was solid enough to be included among the giants of American business. Soon, it was in the process of turning over 80 per cent of its equity to a trust representing people who had sued the company for liability in connection with one of its principal former products, asbestos.

For all practical purposes, the company was brought down by questions of corporate ethics.

Decades ago, information began to reach Johns Manville's medical department and through it, the company's top executives-implicating asbestos inhalation as a cause of asbestosis, a debilitating lung disease, as well as lung cancer and mesothelioma, an invariably fatal lung disease. Manville's managers suppressed the research. Moreover, as a matter of policy, they decided to conceal the information from the affected employees. The company's medical staff collaborated in the cover-up, for reasons that are not hard to guess.

Money clearly must have been the major motive. In one particularly chilling piece of evidence, a lawyer recalled how 40 years ago he had confronted Manville's corporate counsel about the company policy of concealing chest X-Ray results from the employees. The lawyer had asked, "Do you mean to tell me that you would let them work till they dropped dead?"

The reply was "Yes, you save a lot of money that way."

Based on such testimony, a California court found that Manville had hidden the asbestos danger from its employees rather than looking for a safer way to handle it. It was less expensive to pay workers' compensation than to develop safer working conditions.

A New Jersey court was even blunter: it found that Manville had made a conscious cold-blooded business decision to take no protective or remedial action, in flagrant disregard of the rights of others.

The truth of why this happened is less glamorous. The people involved found themselves in a dilemma, and they solved it in a way that seemed to be least troublesome, deciding not to disclose information that could hurt their product. The consequences of what they chose to do both to thousands of innocent people and, ultimately to the corporation, probably never occurred to them.

BHOPAL GAS TRAGEDY: THE BIGGEST HUMAN DISASTER

The Bhopal disaster refers to a chemical leak in 1984 in the city of Bhopal, India. At the time, it was called the worst industrial accident in history. To call it an accident would be wrong, for it was a result of neglect and gross mismanagement of an enterprise that was dealing with deadly chemicals.

On December 3, 1984, about 45 tons of the dangerous gas methyl isocyanate

(MIC) escaped from an insecticide plant that was owned by the Indian subsidiary of the American firm Union Carbide Corporation. The gas drifted over the densely populated neighbourhoods around the plant, killing 3000 people that night and creating a panic as tens of thousands of others attempted to flee Bhopal. The final death toll was estimated to be between 15,000 and 20,000. Some half a million survivors suffered respiratory problems, eye irritation or blindness, and other maladies resulting from exposure to the toxic gas; many were awarded compensation of a few hundred dollars. Investigations later established that substandard operating and safety procedures at the understaffed plant had led to the catastrophe. In 1998 the former factory site was turned over to the state of Madhya Pradesh.

Earlier too, complaints were being made about the maintainability of the plant, of how MIC was leaking in small amounts. The previous incidents of leakage had also caused the death of some people and left others severely injured. But the authorities paid no attention to it. The machines were worn out but no replacement was done.

There are many other reasons which contributed to this unfortunate event.

The following are the reasons that contributed to the Bhopal tragedy:

- An inspection team came from Danbury, United States to the Bhopal plant and found 61 safety problems. Out of these 61 problems, 31 were major.
- The main refrigeration and cooling system was closed down 150 days before the accident.
- To reduce the cost, the number of workers was reduced.
- Specialised training was not given to the unskilled workers to understand the risks and dangers of their work and the consequences of neglect and mistakes.
- Before this major tragedy, there had already been minor leakages which cost the life of one worker and others were injured.
- No supervisor was there for the night shift on the day of the tragedy.
- The pressure control valve of tank E610 from where the gas leaked had not been working properly for over a month.
- There was gross negligence on the part of the maintenance authorities.
- There was no backup plan to deal with emergencies.

The Chief Justice, Bhagwati, while introducing the Doctrine of Absolute Liability in this case gave the following statement:

> "*We are of the view that an enterprise which is engaged in a hazardous or inherently dangerous industry which poses a potential threat to the health and safety of the persons working in the factory and residing in the surrounding areas owes an absolute and non-delegable duty to the community to ensure that no harm results to anyone on account of hazardous or inherently dangerous activity which it has undertaken. The enterprise must be held to be under an obligation to provide that the hazardous or inherently dangerous activity in which it is engaged must be conducted with the highest standards of safety and if any harm results on account of such activity, the enterprise must be absolutely liable to compensate for such harm and it should be no answer for the enterprise to say that it had taken all reasonable care and that the harm occurred without any negligence on its part.*"

On 14th and 15th February 1989, the Supreme Court in *Union Carbide Corporation v. Union of India* ordered UCC to pay a sum of $470 million (Rs 750 crores) to the victims.

In 2010 several former executives of the company that operated the Bhopal plant—all Indian citizens—were convicted of negligence.

Source: Bhopal Gas Tragedy Case Study, Diva Rai, 30 July 2019 https://blog.ipleaders.in/bhopal-gas-tragedy-case-study- accessed on 12 August 2022.

Corporate scandals are a dime a dozen. Reputation or size is no guarantee that someone is a saint. Known as the "Diesel dupe" or "Diesel gate", the Environmental Protection Agency (EPA) found that many Volks Wagon (VW) cars being sold in America had a "defeat device" or software in diesel engines that could detect when they were being tested, changing the performance accordingly to improve results and meet the emission standards. The German car giant has since admitted to cheating emissions tests in the US. Once back on the road, the engines emitted nitrogen oxide pollutants up to 40 times above what is allowed in the US.

VW had admitted that about 11 million cars worldwide, including eight million in Europe, are fitted with the so-called "defeat device".

Martin Winterkorn said his company had "broken the trust of our customers and the public". Winterkorn resigned as a direct result of the scandal and was replaced by Matthias Mueller, the former boss of Porsche.

"My most urgent task is to win back trust for the Volkswagen Group—by leaving no stone unturned," Mr Mueller said on taking up his new post.

Source: https://www.bbc.com/news/business-34324772

Whilst VW was in the limelight, I am certain, they are not the only ones. There must be a whole lot of others in different industries violating the pollution norms in different ways with full knowledge. This is noteworthy because pollution and global warming are serious humanitarian issues that threaten the very existence of humanity. It is the social responsibility of businesses to be socially and globally responsible.

Johnson and Johnson, the much-trusted brand for baby powder for decades has had 48000 lawsuits alleging that its powder is contaminated with asbestos, and has caused cancer in people. J&J denies the allegations. Is there smoke without fire? Nevertheless, J&J has announced that it is replacing the controversial talc with corn starch. According to Fortune reports J&J has paid $3.5 billion in compensation. The company had discontinued North American sales of talc-based baby powder in 2020 but will stop sales of the product globally in 2023. Interesting that they continue the sale of harmful baby powder in other parts of the world.

The point here is, money drives the mare. The richer the mare, the harder he runs after the money, be it individuals or corporate. No one can ever be trusted to operate ethically. The public good is not a concern for anyone. Thus, the need for positive defiance one way or the other.

Let us now look at celebrities who are amongst the richest and the most privileged people in the country through whom the corporate resort to manipulative marketing. The famous Indian actor Amitabh Bachchan was trolled on social media for promoting a tobacco product, Kamala Pasand. He apparently justified by saying that it generates employment. Later, when the anti-tobacco organisation requested him to refrain from endorsing the Kamala Pasand ad to prevent youngsters from getting addicted to tobacco, he terminated the contract. He stated he did not know that it was a surrogate product. Tough to swallow. Many other actors and sportsmen are promoting tobacco-based and other products like Coca-Cola and Pepsi that are believed to be harmful to health. I cite his example because he comes from an illustrious family and himself is among the most respected actors in Bollywood. For them to promote unhealthy products for money and claiming ignorance is grossly irresponsible because they influence a large number of people.

Similarly, Hollywood actor Pierce Brosnan was amidst controversy for endorsing Pan Bahar, a product understood to be harmful to health. He blamed the company for 'grossly manipulating' media organizations into believing he endorsed the tobacco product. He was ignorant of the details of the product and demanded the company remove him from its advertising campaign as he had no prior knowledge of endorsing something that would harm one's health.

We have a fine example of the Indian Badminton Icon Pulela Gopi Chand. A relatively unknown name, he pales in comparison in wealth and popularity as compared to the cricketers and Bollywood stars but towers heads and shoulders over them in values and character. He spurned the offer of a soft drink of brand ambassadorship at the peak of his success on the issue of values. Top celebrities like Sachin Tendulkar, Amitabh Bachchan and Shahrukh Khan endorsed Pepsi and many Bollywood actors and sportsmen still do. Bachchan apparently stopped it when he was questioned by a small girl in a school, as to why he endorsed Pepsi when her teacher told them it was poison.

Let us look at the media; twenty-four-hour channels that churn out crap. They flash-catching headlines, grab your attention and then sell it to the advertisers. This is an era of paid news based on who owns the channel and who pays the most. One veteran officer who appears on a TV channel regularly as a defence expert, when questioned why he does not say on TV what he says on WhatsApp group, replied, "If I do not say what they want me to say, they will stop calling me." Fake, doctored and manipulated news. TRP is all that matters; the truth is for sale. It has become so difficult to separate the truth from the fake in every aspect of life. The worst is yet to come as Artificial Intelligence and Chat GPT make inroads into our lives.

Is it possible to do business ethically?

TATA – A VALUE-DRIVEN ENTERPRISE

It has been our DNA—to serve those who serve us.

Business does not have to be unethical. Few business houses evoke trust and respect. The Tata Group of India is at the top of the ladder which has set very high standards of value-based corporate ethics.

It was founded by Jamshedji Tata in 1868 as a start-up and is a global enterprise today, often referred to as the only value-based corporate house. It has over 800000 employees across the globe.

Taj Mahal Palace and Hotel in Mumbai is an iconic landmark that was built in 1902 well before the Gateway of India (1914), right in front, built to commemorate the coronation celebration of King George V. It became the entry point of British viceroys and governors, and ironically also the exit point of the British colonialist, as its first battalion disembarked from there when colonialism was dismantled from India.

It is said that Jamshedji Tata was inspired to build this hotel after he was refused entry at one of the grandest British hotels—Watson's Hotel, which was restricted to 'whites only'. Jamshedji Tata took this as an insult to all Indians and then decided that he would build a hotel where not only Indians but all foreigners could stay without any restrictions, and that's how India's first super-luxury hotel came into being. Now Taj is a centre of attraction all over the world.

On 26 November 2008, ten members of Lashkar-e-Taiba, an Islamic militant organization based in Pakistan disembarked from boats at the same Gateway of India and proceeded to unleash two days of terror in 12 coordinated shooting and bombing attacks in and around south Mumbai, killing more than 150 Indian and foreign nationals. The Taj Palace was the prime target of the terrorists, where at least 31 lives were lost, including 11 hotel staff and another 28 injured.

Employees of the Taj Mahal Palace and Hotel in Mumbai were well acquainted with the back stairways and exits of the famous hotel. They had a quick way to escape when 10 terrorists launched an attack on November 26, 2008. But many didn't flee, instead choosing to help guests escape and then returning to help more. Telephone operators stayed the night, informing guests and telling them to keep their rooms quiet and dark.

Why did they not leave? Why did they perform above and beyond the call of duty, like soldiers? Can this level of loyalty and dedication be replicated and scaled elsewhere?

A new case study from Harvard Business School, "*Terror at the Taj Bombay: Customer-Centric Leadership*", finds possible answers both in the traditions of the country as well as in the deep customer-centric culture infused by the operators of the Taj: Indian Hotels and Tata Sons.

According to case author Rohit Deshpande, a professor at Harvard Business School and a native of India, at least three factors were in play at the Taj.

- **The right people.** In this case, Indian Hotels CEO Raymond N. Bickson describes how he first looks for "nice people who are not afraid of serving people." He can teach them to be a bellman, a waiter, or a desk clerk, "but I can't teach them to be nice. I can't teach that spirit of ownership."
- **Indian culture.** "Athithi devo bhava," or the "guest is God", is deeply ingrained in Indian culture. In short, the phrase means that honouring guests is equal to honouring God, a message deeply embedded at the Taj.
- **Employee-Employer relations.** In India, there is a strong "paternalistic equation" between employer and employee, an attribute underscored by rewards given by top executives to staffers for their lengths of service. Done right, relationships in Indian companies can feel more like family than us versus them.

In short, the case shows how non-monetary factors such as a company's governance and values can be powerful motivators for employees.

"At a time when we are hearing so many stories of human frailty, mismanagement, and moral turpitude, the Taj research is about ordinary people who became heroes. It's about leadership from everywhere, especially leadership from below," said Deshpande.

The culture of employee empowerment has been ingrained in the Taj workforce for some time now. For instance, the researchers found similar displays of gallantry at the Taj properties in the Maldives at the time of the tsunami in December 2004. "I realised that just like the character of a human being is the sum of choices made over the years, the culture of an organisation is the sum of values, policies and practices consciously fostered over the years," said Raina.

Deshpande says, "The other thing is that I grew up there. So, the Taj is part of my memories, too. As one of the interview subjects said, the Taj is their Taj, meaning anyone who has ever walked through its doors. It's a place that means many things to many people."

In one interview, Taj general manager Karambir Singh Kang describes his father, a military man, telling him that his job is like being the captain of a ship. "I think that's the way everyone else felt, too," says Kang. "A sense of loyalty to the hotel, a sense of responsibility to the guests." Several hours into the siege, Kang's wife and two young sons died in a fire that swept through their apartment on the hotel's top floor. Even after receiving the news, he insisted on staying at his post to help direct the response to the ongoing attack. (The battle for control at the Taj would continue a full two days after other locations had been secured.)

Nothing in the employees' training could have prepared them for such an unprecedented situation, Deshpandé says. Yet, further interviews and text documents from the case provide background on the unique culture of Tata Sons, Taj's parent company, while also revealing the exacting process for selecting, training, and rewarding Taj employees for their work.

The question of why the Taj employees demonstrated such loyalty elicited a variety of responses from students, Deshpandé says.

"For example, some suggested that it has to do with governance of the Tatas; two-thirds of their profits are donated to charitable causes, so the employees feel that they are working for a higher good." But the IT firm Tata Consultancy Services has had many of the same difficulties with employee retention that other Indian IT firms experience. "In that case, the loyalty might be more to self rather than to the organization," he says.

A definitive answer to the question of why the Taj employees behaved as they did may not be possible; but managers who read and view the case will likely come away with a clearer sense of what it takes to build a particular culture and value system and how to recruit, train, and reward employees in non-monetary ways.

Source: https://hbswk.hbs.edu/item/terror-at-the-taj

THE SPIRIT OF DEFIANCE

Opened to guests in 1902 for the first time, Mumbai's Taj Mahal Palace Hotel is a unique institution and the terrorist attack on November 26, 2008, impacted the psyche of Indians, especially Mumbaikars. However, Ratan Tata was determined to not only restore the structure but also send out a message that the terrorists had failed to kill the spirit of Mumbai.

Even though the Taj was reopened a month after it was attacked, it took 21 months to restore the iconic hotel to its glory. The cost of reconstruction is estimated to be $38 million. The 26/11 attack severely damaged the heritage wing of the hotel.

In an interview before the reopening of the Taj Mahal Palace, Ratan Tata who had promised to build every inch of the hotel said: "This flagship property, this venerable Old Lady, is going to reopen in the same glory, the same splendour of more than 100 years."

Ratan Tata dedicated the restored hotel to those who were killed in the 26/11 attack. In 2009, he unveiled a 12-foot-high memorial which bears the names of the 31 employees and guests killed in the attack.

After the three-day-long siege in 2008, the Taj stood in ruins. But when the Taj resumed operations, it opened with more radiance than ever, making it loud and clear that the people of India cannot be knocked down so easily.

Ratan Tata did ensure the "venerable Old Lady" reopened with the same glory and splendour it radiated for over 100 years.

Source: Saumya Bhattacharya
https://economictimes.indiatimes.com/news/company/corporate-trends/26/11-mumbai-attack-hr-practices-converted-ordinary-taj-employees-into-heroes/articleshow/10849491.cms

Not so Noble Profession—Medicine

For a man staring at death due to illness, a doctor is closest to God. Not anymore, for the profession is less than noble. The Covid pandemic saw some of the worst practices by pharmaceutical companies around the world. Reportedly, some hospitals in India were selling hospital beds during the Covid pandemic by keeping them occupied by fake patients. One dose of Remdesivir medicine believed to be an effective drug against Covid, costing a few hundred rupees (a few dollars) was sold for over rupees one lac (dollars 2000) and fakes too.

Peter C Gotzsche, MD, the courageous author of the book *Deadly Medicines and Organised Crimes* exposes the criminal nature of the pharmaceutical companies and the doctors. He says,

> *"It is not popular to tell the truth in health care. Very few people are independent of money in healthcare. In my country (Denmark) there is very little corruption, there are thousands of doctors on the industry payroll, even though we have only 20,000 doctors.*
>
> *Much of what the drug industry does, fulfils the criteria of organised crime in the US Law. They behave in many ways that Mafia does.*

> *They corrupt everyone they can corrupt. They have bought every type of person including ministers of health in some countries."*

Was he harassed for exposing the truth? Yes, he was, but he had a reason to 'rebel with a cause'—the future of humanity.

Author's Notes

The frauds are a dime a dozen, I have mentioned just a few. Personal and corporate greed are the hallmark of such scams and will continue to happen. In all such scams, it is the senior executives who make the big money and are entirely responsible. Simple employees are squeezed to get them to do the unethical as the Wells Fargo scam shows, opening a million fake accounts to shore up their brand value and share market price. The senior management had shares in millions and through manipulations made fortunes till the bubble busted.

Greed is one thing, when senior management wilfully risks the lives of their employees to make money is an unpardonable human sin. The Manville Corporation and the Bhopal Gas Tragedy are two glaring examples of this practice.

We need to draw a comparison of these case studies. Enron violated every rule in the book to fool the stakeholders for incredible profits. The Manville Corporation were prepared to see their employees drop dead of asbestosis for more profits, pharmaceuticals and doctors collude to let people die. On the other hand, there is Tata, where the employees voluntarily risked their lives and died for the honour of their company. They displayed a sense of duty, only seen in the military.

I have delivered talks at many companies, Indian and foreign. Values and ethics are the buzzwords, more in theory and less in practice.

The message that Tata's story conveys is that the only thing that will sustain a company over a long period is the value-based culture and the congruence in the stated and practised values. No company will ever progress by disregarding the well-being of the people who power the wheels of the company. While some cheats may getaway, you may not be the lucky one. For corporate, sooner than later, bad deeds will catch up.

After the terrorist attack, Ratan Tata visited the families of the employees who had died and were injured. He met a woman who pointed to the garlanded figure of her late husband and said: "My children never realised their father was a hero." It took Tata by surprise, as he expected to encounter anger and sorrow.

Tata Group took upon themselves that the families were well taken care of in every way, financially, housing, children's education and employment. This is quite in contrast to what Enron and Manville Corporation did.

Another Indian enterprise Infosys, a tech giant has a reputation for corporate ethics. They have consistently refused to bribe the officials to get their files moving, whatever the cost, and in the end prevailed. He discouraged employees from working beyond office hours. Their founder Mr Narayan Murthy was even thought of as a suitable presidential candidate by many well-informed people in the country for his character and values. So, business does not have to be unethical. You can still be the leader while remaining a value-based company and defying the generally accepted beliefs of what it takes to be successful in business.

What are the lessons and how difficult is defiance for the CEOs or the directors in the interest of the company? It is indeed difficult, for the chances are that the owners or the investors will shoot the messenger first. The story of Enron, Manville, Volks Wagon and many others, on the contrary, demonstrate that when people fail to stand up to corrupt and unethical practices, the company will be doomed. A well-articulated and justified dissent will get someone to see the long-term consequences for the company and take corrective action. Possibly, these companies would have survived to see another day, if someone in the right place had defied the status quo and spoken up.

When the lives of the employees and those of people around are involved, defiance remains a justified approach that in the end will benefit all stakeholders—company owners and the rest.

Today, when the world is faced with an unpredictable future because of environmental degradation and global warming, every corporate house has a social responsibility to voluntarily play its part and make this world a safer place for future generations. It includes their children too.

Rationalisations

Why do managers act unethically that ultimately inflict great harm on their companies, themselves, and people on whose patronage or tolerance their organizations depend? An examination of the black demos of Enron, Manville Corporation and the Union Carbide in Bhopal tells us the following.

- A belief that the activity is within reasonable ethical and legal limits—that is not really illegal or immoral.
- A belief that the activity is in the individual (professional growth) or the corporation's best interests—that the individual would somehow be expected to undertake that activity.
- A belief that the activity is 'safe' and it will never be found out or publicised.
- A belief that the activity helps the company and the company will condone it, and even protect the person who indulges in it.
- Personal ambitions or corporate greed.
- Pressures of business competition.

SURVIVING THE ETHICAL DILEMMA

If the above are the reasons why CEOs act unethically, it will help to ponder what makes you think that you will not be caught. Some of the Enron executives who made hundreds of millions of dollars never lived to enjoy that money. How was the sight of these men, who once walked tall with the high and mighty, walking handcuffed trailed by their wives?

Do you need 300 million dollars to live happily? Did that huge ill-gotten wealth bring them happiness? It brought them death, humiliation and shame, not only to themselves but to their families who would not know where to hide. Ask yourself this question. Assuming you are caught, will this be worth the trouble, indignity and shame?

When human lives are endangered, people must stand up in defiance. Blood money could buy one a big house but not a peaceful sleep.

Business houses the world over need to learn from the Tatas of India. When Tata Steel was downsized from 78000 to 40000, they did not dump those employees like Elon Musk and many others did. Tatas ensured to pay them their present-day wages until retirement age. That has been their DNA. Compare this with Manville Corporation who were prepared to see their employees fall dead for profit.

The best compliment that one could get? I was travelling in an Ola cab once; I was surprised that even the cab driver knew what Tata stood for and respected them.

MAHATMA GANDHI'S SEVEN SINS

It will help to remember them.

- Wealth without work.
- Pleasure without conscience.
- Knowledge without character.
- Commerce without morality.
- Science without humanity.
- Religion without sacrifice.
- Politics without principle.

♦ ♦ ♦

Chapter Thirteen

Bureaucracy: Resurrect the Rusted Steel Frame

Zindagi bhar ghungroo bandh ke naachte rahe, aur kab tak naache te rahenge....

—***IAS Officer on retirement***

This chapter is written with reference to the Indian Civil Services; however, I do believe this will be applicable almost everywhere.

As we come to the end of the book, it is important to discuss the civil services, the Indian Administrative Service (IAS) in particular. In every aspect that has been discussed in the book, civil servants are involved in advisory, planning or implementation capacity. They thus have to measure up to the dream of Sardar Vallabh Bhai Patel who saw the civil services as the steel frame of Indian governance. The perception is that the steel frame is badly rusted as we shall see later. This chapter examines the ills that have come to permeate this important steel frame and recommendations are made to fix the basic foundation.

Bureaucracy in common parlance is not an inspiring term. It refers to a lethargic, inefficient, slow-moving system involving complicated rules that are often unnecessary. Common people view bureaucracy more as a corrupt hindrance than a solution.

No discussion of politics and politicians can be complete without civil servants. Given the varying nature of the two entities, it is a marriage of inconvenience turned into an alliance of convenience by both, more by the latter.

As is well known, the majority of the IAS officers manage some post-retirement job somewhere or the other. It is a juicy carrot that keeps them toeing the political line that has come to create what is known as the committed bureaucracy. The rule makers and political executives have little time or inclination to monitor anything except what matters to them, for their focus is on the elections and vote banks. One wonders, why it has to be a generalist IAS officer to be the head of every other service without any experience, which the present government has attempted to redress.

One senior IAS officer whom I know narrated this incident. He asked a batchmate of his who was retiring.

"Have you not tried to get a post-retirement job?"

His friend replied, "*Zindagi bhar toh ghungru bandh kar naachte rahe, aur kab tak naachte rahenge.*" [Whole life we have been dancing (*to the tune of the politicians*) with the musical anklets on our feet. How long will we keep dancing?] While plenty of civil servants are turning the wheels of progress in India through their diligence and this will not be applicable across the board, this self-declaration by a senior IAS officer reveals an important facet of civil servants.

The political executives with great authority call themselves the voice of the people and that people have given them the authority to frame policies. Let us look at Israel, another democracy. The Netanyahu government in 2023 wanted to change the policy for the appointment of Supreme Court judges. The people understood the intention and the dangers and protested on the streets forcing the government (people's representatives and their voice) to change their minds. It was exactly like the National Judicial Appointments Committee (NJAC) in India. The government wanted to have the sole authority to appoint judges, as opposed to the collegium system in vogue presently, where the judiciary appoints judges. Seeing the pitfalls, the judiciary struck down the proposal of NJAC, maintaining the status quo. In India, there is very limited scope for the voice of the common man to breach the high walls of the parliament. Anna Hazare's Lokpal movement proved that in good measure and while that institution exists, it has been rendered toothless by the polity.

Politicians make policies to safeguard their interests and suit themselves. The criminalisation of politics is rampant and the most powerful entity in a democracy, the people remain mute spectators. In India as of 2023, forty-three per cent of members of parliament have criminal cases against them and they continue on the grounds of being innocent till proven guilty. Given the pendency of cases, it is an academic exercise and they will continue forever. In the Punjab state of India, politicians had given themselves a pension for every term as a member of the state legislative assembly/council. Some were getting ten pensions, all from the taxpayers' money. Thankfully and surprisingly the present government has promised to strike that down and reduce it to one pension. So much for people's voices.

Corruption is a way of life in politics and governance in India. The parliamentarians increase their own pay and perks without a single dissent or debate. Is it correct for them to fix their own pay and perks which violate all the norms applicable to the rest of the country? There are civil society groups and individual crusaders who contest this misuse of power, which often is an uphill battle against the system. The Police and Administrative Reforms passed by the Supreme Court to make the police effective have not been implemented in many states.

What role and responsibilities do the civil servants (public servants) have as advisers? Is it realistic to expect something from them?

> *Has IAS failed the nation? Yes, and it's not all politicians' fault. The service rewards mediocrity & risk aversion*
>
> ***—Duvvuri Subbarao, Times of India, 25 March 2022***

Source: https://timesofindia.indiatimes.com/blogs/toi-edit-page/has-ias-failed-the-nation-yes-and-its-not-all-politicians-fault-the-service-rewards-mediocrity-risk-aversion/

In an interview with Karan Thapar on the Wire, Duvvuri Subbarao, IAS (Retired), former governor of the Reserve Bank of India reiterated the following observations on the IAS.

- The public perception of the IAS today is of an elitist, self-serving, status quo-perpetuating set of bureaucrats who are out of touch with reality, who wallow in their privileges and social status **and have lost the courage of conviction to stand up for what's right.**
- Once upon a time, the IAS had a "formidable reputation for competence, commitment and integrity", but that's "unravelled". Today "the IAS has lost its ethos and its way. Ineptitude, indifference and corruption have crept in".
- On the matter of competence, Dr Subbarao said "It is not as competent as it should be or it used to be". He said talent gets atrophied and people fail to perform.
- Citing an unnamed chief minister, he said this gentleman had told him how deep the rot runs through the IAS. The CM claimed 25% are "callous, corrupt or incompetent". Another 50% have turned their jobs into sinecures. Only 25% can be relied upon to get work done.
- The problem, Dr Subbarao said, is the culture within which the IAS operates. He called it "the biggest problem". He described it as "a deeply flawed system of incentives and penalties".
- Explaining further, Dr Subbarao said, "Almost everybody gets promoted... almost everybody gets outstanding grading in performance." As a result, he said, "There is no encouragement of talent and no penalisation of laziness and corruption."
- He said, "Young recruits come in with sharp minds and full of enthusiasm...but soon they become cogs in the wheels of complacency and acquiescence, turn lazy and cynical, and worse, lose their moral compass." As a result, "there is no motivation for officers to upgrade their knowledge and skills ... (and we have) a system that promotes mediocrity."
- The cure, Dr Subbarao said, is that "the IAS has to be reformed into a meritocracy". He said that we need a proper system of lateral entry based on examinations and requiring every lateral entrant to spend five years of his first 10 years in field postings. Second, IAS officers, who spend their initial years as generalists, must acquire specialist domain knowledge. However, he added, "Specialisation need not be mandatory". What one needs is a mixture of specialists and generalists.

- He makes a very telling comparison between how civil servants and the police are viewed in Britain, where they investigated the prime minister, and how they are viewed in India, where it would be "unimaginable" to think they could investigate the prime minister.

Source: https://thewire.in/government/watch-the-ias-has-failed-india-and-must-change-ex-rbi-governor-duvvuri-subbarao

Let us look at another frontal assault on the IAS by a 1994 batch lady officer expressed in her article titled *The Belief System and some truths, Dipali Rastogi, IAS*

Earlier in the book, I stated that it is tough to fight the enemy, but even tougher to fight your own inept system. This lady officer seems to be a rare shining steel rod in the rusted 'Steel Frame' that the IAS was meant to be. She has shown great courage and integrity in giving the IAS a reality check. This would not have pleased either the IAS or the government.

In her article above, she paints a sorry picture of the service which she has seen so closely. Here are the extracts:

- We are in this service to serve. The truth is, we scarcely behave as servants.
- We have a very high opinion of ourselves and our intelligence and experience, and think people respect us for what we are. In reality, people genuflect before us due to the power we wield to do either benefit or damage.
- We are paid to manage things efficiently and create systems. In actuality, we thrive on mismanagement and chaos because that gives us the power to choose some over others.
- We are supposedly the steel frame, in reality, we have no vision. We take ad-hoc decisions looking at what the authority above us wants.
- We exploit the system for preferential treatment for ourselves and the people known to us. We are hypocritical enough to say, we do it 'help' people.
- Worst of all, we are the most pompous, officious and ill-bred set of people. And we have the nerve to say, we work for the people of this country.
- In reality, we have no stakes for the country-our children often study abroad and we have created a niche cocoon of the luxuries this system can give us.

- We have no empathy with the larger populace, though we are always careful to make the right noises.
- Finally, if there were any justice, we would have long been extinct. But we are too powerful to let ourselves be annihilated. We are the IAS.

What does one make of Subbarao's and Rastogi's views? One can choose to agree or disagree. Their views have to be taken seriously. They come from successful insiders of immense experience and not disgruntled individuals and they have been made openly with full ownership. Finally, the starting point of transformation is to accept that a problem exists. These courageous officers have done the nation a favour. Their courage and commitment will be worth it only if the government has the courage to fix what is broke. Like the unimplemented police reforms directed by the Supreme Court, the status quo is more likely to prevail.

Let me share my experiences, even though a brief one that validates this criticism.

In my last assignment in the Army Headquarters of over two years as the Additional Director General and officiating Director General, I interacted with the Ministry of Defence (MOD) bureaucracy at close quarters. I concluded that with an eye on their future, the effort was to play safe and avoid making decisions. Important files were universally kept in a loop till their tenure was over. The cycle would start all over again when the new incumbent arrived. As a result, no decisions were ever reached on critical issues and the cases kept rolling forward for decades to come back to zero, for by then the circumstances would change. Worse, there is no accountability for the incompetence, irresponsibility and lackadaisical attitude. No bureaucrat in the MOD can be held accountable for procurement cases failing because the system has been so engineered.

During the Army Commanders' Conference at the Army Headquarters, there is a MOD interaction session. All the joint secretaries headed by the Defence Secretary attend this session along with the top army hierarchy. The major business is to discuss and expedite long pending cases that have not seen progress.

Most of the cases that are brought there have been languishing in the MOD for over a decade. I am given to understand that the interaction agenda used to be screened by the MOD. What was embarrassing due to inaction at the MOD was removed from the list. If the Army has included an agenda in the list for the

MOD interaction, it is obviously critical. And the Army must insist that the item cannot be removed from the list unless it is brought to a satisfactory conclusion before the event.

In my view, from what I witnessed, the methodology of MOD interaction was a complete waste. What was being discussed were individual issues, whereas, what must be streamlined are the processes, policies and procedural issues that make functioning effective, expeditious and accountable so that files do not keep going around for decades.

Where the Army must take the blame is that it allows this rare MOD interaction to become just another event, rather than seeking accountability for inaction. I got a clear impression that the Army is almost pleading for its long pending cases to be expedited as if it was asking for a favour. I was aghast at the submissive tone of very senior officers who presented their cases before me.

I had to present one simple case relating to the authorisation of training scales of ammunition for tank T 90, which was languishing for twelve long years. Precedence of authorisation of tank T 72 (earlier make) ammunition already existed, duly approved, as such it should have been addressed without too much fuss.

I made it clear addressing the Defence Secretary, that the issues that we discuss here are neither individual directorate issues nor army issues. They all affect the country's security and therefore, are the country's issues. I said this case has been languishing for twelve long years. On two occasions the file was with the Joint Secretary (ON) for more than twelve long months without any action whatsoever. I stated I am not worried about my case. What I want to question is the systemic problem of delays, lack of urgency and total lack of accountability of officers in the MOD for inaction. How has that joint secretary been held accountable for sitting on the file for the whole year twice, without justification?

So, my experience only validates Dr Subbarao's opinion.

Bureaucracy and Constructive Disobedience

Let us look at the recent episode of 23 April 2023. A group of Indian women wrestlers publicly protested against the president of the Wrestling Federation of India (WFI) for sexual harassment when their normal efforts over three months failed to get a First Information Report (FIR) registered against him. The Delhi police dilly-dallied filing an FIR on this cognisable offence till the intervention of the Supreme Court. The reason, the WFI president is a heavy weight of the ruling party and the Delhi police is under the central government and not the Delhi state government. So, here again, comes the issue of the moral compass—the character and commitment of the IPS officers in question. This is when the complainants are national athletes of repute who have brought honour to the country.

What would happen to a common man is anybody's guess.

Now, the readers must refer to the answers that the civil service aspirants give in the interview when they are asked what they would do if they found a chief minister without a seatbelt in a car!!

Why are these officers so helpless and impotent? Is it all the politicians' fault? Duvvuri Subbarao, himself a retired IAS officer and former Governor of the Reserve Bank of India doesn't agree.

Here I would like to cite the case of *Anoop Jaiswal Vs the Union of India*. He was withdrawn from the police academy on some alleged disciplinary grounds. He personally legislated his case in the Supreme Court. He was reinstated and later retired as a DGP of a state. In his defence, he said, 'My Lord, the IPS academy wanted me to be subservient. I am prepared to be disciplined but I am not prepared to be subservient." So, you see where the rot starts. It can actually be traced to the selection process itself.

He was asked about the much talked of political interference in the police. His reply was, "Politicians will not interfere if they know you brook no interference. An upright IPS officer with the legal power of the CrPC and the safeguards of the constitution cannot be touched. The politicians understand that they are vulnerable. The politician knows that he may or may not be here after the next election, the IPS officer is here to stay for the next three decades. So, it is all up to the individual."

In 2017, Deepali Rastogi had gone public picking holes in the 'Centre's Open Defecation Free campaign' to provide toilets to every household, even where a pot of drinking water had to be fetched from a distance. She wrote, "Don't get me wrong, I'm all for toilets. After all, I am a city-dweller. I'm just uncomfortable with the way we are pushing it,". I certainly see the merit in her observations applicable to water-stressed areas.

Rather than examining her observations dispassionately and recalibrating their policy for water-stressed areas, the state government reportedly served her a show cause notice for alleged violation of All India Services (Conduct) Rules for her article. This is a brilliant case of shooting the messenger because the message is unpleasant to you.

Source: https://www.financialexpress.com/india-news/ias-officer-deepali-rastogi-gets-notice-for-picking-holes-in-open-defecation-free-drive/625578/

While we are on this, I must recall that when I was doing the Advanced Professional Programme in Public Administration (APPPA) Course at the Indian Institute of Public Administration, Delhi, in 2011, we were briefed on the construction of toilets by Rajasthan cadre civil servants. This was the very question I had asked way back then. They had no answer. I understand toilets constructed in such water-stressed areas of Rajasthan are being used as storehouses or for tying goats because they are unusable for lack of water. It meets the statistics of numbers while failing badly in the purpose. There was another such case of providing heat-conserving cooking stoves to the tribals. These stoves needed wood pieces no bigger than about six inches by three inches. My question was the same; how practical was it to expect tribal families to cut wood to these small sizes for these stoves? They were speechless.

Notwithstanding the peripheral issues, these episodes highlight the need for fearless civil servants who can speak the brutal truth to power and get the best value for the country's resources. That they do not blindly dance to the tune of the political pied piper without using their mind and be fearless in offering well-informed advice for the good of the nation.

When you are a person of character and integrity and your intentions are noble, no one can touch you.

The case of the upright IAS officer Ashok Khemka of the 1991 batch needs to be mentioned here. He is famous for cancelling the mutation of the illegal land deal of the son-in-law of a very prominent political leader. He has been reportedly posted 55 times in his career spanning over three decades by political authority. He is cited as deterrence by others for forthrightness. It is because he is one of the very few crusaders and others are ready to dance to the political tune, both for convenience and personal benefit in different ways. Posting is all that they can do, and what is so scary about getting posted to another place in the state? If others also stand up for their conviction and values, all this will stop.

Scholars of Indian Civil Services KP Krishnan and TV Somanathan opine "Despite legal and constitutional safeguards, the services have not adequately resisted political interference, partly because of the incentive structure. They also observe that civil service has not performed well when it comes to providing effective public services and promoting economic development."

—Quoted in the article Ring out the old, Indian Express, 19 May 2023, by Reena Gupta

Resurrecting the Spine

Let's see another view expressed a year later. *Fear of Falling, hope of rising.* Manish Sabharwal, *Indian Express* dated 20 April 2023 makes the same points. It appears he overheard the conversation that I used to have with other friends one of whom was an ex-army officer who joined civil services and understood both sides well. Manish makes the following points:

Civil servants exist to end poverty and not pay pensions. He is meaning that they must do bigger and more critical things and not occupy themselves with pedestrian stuff that clerks should be doing.

He recommends copying three HR practices from the military. These are:

- **Hiring**. Initial fixed terms for successful candidates on the lines of Agniveer for the armed forces. Candidates are recruited for a tenure of ten years after which a certain percentage is shed off, as in the case of Agniveeer where it is 75 per cent. The argument of generalists lacks conviction in a world where governance is so diverse and the world transforming at a rapid pace that brings a new cognitive and adaptive challenge every day. It is hilarious that every tech graduate justifies his suitability for IAS identically i.e. on the scientific temper that he has cultivated during graduation that will help him to address every problem from finance to animal husbandry or defence. In the military a soldier is a specialist, he can't be an infantryman today, a gunner tomorrow or a tank man day after, if he has to be effective. Even within that arm, he has to learn to fight in the deserts today, two years later unlearn that and learn to fight on the icy mountains, and two years later learn to swim across a 70 metres canal with full battle load and fight in obstacle-ridden terrain, and on another day fight terrorism. He does all this while adapting to changing technology, weapon systems, the terrain and the enemy. So, either the IAS functions are so moronic that they can be done by anyone of average intelligence or the organisation is not getting the best dividend because they are always learning on the job. Surely, the experience and expertise of the Ministry of Animal Husbandry don't make one suitable for the Ministry of Defence or Finance.

- **Structure** (Performance management forced via a frozen pyramid). He says that the 'on paper' performance management system has collapsed: only a microscopic minority do not get to the top grade through indiscriminate promotions. Top heaviness undermines performance and the hierarchical pyramid has become a cylinder in which the donkey and the horse both reach the top. Uttar Pradesh has 80 Director Generals (DG) and Additional Directorate Generals (ADG) for about 2.5 lakh policemen. The Army has 175 Lt Generals for a 12.5 lakh army. The army has only seven army commanders for the whole country.

He says the solution for differentiation is an honest appraisal, but that is unlikely to happen. So, he recommends a structure to de-cylindrify the promotion pyramid—restrict the Secretary rank in the capital to 25, Secretary and DG rank officers in states to two, introduce the retirement ages based on the rank and shrink the ministries and departments. Civil servant selection is highly meritocratic, but their careers are adversely affected by the ossified practices that do not punish bad performers, therefore punish good performers.

An environment where only the meritorious and those who perform progress will create the fear of falling and the hope of rising by raising competition, accountability and uncertainty.

Let me explain this in relation to the HR practices in the military which he has borrowed. Army has the steepest promotional pyramid anywhere in the country. More than 60 per cent get overlooked for promotion in the very first promotion board to Lt Colonel at the young age of 35-37 years, i.e., at the service of 15-16 years. In the IAS, every single soul gets his Non-Functional Upgrade (NFU) pay at about 17 years of service and other Class A services get it two years after the IAS. Almost every civil servant barring an odd exception reaches the position of joint secretary and draws that pay (more than that of a two-star General in the military) for approximately fifteen to twenty years. In the military, less than 2-3 per cent reach that rank and on average, a two-star in the military draws that pay for no more than four years.

Promotion Examinations for Every Promotion. Military officers constantly have to undergo promotion examination for every rank till Lt Colonel. Thereafter, there is an extremely competitive promotion board for every rank up to Lt General. In each of these boards, only about 30 to 35 per cent make it to the next rank. At the pace at which the world transforms, everyone needs to learn, unlearn and relearn and adapt. In civil services, there is no skill upgrade or promotion examination once you are in. The army officer needs to do a course for every next higher level of command responsibility. This is in terms of the Young Officers Course to be a platoon commander, Junior Command Course to become a company commander as a Major or Lt Col, the Senior Command Course to command a battalion as Colonel, Higher Command or Long Defence Management Course to command a brigade as a Brigadier and the National Defence College or the Advance Professional Programme (APPPA) course at IIPA to command a division as Maj General. If one does not get nominated for these courses, which are merit-based, one does not make it to the next rank. What it enforces is competition and meritocracy. Unlike civil services, there are no free lunches in the military. Every promotion is hard-earned where the majority is left by the wayside and retire accordingly.

This concept suitably needs to be introduced in civil services. Below is a graphic comparison of the military and civil services promotion pyramids.

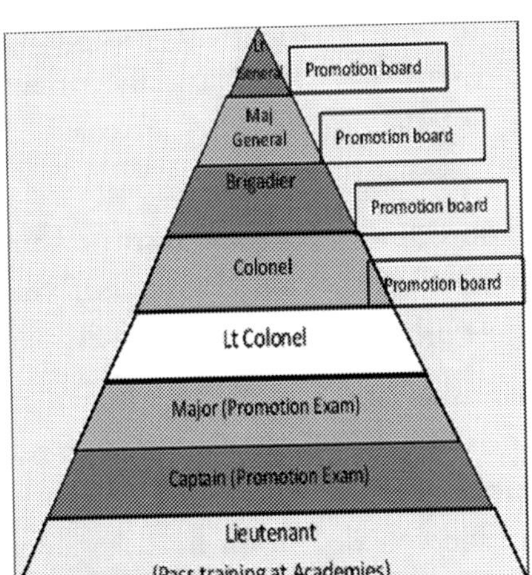

Military Promotion Pyramid
(Approval rate in every board less than 35%)

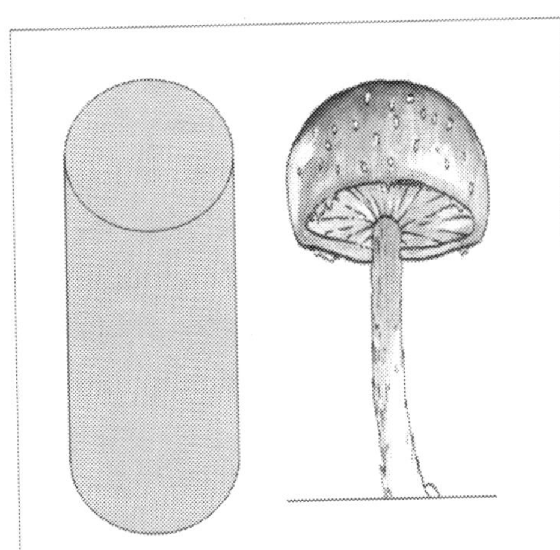

Civil Services Promotion Pyramid

Suitability Versus Eligibility

Decoding the Civil Services Selection Process: Competitive and meritocratic, yes, but there is more to it than meets the eye.

The most critical point Dr Subbarao makes is about losing the moral compass—**the courage of conviction to stand up for what's right. This is all about character** and disastrous for the country, as the politico-bureaucratic combine is charged with the nation's future. So, when the steel framework gets rusted, the structure will crumble. So, let us see where does the trail of disaster start? In my opinion, it starts right at the much-publicised selection process.

Hard to guess, but there must be close to 100 IAS coaching centres in Delhi alone, mostly mushrooming astride the Pusa Road in Karol Bagh. They provide all kinds of coaching for civil services and many other exams. The last thing in the marathon is the mock interview practice that these coaching centres provide the candidates for free. These mock interviews, conducted identically to the actual interview with five panellists, are video recorded and given to the interviewee for self-improvement. The interviews of the selected candidates are then uploaded on YouTube for publicity by these institutes.

What has this got to do with this book?

Each candidate on average takes about eight mock interviews in different coaching centres. By the time candidates reach the actual interview, they are tailormade clones in their mannerisms, views and answers, sculpted by coaching institutes and mock interviews to give legally, ethically and politically correct answers which everyone knows they will never follow in life. They are coached to conceal the chinks in their character and personality.

Let us come to the civil services examinations. These coaching institutes are mainly owned and run by retired civil servants. The written examination has two papers as part of General Studies dealing with ethics and case studies.

Opinion-based questions, controversial issues and ethical situations that should bring out their character, logic and rationality, are answered in an identically tutored manner citing the Constitution, rule of law and ethics. When asked, "As a superintendent of police what will you do, if you find the chief minister travelling without fastening the car seat belt?"

Pat comes the reply from everyone who is asked this question, "I will serve him a challan and fine him." Wow, it will be a great day when someone demonstrates that kind of courage.

The wrestlers' protest narrated earlier and the story of the murdered infamous Uttar Pradesh politician Don Atiq Ahmed, who ran riot unchecked for two decades, make these answers sound comic at best. A former DG Police of Uttar Pradesh narrated his bloody criminal history in an interview. My question as usual is, "What did you do when you were the DG Police of that state?"

Candidates are tutored in the mock interviews to follow the middle path and say nothing that could annoy anyone. They are advised to follow the safest route of aligning with the government's view and taking recourse to the court ruling to dodge giving a personal view. The question is, what do you expect from the interview panellists who have always chosen the path of least resistance by their own admission?

So, what exactly is the purpose of the UPSC interview? What are they trying to assess? Theoretically, the interview is trying to judge if the candidate is ethical, secular and rational. Given the last word coaching, they all come up with neutrally safe, ethically perfect and politically correct answers that give nothing away about the candidate's personality. They all project a put-on personality with a deliberately cultivated submissive persona for the interview. Out of the interview room, they are different persons altogether. Interviews of this nature will fail when it comes to the suitability of the candidates and suitability relates to character and aptitude. At least that is what the ghungroo story and Subbarao's views indicate.

Thus, in effect, the interview becomes an assessment of verbal knowledge and communication skill with the luck factor thrown in big measure. A pliant and submissive demeanour is a big plus. There is little scope for identifying the all-important hidden character traits of the candidate.

Incidents of unethical behaviour and corruption by civil services keep figuring in the news frequently.

Recently, there were two cases, one of a young IPS officer conducting himself brutally with persons in custody and the other of a lady IAS officer whose unaccounted property worth over 80 crores were seized. Both these were supposedly academically brilliant having become IPS and IAS in the first attempt at a very young age. By the UPSC norms, they were amongst the most meritorious and eligible. As we see, they were clearly unsuitable and unworthy of those responsibilities while being most eligible. So, academic excellence as the basis of selection fails muster here. It is not an indicator of character or competence.

As I have pointed out earlier, the present selection process lacks the methodology to gauge what lies under the skin, unlike the Services Selection Board (SSB). They are not isolated cases. They highlight the grave deficit in the selection process that needs to be bridged.

When Subbarao talks of generalists and specialists, he is highlighting this important issue of suitability to keep pace with the rapid changes that have become the new norm.

The process of civil services selection casts a shadow on its effectiveness. Some observations are listed below:

- It is entirely an academic process where, in some categories, candidates can take unlimited attempts with a maximum age limit of 37 years, going up to 47 years for physically handicapped. The majority pass in their fourth attempt or more.
- The fixed syllabus means it is more related to diligence and perseverance rather than intelligence. Ability to cram and regurgitate. If you can persevere, one day you will get through.
- In the military selection of officer cadets, the SSB tests character, officer-like qualities, leadership, trainability etc. Many candidates who fail the SSB many times go on to become IAS and IPS officers holding top positions.
- The candidates have twenty services to choose from. The IAS, IFS and IPS are the top three preferred services, IAS being the first.
- Based on the written examination and the much-flawed interview that I have talked about, a merit list is drawn. Candidates are allotted service based on their merit and reservation.
- In the entire selection process, there is no methodology of any kind to assess his character, psychology, suitability, aptitude or trainability for a service that he is opting for or is allotted. This is explained away by stating that each service has its specific training for the probationers. This training will not change his character, suitability, attitude or aptitude. So, you will have persons most unsuited for the job they land up with.

- Compare this with the military SSB where the brightest and the most eloquent may not make it past the SSB for lack of qualities that I have listed earlier. Skills that ensure civil services selection mean little for the selection of military officers who deal with missions and leadership of the most challenging kind.

Why do people make a beeline for the civil services—status, job security, perks and privileges, medical cover for the dependents, assured career progression and pay till 60 years, authority without accountability, no liability for incompetence and non-delivery, pension etc? Finally, for many, the opportunity to make big money through corruption. The percentage of performers and pedestrians highlighted by Subbarao says it all.

Compare this with corporate, there are targets and deadlines to meet. You have to dig a well every day to assure yourself a drink. The sword of Damocles hangs dangerously over your head. Fail to measure up and you ship out the next day as we have seen around the world. There are no free lunches as in the government services—assured pay even when one does nothing.

RECOMMENDATIONS

Given the nature of polity and politics, a country can ill-afford a pedestrian bureaucracy that is 'His Master's Voice'. We need one with a reasonable spine to support the steel frame Sardar Patel envisioned. We need more of the likes of TN Seshan, KPS Gill, Khemka, Julio Ribeiro and Prakash Singh.

While the legislature and executive must have the last word on policy formulation, the bureaucracy can emphatically provide impartial advice and not acquiesce to ill-intentioned policies and projects. Where they can certainly make a difference is to live by the values of the service, standing up for their convictions and firmly declining to be part of corrupt practices and prevent it from happening in their area of responsibility.

Is it too much of an ask? No, it is not. The constitution provides enough safeguards to civil servants, even for a period after retirement. So, it is just about character and a strong conscience. At the age most civil servants join service, they are hard-boiled and these traits cannot be injected. Good mentors and role models will make some difference to a few, but for most, it is too late.

The solution, therefore, lies in an 'MRI-based selection process' that can see through the façade and identify men of character despite the coaching, as the SSB does. The interview process needs an overhaul.

Character and Moral Courage

Take care of Character, the rest will take care of itself.

In a political system where the political executives could be illiterate, unscrupulous, criminals and guided by single-minded lust for power and money, we cannot have a committed bureaucracy carrying ghungroos in the briefcase. Academic brilliance will not help; character is the key, conscience the watchman and courage the bulwark.

I wish to recall a few incidents narrated by a very senior IAS officer.

- A beetle-chewing minister on a dais is looking for something to spit his beetle muck into. A DGP takes out his handkerchief and collects the spit in his handkerchief.
- In another incident, just a tad worse; a minister in a meeting coughs and looks for something to spit off his cough, a chief secretary stretches his open palm for the minister to spit, which he does.
- The cases of political and mafia dons, and how they run riot at will with the full connivance of the politicians and the police are too well-known to be repeated.

It is not to say that there are no good apples. To me, this is bad enough to destroy the reputation of the service. How can officers of such high rank and responsibility sell their souls and for what?

All the problems highlighted on the IAS by Duvvuri Subbarao and others are a function of one single personal trait—CHARACTER. In the entire civil services examination, there is no methodology to gauge and assess character. The written paper on ethics is an academic exercise as is the interview. Candidates are smart, fully aware of the requirements and tutored to make these irrelevant in this regard.

Thus, there is a need to introduce a suitably designed psychology test on the lines of SSB to select men of character, moral courage and aptitude. This could be the third and final stage of selection before the first layoff comes into effect. This could be done through existing SSB boards suitably structured and augmented by HR experts and psychologists.

Agniveer Scheme for Civil Services

Agniveer Scheme. If the government thinks they introduced a game-changing scheme in the military, it is time to introduce this in the civil services too at all levels, the steel frame for governance. It could be done in the following ways.

- Enrol 25/50 per cent more candidates in every batch who are enrolled for five years. Their emoluments are trimmed suitably so that there is no additional burden on the exchequer due to increased intake.
- Candidates are selected as one pool i.e., without a choice of service. No service is allotted for the first five years. During this period, they are given exposure to three different services/ministries.
- Towards the end of the stipulated term, a psychological and aptitude test is evolved to gauge personality traits and identify their suitability for various services.
- The stipulated percentage of officers is retained based on a matrix that includes written performance, performance reports and psychological evaluation. The rest are released from service.
- Services are allotted after five years based on suitability and aptitude derived from their performance reports and recommendations. The performance report form should be designed appropriately for this purpose including peer review.
- There is another option. Have a small core of service cadre in each service which is selected after five years based on their performance and aptitude as given above. The rest of the civil service remains a common cadre and officers are employed based on their calibre, aptitude and performance. This proposal best combines continuity, talent and suitability for the good of the organisation. Since the IAS officers are generalists and serve in all kinds of ministry, this proposal promises a transformational change. It provides a larger pool to pick the best man for the job and enforces competition and performance.

Military Attachment. All civil services probationers must do 12 months of attachment with the army after the final selection. This will, hopefully, inculcate self-pride, leadership, values and a sense of sacrifice. It will also partially address the officer shortage in the military.

Hire and Fire Policy in Government jobs. Government officers fall short on delivery and commitment because of the security of the job, and assured pay and promotion. Welfare-oriented policies and complex procedures make discarding the incompetent and deadwood difficult, if not impossible. As suggested by Manish, there has to be an efficient system of rewards and punishment including the provision for lay off creating the fear of falling and the hope of rising, by recognition of merit and delivery. Thus, such a ten per cent layoff should occur at 10 and 15 years of service. These vacancies so created be filled by specialists' lateral entry based on an appropriate selection process for different ministries.

Peer Review and 360 Degree Evaluation. This must be introduced suitably to assess the character and integrity of civil servants. This will neutralise patronisation by politicians and expose the corrupt and committed bureaucracy.

Moral Values Audit

Corruption relates to opportunity, and civil servants have many. I have devised what I call a 'Moral Compass Audit', a methodology to nudge you to stay on the right course when at the crossroads of moral dilemmas in life.

Ask yourself these questions:

- Is what I am doing right or wrong?
- Don't I have enough to live with dignity? Will it really change my life?
- Can I go and tell my family and friends what I did without feeling embarrassed?
- Will it be worth the embarrassment if found out, dismissed and locked up in prison?
- Will your children be proud of what you have done or feel embarrassed amongst friends?

Now, the question is which orders to contest. We have seen political behaviour which is guided less by people's interests, and more by political expediency. It is quite simple: there is the Constitution, the law of the land, and civil services ethics as a guide. Most importantly, your conscience will clearly tell you which orders, policies, or behaviours need to be contested. Your character will dictate your response.

> *The voice of conscience is so subtle, that it is easy to ignore it.*
> *Yet, so clear, that it is impossible to mistake it.*

This proposal will transform the laissez-faire culture of the bureaucracy. It will kick in Charles Darwin's theory of survival of the fittest (best). This will make the civil services meritocratic. I have no doubts that it will transform governance like never before.

Character is the Key

What you are shouts so loudly, that I cannot hear what you say.

♦ ♦ ♦

Chapter Fourteen

Positive Defiance: Managing the Turbulence

We do not always choose the times and the circumstances we serve in. We can always choose how we respond, irrespective of the circumstances.

We now come to the most important part. Many would say after reading this book that it is foolish to sacrifice your career and happiness. What difference does it make to you, the world will go on? So, as they say, everyone wants a Martyr Bhagat Singh to fight for their freedom, but they want him in the neighbour's house.

We will address this in a while.

The Nuremberg trials were among the most significant events in modern history because they dealt with the greatest human tragedy, committed deliberately by humans. The most important aspect of these trials was whether 'obeying orders of superiors' was a legitimate defence for committing atrocities. It wasn't and it was possibly the first time when people were punished for obeying orders as many were executed for war crimes. It was the same in the Tokyo trials for the Japanese. This is not a straitjacketed simple issue as it appears.

"It is interesting but it was tragic. If you receive a military order, you must obey. That is where the big difference between a military and a political order comes in. One can sabotage a political order but to disobey a military command is treason."

Source: General Von Kleist to Leon Goldensohn (25 June 1946). Quoted in "The Nuremberg Interviews", Leon Goldensohn, Robert Gellatel (2004).

While what is said above is true in spirit for the military, but cannot be without caveats. The caveats are related to the legitimacy of the order. It is related to the awfulness of a lawful order. The orders related to the extermination of Jews fall in the category of illegitimate orders which go to the lowest depths of humanity. In the military, defying even illegitimate orders has its challenges, especially when the chain of command is a party to that plot, but it must be done for good reasons. In Germany, the problem was that the majority of the people involved with the extermination of Jews, right from the top to the bottom were convinced with it, either because of personal conviction or swayed by the NAZI propaganda. In Europe, in almost every country occupied by Germany during the Second World War, there were willing accomplices to the German crime.

The middle and higher-level officers in the military may have to deal with defiance of military orders when necessary. It is the highest military leadership that has to deal with confronting the political leadership where necessary, as we have seen in some examples in the book. The political approach to even wars could sometimes be guided by their name in history, direct personal benefits, and political expediency rather than national interest. John F Kennedy and Lyndon Johnson are examples of this in the context of the Vietnam War, and George Bush and Tony Blair for the Iraq War. Statistics, half-truths and false narratives are great tools to shape public perceptions and prove what you want to be proven by cherry-picking statistics that suit you. Social media has been a boon for perception warriors. According to a highly placed Indian Army Officer, when the Kargil war was in progress in 1999, the political leadership was focused on the war. The day the election dates were announced, the focus of the government changed overnight from war to elections as if the war didn't exist.

In India, a recruitment policy for the armed forces under the name 'Agni Veer' was announced by the government. The recruits were to be enrolled for four years after which only 25 per cent would be retained. This scheme had serious flaws related to the intangible aspects of the operational effectiveness of the military, both for combat and technical arms that can only be perceived by the military. In a press conference chaired by the defence minister, the three service chiefs unconvincingly tried to justify the unjustifiable and cut a sorry figure. The announcement was followed by nationwide protests which forced the government to review and address the genuine concerns. Observers believed that it was more out of political expediency and budgeting than for the good of the military, as they claimed. When the government starts looking at the military as an employment agency to check political boxes, you have set the stage for its deterioration.

The military hierarchy seemed to be refusing to see the obvious and towing the government line. At the level of the service Chiefs, they must stand by their convictions.

The Chief of Defence Staff (CDS), instituted with much fanfare as the need of modern-day challenges had gone into cold storage after the unfortunate demise of the first CDS in harness in December 2021. It took the government almost a year to appoint one and that happened after a bizarre policy. The new CDS, a former army commander, with no extraordinary credentials, has been forklifted from retirement. So, India has a CDS with a challenging mandate of force transformation who does not have the experience of a service chief but presides over three. What were they looking for in tweaking the selection criteria; pliability rather than competence?

Von Kleist highlights the difference between defiance of military order and political order. The risk to the soldier who defies a military order can be grave. Hence, we have to examine the possible cost of defiance to the individual and how to minimise it.

The politico-diplomatic canvas is much wider that subsumes military and the military leadership needs to understand that. It is important to see your role from a position or two higher for a better perspective of your role. Nevertheless, given a critical situation that demands positive defiance, the challenge is that the debate on who is right will be effectively settled only after the event. A good example is, when Hitler was planning the annexation of German-speaking areas in Austria and Czechoslovakia, senior military commanders were concerned that it could lead to war with European countries. It did not happen and these areas were annexed without firing a shot. UK and France, with no appetite for another war, acceded to these annexations under the Munich Pact through a policy of appeasement. This raised Hitler's status, emboldened him and silenced the sane voices. Eventually, that led to the German disaster when Hitler got carried away with these successes. When the German Wehrmacht realised where Hitler was leading the country, they tried to assassinate him many times, nearly succeeding—a case of positive defiance. In that endeavour, many German officers including Generals were executed. Thus, it is a tough, yet sometimes necessary call that needs very fine judgment and courage.

That said, some events and decisions need no rocket science to figure out that they are gravely harmful. One such example is the new criteria for the selection of the CDS promulgated by the Indian government, which defies logic.

The other aspect is that sometimes the political leadership may have noble intentions, but their ignorance of military nuances can lead to catastrophe. It happened in India in the India-China War of 1962. So, against the view that the military has no constitutional authority to question the decision of the chief executive, it is fair to assume that, as in the case of Donald Trump, in the case of Prime Minster Nehru too, the institutional mechanism was rendered redundant to question the well-intentioned, but disastrous policy for which the military had not been prepared. When Nehru ordered the army to throw the Chinese out, he clearly had no idea what that meant, what it involved and what could be the consequences. He was the one who thought India did not need an army and wanted to scrap it. Since independence, he had marginalised the army in every way and never prepared them for war. It reflected in the India-China 1962 War.

Going by the logic of the proponents of civil supremacy over the military, the latter must remain quiet, be mute observers and be blindly obedient even when the house is on fire. This obviously is the flawed logic of chair-bound theorists who have no responsibility of any kind in this context.

> *Where was the institutional mechanism in India when PM Nehru, despite the existential national security challenges neglected the armed forces which led to the debacle of 62 War?*

I Accuse: The Dreyfus Affair

> "*The most striking contradiction of our civilization is the fundamental reverence for truth which we profess and the thorough-going disregard for it which we practice.*"
>
> **—*Vilhjalmur Stefansson, Adventures in Error, 1936***

Alfred Dreyfus (1859-1935) was a French army officer whose trial for treason began a 12-year controversy, known as the Dreyfus Affair, which deeply marked the political and social history of the French Third Republic.

Dreyfus was the son of a wealthy Jewish textile manufacturer and decided on a military career. Captain Dreyfus was assigned to the War Ministry when, in 1894, he was accused of selling military secrets to the German military attaché. He was arrested on October 15, and in seven days he was convicted and sentenced to life imprisonment. He was sent to the infamous penal colony of Devils Island, off the coast of French Guiana, on 13 April 1895.

The legal proceedings, which were based on specious evidence, were highly irregular. Although he denied his guilt and his family consistently supported his plea of innocence, public opinion and the French press as a whole, led by its virulently anti-Semitic faction, welcomed the verdict and the sentence. In particular, the newspaper *La Libre Parole* used Dreyfus to symbolize the supposed disloyalty of French Jews.

Soon doubts began to grow. Lt Colonel Georges Picquart found evidence that Major Ferdinand Walsin-Esterhazy was engaged in espionage and that it was Esterhazy's handwriting found on the letter that had incriminated Dreyfus. Picquart was removed from his post as it was believed that his discovery was too inconvenient for his superiors. The pro-Dreyfus side slowly gained prominent adherents, among them was Georges Clemenceau—the future World War I premier.

Officers involved in fabricating false evidence and spreading rumours that implicated Dreyfus were acquitted while Picquart was arrested to cover their own mistakes. This precipitated an event that was to crystallize the whole movement for revision of Dreyfus's trial.

On 13 January 1898, the novelist Émile Zola wrote an open letter published on the front page of *Aurore*, Clemenceau's paper, under the headline "J'Accuse." (I Accuse). By the evening of that day, 200,000 copies had been sold. Zola accused the army of covering up its mistaken conviction of Dreyfus and acquitting inventors of fabricated evidence against Dreyfus on the orders of the Ministry of War, a very serious charge on two very powerful institutions.

By the time of the Zola letter, the Dreyfus case had attracted widespread public attention and had split France into two opposing camps. The issues were regarded as far exceeding the personal matter of the guilt or innocence of Dreyfus. The anti-Dreyfusards (those against reopening the case), nationalist and authoritarian, viewed the controversy as an attempt by the nation's enemies to discredit the army. It also saw it as a case of national security against international socialism and the Jewry of France against Germany. The Dreyfusards (those seeking the exoneration of Captain Dreyfus) saw the issue as the principle of the freedom of the individual subordinated to that of national security and as republican civilian authority pitted against a military authority that acted independently of the state.

Amid uproar in the parliament, the government was pressed by the nationalists to bring Zola to justice, while anti-Semitic riots broke out in the provinces. A petition demanding revision of the Dreyfus trial was signed by some 3,000 persons, including a host of prominent intellectuals. The trial of Zola began on 7 February; he was found guilty of libel and sentenced to a year's imprisonment and a fine of 3,000 francs.

From 1898 to 1899 the Dreyfusard cause gained in strength. Major Henry committed suicide at the end of August 1898, after confessing his forgeries. Esterhazy, another conspirator, fled the country. The confession of Henry opened a new phase in the affair, for it ensured that the appeal of the Dreyfus family for a retrial would now be irresistible.

A new ministry took office in June 1899 and resolved to bring the affair to an end at last. Dreyfus, brought back from Devils Island for retrial appeared before a new court-martial. It found him guilty, but the president of the republic, to resolve the issue, pardoned him. Dreyfus accepted the act of clemency but reserved the right to do all in his power to establish his innocence.

In 1904, a retrial was granted and in July 1906 a civilian court of appeals cleared Dreyfus and reversed all previous convictions. The parliament passed a bill reinstating Dreyfus. On July 22 he was formally reinstated and decorated with the Legion of Honour. The army did not publicly declare his innocence until 1995.

The Dreyfus case or *l'Affaire*, as it came to be called was an important landmark in the history of the Third Republic and modern France. From this turmoil emerged such drastic anticlerical measures as the separation of church and state in 1905 to a cleavage between right-wing nationalists and left-wing anti-militarists that haunted French life until 1914 and even later. On each side were mobilized France's most eminent literary men, and the violent controversy destroyed the cohesion of French life for more than a generation after. A conjunction of mistaken loyalties, repeated stupidity, base forgeries, and excited extremisms inflamed the situation into a national crisis. At best, it evoked a passionate repudiation of anti-Semitism, which did France honour; at worst, it revealed and intensified a chronic internal division that was to be a major source of national weakness.

Colonel Georges Picquart annoyed the entire military hierarchy when he decided to follow the dictates of his conscience and stood for justice. He was repeatedly told by them not to expose the facts of the forgery of documents to falsely implicate Dreyfus.

When these facts were exposed by his lawyer, he was court-martialled. He could have conveniently avoided this humiliation and misery by just keeping quiet. Why did he choose the harder right at a great personal cost?

Author's Notes

There are three aspects that I wish to highlight that are not peculiar to this case alone. One, that inadvertent injustice is one thing, not redressing the mistake when the truth is laid bare is unethical and can lead to serious consequences as we see here. It is against the values and ethos of the military but happens so often. Two, that the higher authority is least likely to accept its mistakes. In covering up, they will be happy to hang the likes of righteous officers like Colonel Picquart. That Emile Zola was also convicted of libel for uncovering military complicity is a tragic irony that only reflects reality.

The third is the positive defiance of Emile Zola and Colonel Picquart which made all this possible. The case divided a nation and changed the course of history for France. It would not have happened without their courage. The whole tragedy would have been averted if there was one senior military officer in France who could defy the authority and stand for truth and justice.

It was the unethical conduct of the army leadership and war ministry combine-Generals and politicians that changed France. As reflected in the survey, one can never trust politicians and how much can one trust the military hierarchy is a matter of who is at the helm at a point in time. These times come occasionally. It is such travesties that need to be challenged and defied whenever, wherever and however, as Picquart and Emile Zola did at personal cost—a price worth the cause for the greater good.

In organisations other than the military, the consequences of positive defiance are not that serious. In the corporate, one would at best be looking for another job. A competent man is rarely out of a job. We have seen that a person who stands up to his convictions in the military will find himself fighting the system, because, in doing so, the superiors are invariably drawn into the net of accountability as we saw with Lt Colonel Scheller. The superiors then take an adversarial position and try to fix the whistle-blower. If the person is not careful, he could be violating some rules of conduct or instructions on the way and that leaves him legally vulnerable that is exploited.

The safeguard is that we have recourse to the civil judiciary, not that they have the reputation of being saints. The process and the duration that cases take are punishments bad enough.

What is so peculiar about the people who challenge authority? As Colonel Scheller said, when he decided to go public, he clearly knew the price he would be paying for it, and so did Corporal Glenton. Scheller had a promising career and pension waiting. These are people whose inner voice would make them miserable if they did not answer the call of their conscience. I have personally experienced that and that was the reason why I defied authority whenever I was convinced of the issue.

A careerist will never stand up for anything but himself and there is little good that he will do to the organisation or his subordinates.

Corporal Glenton was hounded, yet, could only be punished for desertion because the government and the military knew his case will kick up a politico-military storm that no government wants. He had violated service regulations on the way in going public. He quit the army of his own accord. Captain Jason Wright simply resigned, unable to defy his conscience. In doing so, he avoided the system's wrath and could leave without hurting his cause, yet made a strong point. Colonel Scheller was court-martialled for violating many military regulations in going public with his critical social media video. He left the Marine Corps at a great personal cost. Julian Assange has been hounded since and has lived a difficult life. Edward Snowden is living in exile in Russia. The last two, because the US projected their acts as espionage.

Has anything changed after their defiance in the US? The issue of how much the government can intrude on the privacy of citizens is public in the US and Europe. The efforts of these heroes have raised awareness in public and put a check on the government in some ways. The senior military hierarchy rarely has the courage to accept responsibility for their incompetence and failures. The politicians are past masters in passing the buck. When the dust of such developments settles, and surprisingly it often does pretty quickly, it is business as usual for everyone. Why then should the US have the same experience in Vietnam, Iraq and Afghanistan? These acts of defiance get at least some people to introspect. In India, despite the experience of the 1962 War, the Indian military continues to struggle in different ways from a lack of institutional support in addressing national security challenges. The defence minister is the most convenient office to be rotated for political expediency. For politicians, everything revolves around power, votes and elections; little else.

Does that mean there is no place for positive defiance in the military? I do not think so. I had defied authority every time I was convinced after a cool deliberation that defiance was warranted. And, here I am, a Major General and still inspiring officers six years after superannuation.

We now come to the important part. In the corporate world, an inconvenient director will be side-lined or at best sent home. He has little to lose in sailing with the wind but could lose his job if he confronts the board of directors against their unethical practices. The management, the directors and the CEOs are overly paid people, so they have no incentive to rock the boat. For the rest, it is about survival. However, as we saw in the case of Manville Corporation, the management was prepared to see their employees drop dead from asbestosis in pursuit of profit or Union Carbide to be so lackadaisical with safety when dealing with such dangerous chemicals that resulted in the deaths of thousands. There can be no case for a man of conscience not to rock the boat when human lives are in danger, no matter the consequences. In the worst case, they can only sack you, they can't hang you. This could save you a lot of trouble as in ENRON and lives too.

So, what is the way out here? While it may look unethical on the face of it, there is always a way out by 'anonymous whistleblowing' when the company's pursuit of profit threatens human lives or endangers society or the environment. In my opinion, anonymous whistleblowing that saves human lives is ethical.

The lives of people are worth an unethical act for good reason.

Nurturing Positive Defiance

I have discussed this concept with some. While everyone agrees on the need for positive defiance, they raise some observations:

- The difficulty in drawing the line. To what level should this be acceptable? If everyone who disagreed with his superior's orders started defying, no organisation would function.

- Who is right will effectively be known only after the event is over.
- The onus of taking the final decision lies with the political/higher authority with inputs of various agencies, including the military where relevant, so where is the scope for defiance?
- It is a wish list; implying it will not happen even though it is so necessary.

My arguments in the book address these issues. We are talking of positive defiance on issues where glaring consequences stare you in the face. It is about issues of great significance that impact national/organisational interest or human lives, where the institutional oversight mechanisms have become redundant, have been manipulated or simply failed. In my opinion, no level can be laid down. Holocaust and My Lai massacre demonstrate that there was a case for positive defiance of orders even by a Private/junior most soldier and a warrant officer actually did and there were Nazis who saved Jews, Schindler being the most famous of them all. It is all related to the lawfulness and awfulness of command and not the level.

This would not be desirable at the lower levels in the interest of discipline. The only way to prevent this is a culture of free expression and constructive dissent. In the military, men need to be encouraged to speak up and be heard when they have an issue. Above all, in the interest of the organisation, men should be shielded from this dilemma by their superiors by doing the needful themselves and ensuring that no unlawful or awful orders trickle down to the men.

Now we come to the important aspect of how we institutionalise constructive dissent and constructive disobedience/positive defiance as necessary leadership traits. How do we begin to look at it as a positive thought rather than a disruptive idea? In other words, how does it get internalised as part of the organisational culture?

This is not so challenging when seen dispassionately and without a sense of insecurity. The insecurity comes from incompetence and lack of integrity. Positive defiance is a close cousin of moral courage and integrity in soul and spirit. These two are universally acknowledged as the most important leadership traits and expect leaders to stand up for their convictions or for what is right, irrespective of the consequences. Positive defiance is one way to demonstrate integrity and moral courage in the best interest of the organisation.

I strongly believe, at the outset, this concept will face stiff opposition from higher ranks, particularly within the military, for the same reasons as they oppose a 360-degree evaluation where subordinates also evaluate their seniors.

I am certain when the 360-degree concept was first floated, there must have been a tsunami of opposition in most organisations. All kinds of arguments against it must have been forwarded, the basic being how can a subordinate evaluate his superior or that it will lead to populism and dilution of authority etc. Today, this is an extensively practised concept with its benefits that enforces accountability and fairness on the superiors.

The Indian Army continues to oppose this because of a sense of insecurity among senior officers. That 70 to 80 per cent of officers of the Indian Army are graded outstanding is a reflection of a lack of courage to tell a subordinate where he stands. No conscientious, selfless and competent officer will ever have a problem with 360-degree evaluation. I do not have and have long been a proponent of this concept in the military.

Let me explain this way; leaders who allow for dissent get the best plans at the end of it because personal biases, preconceived ideas and dogmas get war-gamed. Leaders who are prepared to receive bad news as easily as good news, allow themselves better opportunity to deal with crises before it blows. It allows their team to experiment with new ideas and generate momentum towards the organisational goals. It promotes trust and ownership, the two pillars of growth.

The Organisational Climate

There is always resistance to change and this appears to be a big disruptive concept on the face of it. This needs transformation of the mind at the top of the organisation, to begin with. The higher leadership of the organisation must deeply introspect over this concept. They will realise that it is not a disruptive concept. Actually, it is an enabling concept that raises the standards of leadership and accountability, thus, enhancing performance, quite like the 360-degree concept, if followed honestly. It will raise the efficiency of the organisations. It will prevent disasters. It is not defiance of legitimate authority or legal orders; it is defiance of incompetence or unethical conduct, unlawful command or a lawful but awful order that is detrimental to the organisation's values and future.

So, why should a superior give an unlawful command if his heart and mind are in the right place? Unbecoming conduct by a superior needs to be questioned by all means and that is what the regulations and ethics expect people to do, don't they? Doesn't the NDA prayer say so, as we saw earlier? Doesn't 'Integrity' as a leadership trait means 'choosing the harder right rather than the easier wrong' and standing up for your convictions and your values?

Corporate offices are swanky and impressive with their vision and organizational values displayed prominently. Often, there is no congruence between the stated and the practised values. If this was not the case, why should we have Enron or Wells Fargo debacles? So, the solution starts with the realisation and acceptance by the senior leaders of the benefits of this concept by overcoming their preconceived resistance and insecurities. Once that happens, they have to work towards creating an organisational climate where constructive disobedience as a leadership trait is nurtured and celebrated. Sounds utopian, I guess. The senior leadership will have to walk the talk and accept constructive disobedience when justified without penalising the person in any manner, in fact rewarding him. It will take some convincing that the subordinates feel it is safe to do so. It may involve subtle exercises, deliberately passing illegal orders that demand positive defiance and using this as a learning tool.

Positive defiance sounds timely alarm bells against fatal decisions before irreversible damage is done by enforcing accountability on superiors and making the organization more effective and value-based. It will also ensure that human tragedies and embarrassments caused due to self-serving and corrupt political leadership are prevented by timely mid-course corrections.

> *I believe that constructive disobedience will encourage constructive dissent, and that will prevent the need for constructive disobedience or defiance.*

Why Things Remain the Same: The Laws of Stupidity

In 1976, Carlo M Cipolla, a professor of economic history at the University of California, Berkeley, published an essay outlining the fundamental laws of a force he perceived as humanity's greatest existential threat: Stupidity.

Stupid people, he explained, share several identifying traits: they are abundant, they are irrational, and they cause problems for others without apparent benefit to themselves, thereby lowering society's total well-being. There are no defences against stupidity, argued the Italian-born professor. The only way a society can avoid being crushed by the burden of its idiots is if the non-stupid work even harder to offset the losses of their stupid brethren.

Source: The March of Folly, From Troy to Vietnam, Barbara W Tuchman

We have seen the results of the survey on the trustworthiness of politicians in general. Politicians are very smart people, or how else could they fool so many for so long and so often? They are clever and smart politically, for themselves and in ways that help them to stay in power and stay out of trouble. In India, politicians with criminal and corruption records keep getting elected and manage to stay out of jail for decades.

Where does the stupidity lie here? Does that convince you that the voter knows best always, or is it the choice between the devil and the deep sea? History suggests as Liddell Hart said, it is these people and their egos that have been the cause of most wars. A study of wars in the last 100 years will validate this view.

President Roosevelt's disgust with colonialism was strong. He believed the French misrule of Indochina represented colonialism in its worst form. Indo-China "should not go back to France," he had told the Secretary of State Cordell Hull in January 1943; "the case is perfectly clear. France has had the country—thirty million inhabitants for nearly a hundred years and the people are worse off than they were at the beginning. They are entitled to something better than that." Britain was no better. They did the same in India and elsewhere in their colonies. Their departure has left the colonies struggling socially, economically and politically.

We know where the US landed; first supporting France back to Indo-China after the War despite their stated position on colonies, then, financing the French war effort in Indo-China which at its peak reached 80 per cent of the expenditure. Then, supplanting the French after their defeat at Dien Bien Phu in 1954. The French had lost 50000 soldiers killed and 100,000 injured. The US suffered more than 58000 killed, 1,50,000 injured and 1600 missing and an estimated two million Vietnamese and hundreds of thousands of Cambodians and Laotians died.

Based on the French defeat, it was clear that the US would go the same way; it was a matter of time. It was quite the same in Afghanistan. What made the US think it would be different for them from the Russians in the graveyard of empires?

Many senior advisors sent for ground assessment to Vietnam returned with the same gloomy prognosis, which included JK Galbraith who advised a negotiated way out. All the sane counsel was disregarded with the 'don't confuse me with facts' approach. McNamara assessed everything on technology and his quantitative model. Everything in battle cannot be put to quantitative analysis—some intangibles are more powerful than tangibles. There are things that no technology could solve then as now, contrary to what he believed.

Project 100,000: McNamara's Morons

Image: Compiled from Internet

To make up for the escalating demands of manpower in Vietnam, McNamara came up with a despicable plan. He lowered the recruitment standards to recruit low-IQ candidates who were mentally and physically unfit to be soldiers. They came to be known as 'McNamara's Morons'. They even included some men with autistic disabilities etc. who could not even read or write but passed the written tests!

McNamara believed he could win the war in Vietnam through the use of advanced technology and computerized analysis. Hamilton Gregory, author of *McNamara's Folly: The Use of Low-IQ Troops in the Vietnam War* writes, he thought one could turn below-average soldiers into above-average soldiers through the use of technology and learning by use of videotapes. The casualty rates of these troops were three times higher than the regular troops.

When half a million able-bodied trained soldiers could not defeat Vietnam, what could be expected of these men, some of whom found even tying their bootlaces a challenge? As much vulnerable themselves, they endangered their fellow soldiers, weighed them down and put them at risk. There was one reported case where one such soldier on sentry duty shot his own officer because he simply could not learn the simple challenging procedure. Cannon fodder, were they?

Where was the wisdom of those leading the US politically and militarily? It is hard to imagine that the military leadership, especially the Army and the Marine Corps accepted these troops who would be employed in actual combat. When this stage was reached, was there a case for positive defiance by the US military leadership?

Rather than the missing wisdom, it is a manifestation of the 'Laws of Stupidity'. McNamara, for sure, must have been a smart man in his own way to be the Secretary of Defence, but Project 100,000 shows, from the military perspective, he was anything but that. The tragedy is that the military let it happen. Worse, lessons are never learnt and the McNamara's Folly was repeated in the Iraq War. One such recruit was shot and died in Iraq when on observation duty because of his deficiencies. Tragically, his fellow soldiers used to call him Forrest Gump, a soldier by this name who was drafted in Vietnam as part of 'Project 100,000' after whom the famous film Forrest Gump was made, the film itself is far from the reality of Private Forest Gump.

Why do people in authority allow such stupid ideas to be implemented?

Why this is so alarming is that as author Hamilton Gregory points out, enough loopholes were left to enable the politically influential middle class to avoid the draft for political expediency. As he says, one senator's son was medically exempted draft for wearing braces on his teeth! This project, suitably sugar-coated, targeted the poor class who could not complain or protest. Their lot after the war was no better than promised. I hope the Indian Agniveers scheme does not land up with the same fate.

American General, Westmoreland, who was the commander in Vietnam for four crucial years, followed a strategy that was destined to fail. When it was not working, he failed to see the reality and listen to his advisors. He fudged and manipulated statistics to prove that the war was progressing well and was ever ready to abandon truth when it came in the way of his ambitions and personal interest. (Source: *Westmoreland. The General Who Lost Vietnam*, by Lewis Sorley)

Clearly, Westmoreland understood neither the nature of the war he was fighting, the people and their history nor the environment. And what is most amazing as per this author is that General Westmoreland never read about the French experience in Vietnam and their defeat at Dien Bien Phu. Quite incredible! This a clear case where the second rung of military leadership in Vietnam should have questioned him and his operational philosophy.

This explains why the French and the US went the way they did in Indo-China. Take it further, how different were Iraq and Afghanistan? Millions died, and millions were displaced and became refugees. Tens of millions were left more miserable than they were before and the US gained nothing from any of these wars. As for the world, it now faces a new resurgent threat that refuses to die down—Islamic fundamentalism. What is happening in Ukraine-the US helping the Ukrainians to fight the Russians to the last Ukrainian for their interests?

The political leadership needs to appreciate that wars rarely bring lasting peace; Ukraine, Iraq, Afghanistan, Syria, African conflicts, Libya, Yemen etc. are examples from this century alone. Violence begets more violence.

Resignation as a Tool of Positive Defiance

The senior military leadership needs to carefully chalk out the approach to manage damage control in a situation that is getting dangerous because of political expediency or ignorance. Here, I would recommend a theory of indirect approach. The best way is to find a supporter of your cause amongst the close advisors of the political executive to legislate your view as if it was theirs. That could often be difficult because they are likely to be part of the problem. Fair chance that you would find a sane mind or two who see the merit of your case and are prepared to take it forward and you could plant your idea from the inside.

A confrontationist approach leads to the hardening of positions and makes communication difficult.

A commander has the option to resign in a predicament. There are two aspects to resignation; one, the commander goes away quietly without the problem getting resolved. Two, that it is one-day news and the political authority will be happy to get the perceived obstructionist out of the way and paint him as the villain. Resignation will have the desired result when there is active media, strong opposition and a functional institutional system in place. Only then will the focus come back on the issue. In the normal course, it makes no headlines as happened when the Indian Naval Chief, Admiral DK Joshi resigned in 2014. The Chief had resigned after repeated accidents involving naval vessels, including a submarine that sank as a result of a fire accident because of dysfunctional batteries, for which he accepted moral responsibility. It is important to examine the details of this episode.

He said, the root cause of his resignation was the "dysfunctional and inefficient" operating environment in the Ministry of Defence and that he was surprised at the haste with which the government accepted his resignation without a ripple. The speed clearly indicated that it did not go through the institutional process. The government was in a hurry to pin it on someone to deflect the spotlight from itself. It was done under a defence minister who was one of the most inefficient office incumbents. Admiral Joshi stated in an interview with the *Times of India*, "Where there is authority, there is no accountability. And where there is responsibility, there is no authority." He added, "I felt being a service chief is not just about preening about on national TV, taking a salute on Republic Day. In actual fact, you are unable to get a set of batteries for your submarines and to my mind, that was a completely untenable situation for continuation as a chief, it had been building up."

The next option is to stick to your stand for the national or organisational good and let the government sack you. That will demonstrate that you stood for something and the next incumbent will be obliged to take note. So, when the situation is this critical, the three service chiefs must be on board and present a unified front. No government can disregard the views of three service chiefs for the national good.

The other methodology, as General Milley said is "to fight from the inside". The advantage here is, that while resigning clears the government's path by getting the defiant General out of the way, fighting from inside enables one to prevent further damage by being part of the system. This can be done by framing directions in response to the government's 'lawful but awful orders' to reduce further damage.

And, when none of this works, the three chiefs could seek the audience of the Cabinet Committee on Security or the Supreme Commander himself. In the worst case, regret their inability to carry out the order in that form because it is certain to bring disgrace to the country.

This discourse on positive defiance must end with the debacle of the India-China War in 1962. The man in the hottest seat was Brig JP Dalvi, the commander of the 7 Infantry Brigade. This brigade was holding defences in the farthest and the most sensitive Namka Chu area, the trijunction of India, Bhutan and Tibet in the North East Frontier Agency, now Arunachal Pradesh. They were occupying the Dhola Post in the disputed zone which became the trigger for the War. He minced no words in conveying to his superior commanders the desperate state of his men, equipment and defences and the disaster just waiting to happen if the Chinese attacked. When no one in the chain of command paid heed, he felt the only way to bring the hierarchy to senses and prevent a national disaster was to resign. Eventually, he did not. He was certain that the Chinese offensive was just a matter of time. If he resigned, the new incumbent will not have the time to get to grips with the situation, the challenges and the leadership environment. He understood that this will put his men in grave danger. He did not want to leave his men to their fate and chose to continue. The defences made from local resources were ripped apart in no time under the onslaught of Chinese artillery fire. The brigade suffered enormous casualties and ceased to exist. The commander was taken prisoner of war. He was never the same man again and died a troubled man. One could argue that he should have resigned and maybe that could have saved the day for India. As a commander on the ground, he made a completely selfless decision. He could have easily taken himself out of the blistering hot seat but stayed on for his men in a situation where disaster was not in doubt. Such decisions could easily be portrayed as cowardice by the superiors. It was the higher political and military leadership that failed the nation.

Turbulence, a Two-way Traffic

When we are in a situation of constructive disobedience, the turbulence could affect the environment and the superior no less. It will seem to challenge his authority and he could feel that it could snowball into mass disobedience, as we are seeing in Israel today against the government's decision to reform the judiciary. Even reservist soldiers in thousands are defying the recall orders to join duty.

Clearly, it must sound alarm bells in the leadership before it turns fatal.

In most cases, this would result in ego battles and the hardening of positions by both or by the superior. A man marred by ego or drunk with power or for personal interests will tend to lose the sense of balance and use his authority to demonstrate who is the boss. In the case of civil-military issues, the political authority could fire the military officer. It could also result in what happened in Pakistan in 1999 after the Kargil fiasco. General Musharraf, the Chairman of the Joint Chiefs of Staff Committee, and the mastermind of the disastrous Kargil misadventure staged a coup and overthrew the elected Prime Minister Nawaz Sharif who was holding him accountable.

What is the best course of action in this turbulence? It needs statesmanship of a high order. The boss, whether political or the organisational head must zoom out and see the issue dispassionately from the perspective of the other man. He must appoint a neutral committee of men of integrity and wisdom to examine the issue afresh in light of the objections.

If you allow the issue to be illuminated by the light of law, values and ethics, norms and the good of the organisation, the best course of action will emerge. Bring in the ego and that will sabotage all solutions.

This SOCS approach will be useful.

SOCS stands for SITUATION – OPTIONS – CONSEQUENCES – SOLUTION.

Situation – What is the issue? What was your role in the development? If the situation is created by your intention or ambitions, is it legally tenable and measures up to the values and ethical audit? Is it good for the organisation in the long run?

Options – Consider all the options to resolve the conflict or the situation.

Consequences – Consider the consequences of all the options.

Solution – Implement the option that has the best long-term consequences for the organization and not you personally.

—*Emotional Intelligence, Daniel Coleman*

♦ ♦ ♦

Chapter Fifteen

Positive Defiance: Ensuring a Safe Landing

How constructive disobedience is received may vary depending on the context, organisational culture and the superiors involved.

In some cases, constructive disobedience may be welcomed as a catalyst for progress by drawing attention to important issues, outdated practices or orders that have catastrophic potential and lead to reforms.

It is more likely that constructive disobedience will be met with resistance, opposition, or even repression. Those in positions of authority or with vested interests in maintaining the status quo or simply because of their ego may perceive acts of constructive disobedience as threats and respond with punitive measures. This can include legal consequences, social ostracism or attempts to discredit the dissenting voices. While most constitutions provide for free speech and expression, we have seen in many countries that people who criticise governments and political leaders are arrested and convicted.

In Indian society, the deep-rooted cultural aspect of respecting the elders and people in authority leads to an environment where far more deference is expected from their subordinates. This can easily transform into an expectation of implicit obedience and subservience. Here any kind of positive dissent or constructive disobedience is likely to be seen as indiscipline and insubordination and treated accordingly. It is therefore important that the practice of this philosophy is done in a manner that the larger aim is achieved without crash landing personally.

We have seen the predicament of General Milley in dealing with an erratic President Trump. We have seen that there will always be people who push academic arguments that do not help. In the context of the above, positive defiance is a necessity for the good of the country, the world and humanity. So, while the need for positive defiance is well established, it is important to do it in a manner that assures a safe landing.

The need for defiance may arise because of one or more of the following reasons:

- Ethical grounds—Unethical or unlawfulness of the lawful order.
- Operational reasons. There are serious problems in accomplishing the task with the terms of reference laid down.
- Disagreement on the mission itself because of its repercussions that the higher authority is ignoring or failing to see.
- Disagreement with a policy decision that has serious consequences for the organisation.
- Government policies that seriously affect military values and ethos.
- At the lower levels, it may be because of amoral, illegal or unjust orders.
- In corporate, practices or oversights that are seriously threatening the employees/stakeholders, the environment or the value system of the organisations.

In any organization, one renders himself vulnerable when one violates the regulations in doing so. In the military, it is worse since you have regulations for the smallest of things and defaulting is a high probability. When one confronts the authority, omissions or commissions that would normally be overlooked are picked up to target the individual. So, some caveats would help to avoid a crash landing:

- What is it that you are trying to achieve and why? It has to be important enough and worth putting your neck on the line.
- Be certain that you have a strong argument with irrefutable logic as per the values and norms of the organization you are part of.
- Avoid giving an impression of confrontation, put a positive sentiment to your case. Build a consensus with your peers who share your views. Try to achieve your objective with the least turbulent methodology. Get the intermediaries to see the merit in your argument and get them to legislate your case with the superior.
- Issues must be raised within the regulations of the military/organisation

and with the confidentiality that the issue warrants.

- Positive defiance must follow the escalatory ladder of discussion, debate, constructive dissent, representation in writing and constructive disobedience. It is typical of bureaucracy to avoid committing on file to avoid accountability. Up the chain, notings initiated at the lowest level are simply initialled without a comment. Must get them to endorse their critical decisions, agreement or disagreement on file so that accountability can be established, if necessary. In the case of the India-China debacle of 1962, every major functionary in the advisory group wrote a book to blame everybody else and glorify himself.
- Finally, when nothing works and you are convinced that you have a 'life and death' case that must be pursued, take it up in writing.
- When even that does not work, seek permission to approach the next higher commander. If permission is not given, tell your boss that you are proceeding anyway. Put up your case in writing with a copy to your immediate senior.
- Finally, take your call on how far are you prepared to go and what are you prepared to risk.
- Do not get on the wrong side of the law.
- If your conscience gives you a call, be prepared to answer it for the larger cause.

The following guidelines will help in avoiding undesirable turbulence:

Respectful communication. Constructive dissent and disobedience must involve expressing dissenting opinions respectfully and professionally which encourages a healthy exchange of ideas and minimizes hostility.

Constructive criticism. The protagonists must provide well-reasoned arguments and evidence to support their counter viewpoints aimed at improving the quality of decisions or actions, rather than simply opposing for the sake of opposition.

Seeking common ground. The protagonists must actively seek areas of agreement and compromise and aim to find solutions that address concerns from different perspectives and bridge gaps between opposing views.

Offering alternatives. Dissenters must propose viable alternatives or modifications to existing plans or policies. They offer constructive suggestions that align with their core concerns and values, thereby contributing to the improvement of the overall outcome.

Commitment to the collective interest. The protagonists must prioritize the greater good and the long-term success of the organization or society. They genuinely believe with the justification that their viewpoint will lead to better outcomes and benefit the nation, community or the organisation as a whole.

Based on my experience, I can say that one must take up issues that cross your red lines. If everyone accepts laissez-faire and does not seek accountability from subordinates and superiors alike, the organisation is doomed. If you do it the right way, there is nothing to fear. Even if there is a price to pay for your organisation and your country, it is worth it. Great things were achieved by courage and sacrifice by someone—often alone to begin with.

There will be times when the issues at stake are of monumental importance to humanity itself, as we saw in Germany, Vietnam, Iraq, and Afghanistan. In such cases, the bull must be taken by the horns and be prepared to face the consequences. This is our obligation to the organization that we have pledged to serve. If you do not, you would have shown disloyalty to the cause and the organisation.

Common people like Rosa Parks, Julian Assange, Edward Snowden, Corporal Glenton and countless others have made the world sit up and take notice. If they had also waited for someone else to dirty their hands, nothing would have changed.

I never shied away from positive defiance and I retired as Major General with a sterling professional and personal reputation. The reason was that there was never a personal interest or agenda involved.

Be the man who can proudly look at himself in the mirror and walk into the sunset with your pride and head held high. Be the man for whom the applause continues well after the curtains are drawn on your stage. Be the man who will be given coffee in a ceramic cup and not a Styrofoam cup well after you relinquish your official position. Be the ordinary man, who did extraordinary things. You will leave a legacy that the next generation will be proud of.

If you do it the right way for the right cause, you do not have to fear the consequences.

An officer's strongest asset is his brain. If he fails to use it, he is no better than a dummy on a bayonet fighting range. We saw the consequences of unreflective obedience at Jelep La and the benefit of positive defiance at Nathu La in the Watershed War 1967. I will strongly recommend that 'Constructive Disobedience' be nurtured as a leadership trait amongst commanders at all levels of command in the military. In the government and civil organisations, it should form part of the organisational values and leadership development programme.

Many unsung warriors listened to the voice of conscience, challenged authority and made this world a better place, often at great personal cost.

> *In the normal course of life's dilemmas, our conscience only sounds a whisper. When your conscience speaks loud and your inaction is inflicting pain and guilt on you, it is time for disobedience. Unfortunately, people have different levels of conscience thresholds and they can turn a deaf ear to the loudest voices of conscience. That is the tragedy that must be fought.*

IF EVERYONE SANG FROM THE SAME SONG SHEET AS THEIR BOSS, THE ORGANISATION IS DOOMED.

♦ ♦ ♦

Chapter Sixteen

Epilogue

The future of humanity is everybody's business. Only people can make the difference—by Action and not Inaction—by Positive Defiance and not by Indifference—by Constructive Disobedience and not by Blind Obedience. There is no possibility that help will come from outer space.

Carlo M Cipolla's 'Laws of Stupidity' can be seen as a manifestation of Pareto's Principle. This small percentage of people is the cause of 80 per cent of human suffering and charts the destiny of humanity—governance, judiciary, religion, military or corporate etc. The small minority succeeds because of the silence or inaction of the majority. We have seen that the stupid repeatedly commit 'Follies' that harms others while doing no good to themselves. A leash on a dog makes him safe for others and a rider on a horse harnesses its immense energy which would otherwise run wild.

Positive defiance is not a disruptive concept. It is a concept that ensures the best interests of the organisation and all its stakeholders by seeking accountability from those responsible. Internalising this concept will enforce efficiency, transparency and integrity and pre-empt disastrous decisions before they become fatal.

Power corrupts, absolute power corrupts absolutely. I have enumerated examples from different walks of life that prove that an average human being is corruptible, self-centric and untrustworthy. Pharmaceutical companies and hospitals, supposedly noble ventures have become business houses, no better than any other. We have seen the example of Manville Corporation which was prepared to have their employees fall dead for profit. Most people can be bought, only the price varies. The research clearly shows the lack of trust that politicians the world over enjoy. Corruption and politics are congenital twins. A rather high percentage of politicians have criminal records of some kind and often ill-educated, sit in parliaments or state assemblies.

The world is on the brink of ecological disaster because of global warming. The crisis has only seen conferences, photo ops and empty promises but no concrete action. Young kids are demonstrating a better understanding of the catastrophe and challenging the global leadership into action.

Holocaust was a horrific human tragedy, but there are many which compete for the ignoble title of being the worst of them all. Neither was Holocaust the first German-curated human tragedy. Throughout history, the white man colonialism has massacred, exploited and dehumanised humanity all across the globe. Barring odd exceptions, all colonies are struggling to shake out of the devastating effects of colonisation. All because of too much obedience and too quietly.

While there is little to choose between colonisers, the Belgian colonisation of Congo under King Leopold II is symbolic of universal colonial brutality and exploitation. Amputation of hands and legs was the retribution of the locals for not meeting the daily rubber plantation targets. Belgian colonialism resulted in the deaths of millions in Congo, as did other colonies. In India, in 1943, the avoidable Bengal famine under British rule resulted in the deaths of over three million people. The British starved Indians to feed their people.

They continue to do so even today in different forms. It is tragic that even today, people like Bruce Gilley defend and propagate the idea of colonialism to uplift poor countries, having sucked them dry during centuries of exploitation and dehumanising them. Europe is prosperous today because of the exploitation of the rest of the world in the period gone by. Former colonies are poor and many are at war primarily as a direct and indirect consequence of colonisation. For 1700 hundred years till the 18th Century, India was the richest country in the world, accounting for 25 per cent of the world GDP for long periods. The Britishers left it in ruins through the brutal exploitation of its wealth and destruction of its systems for their benefit. The famous Kohinoor diamond that adorns the crown of the British Monarch is a testimony of Britain's exploitation of India.

In recent times millions have been killed by Western-led wars across the globe. Ukraine is the latest man-made humanitarian crisis; for US interests. Even Pope understood that it was the US-led NATO barking at the Russian doorstep that triggered the Ukraine war. Long after the Warsaw Pact dissolved, NATO continued to expand all around Russia including the erstwhile Soviet Union-era countries. The whole of Europe led by the US is now fighting Russia to the last Ukrainian. The former German Chancellor Angela Merkel had warned of the consequences of NATO expansion and her sane voice was brushed aside as the US does so often in pursuit of its interests.

The Western world, led by the US is constantly at war in some parts of the world killing hundreds of thousands who have nothing to do with any kind of violence or the cause of war. These wars serve the military-industrial complexes in the West which grease the government machinery and influence government policies. A glaring example is the gun lobby in the US despite repeated shootings that kill hundreds of innocents including children every year. A Blackrock executive rightly said "War is good for fuc*ng business. It is the business houses that decide the policies, not the governments" Everyone is up for sale.

Citizens must take responsibility for their future, demand accountability and prevent fatal decisions.

The militaries need to be questioned too. Notwithstanding the business of civil control over the military, military leadership has the responsibility that over-ambitious, reckless or simply ignorant political executives' decisions do not trigger human tragedy or lead their country to disaster. When they fail, junior ranks like Colonel Scheller and Corporal Glenton step up and seek accountability from the leadership.

Rather than introspecting and putting their house in order, they court-martial these courageous men. The world is governed with very little wisdom as Count Axel Oxenstierna, Chancellor of Sweden said in the seventeenth century. Little has changed in 300 years.

Within the organisations including the militaries, personal interests override organisational interests. Moral courage is conspicuous by its absence. Self-preservation, money, promotions, and ambitions drive those in power or positions of authority. This pushes the onus of constructive disobedience and positive defiance on the middle and junior levels of leadership. Dog-like loyalty is suicidal for humanity. Humans are endowed with the power of analytical thinking and they must use their brains and act rationally for the good of humanity and the organisation.

We need to remember that the future of the world is everybody's business, and so are human lives, and all lives irrespective of colour or creed are equally valuable. Positive defiance may cause turbulence in one's life but this world that we enjoy today was changed by those who were prepared to deal with this turbulence. If one wants better accountability from those in authority, one will have to take up the gauntlet.

If Rosa Parks had also waited for a martyr to be born in the neighbour's house, African Americans would still be travelling at the back of the buses. It was the fearless defiance of Indian women wrestlers against sexual harassment by a political heavyweight of the ruling government that brought the government to its senses. For sure, some of them may pay the price in terms of their sports career. For them, there was a bigger purpose that inspired them to 'rebel with a cause'. Positive defiance does not demand anyone's life. It only means convincingly bringing the spotlight on the critical issues. If that is done in the right manner, the way I have suggested, one does not have to fear anything.

The political leadership has to be held accountable. For them, all that matters is power and votes, people matter only to that extent. We need to take charge of our destiny, elect those people who measure up to our values and ethics and deliver and recall those who fail to. The power lies with people and that must be used with discretion and not on narrow considerations.

The militaries all over the world are the most trusted and value-based organisations. They need to stand up when required and ensure that the ignorance and political expediency of the political leaders do not bring dishonour to the country or bring tragedy to humanity.

People who hold the cards of humanity's destiny, be they political executives, bureaucrats, corporate heads, the military or any other organisation, need to be kept under the leash of accountability through constructive disobedience, and if necessary, through positive defiance when necessary.

> "*At his best, man is the noblest of all animals; separated from law and justice he is the worst.*"
>
> —***Aristotle***

Organisations that nurture a culture of constructive dissent do not have to face constructive disobedience. Constructive disobedience is an essential leadership trait and is an extension of moral courage and integrity, especially at higher levels. It must be internalised in the organisational culture. It will prevent disastrous and fatal decisions that will ensure the long-term sustainability of the organisations.

The future of humanity is everybody's business.

♦ ♦ ♦

Index